FROM THE ANSCHLUSS TO THE ARCADES

THE EVOLUTION OF A FAMILY STORE

by

STEVEN SALAMON

Grosvenor House
Publishing Limited

The right of Steven Salamon to be identified as the author of this
work has been asserted in accordance with Section 78
of the Copyright, Designs and Patents Act 1988

The book cover is copyright to Steven Salamon

This book is published by
Grosvenor House Publishing Ltd
Link House
140 The Broadway, Tolworth, Surrey, KT6 7HT.
www.grosvenorhousepublishing.co.uk

A CIP record for this book
is available from the British Library

Paperback ISBN 978-1-83615-395-5

In Memoriam

In memory of family victims of the Holocaust 1939-45

Jozef Salamon	Sosnowiec Ghetto 1942
Karolina Salamon	Suchej, Poland 1940
Joachim Reichenbaum	Auschwitz 1942
Jakob Reichenbaum	Auschwitz 1942
Ernst Reichenbaum	Auschwitz 1940
Eduard Reichenbaum	Hamburg 1945
Moses Salamon	Sosnowiec Ghetto 1942
Mania Salamon	Suchej, Poland 1940
Josefina Salamon	Suchej, Poland 1940
Anna Salamon	Suchej, Poland 1940
Sabena Salamon	Suchej, Poland 1940
Moses Stein	Transnistria Camp, Ukraine 1943
Rosa Stein	Transnistria Camp, Ukraine 1942

Contents

Part Three: The Son
Steven Salamon 1963

Preface

Growing up, I had little understanding of my father's family background. Dad seldom spoke about his upbringing, the family's life before the Second World War, or how they survived the Holocaust. He was likely unaware of many details, as much of the information he later shared turned out to be inaccurate.

However, there was family folklore. We knew snippets: Ignatz, my grandfather, was Polish, and Frieda, my grandmother, was Romanian; they met while he was serving in the Polish army; their children were born in Austria; they opened a shop in Rohrbach an der Teich, a small village in the Austrian state of Burgenland; they fled to Wales from Austria in late 1939, just before the onset of the Second World War; my grandfather worked at a factory called Aero Zipp Fasteners, established by fellow refugees on the Treforest Trading Estate; my grandmother arrived on a domestic service visa; a family of railway workers took in my father and his brothers; and my grandparents later opened a shop in Cardiff. We heard rumours that my grandfather was in an internment camp and subsequently joined the Polish Corps of the British Army.

Dad, however, was the custodian of boxes containing important clues about the family's story, which Mum entrusted to my sister, Rochelle, after his passing. These held numerous original documents and letters, enabling Rochelle to piece together a timeline and narrative of their lives. The boxes served as a time capsule, allowing us to glimpse their world and the events surrounding them when decisions were made without the benefit of foresight.

This sparked an interest in genealogy, and Rochelle began working on a more extensive family tree. Through meticulous research, she compiled names, places, and dates of births and deaths for many family members across several generations, tracing back as far as our great-great-great-grandparents at the turn of the 18th century. She received assistance from cousins who had documents and photographs from their parents and shared their recollections.

Rochelle was the first in my generation to travel to Austria. She went with our cousin Debbie, who lives in the US and is the daughter of Uncle Sigi, my father's eldest brother. They visited the family addresses they had in Vienna and then travelled to Rohrbach.

Not much more was learned about the family after that until Rochelle attended a Holocaust Memorial Day event in London in 2015 with two of her sons, at which one of the speakers discussed Kitchener Camp – the transit camp in Kent where our grandfather stayed after arriving in the UK – and its role in housing Jewish refugees. This was a lightbulb moment for Rochelle; she had read about Kitchener Camp in family documents but had never connected the dots to understand how our grandfather escaped Austria. Rochelle began to investigate this part of the story further and uploaded dozens of documents and photos to the Kitchener Camp website, just in time for an exhibition at the Jewish Museum in London, which I attended, mingling with other Kitchener descendants from around the world.

> "I was able to provide all the information I had about my family. When we went to the exhibition, the first picture you saw upon entering was my grandfather in his truck," Rochelle recounts in an interview for this book. "They had a huge screen, and they kept displaying the pictures of my family – my grandparents with the three little boys, and them in Vienna when they were trying to leave. It was wonderful to see, because in Jewish tradition there is the idea that someone's soul continues for as long as their name is still spoken."

A smaller, permanent version of the exhibition is now housed at the Wiener Holocaust Library in London.

In January 2023, my older sister, Belinda, informed me that our cousin in Israel, Yuval Stein, the grandson of my grandmother's brother, had recently visited Neuberg, a village in Austria where his grandparents had lived before the Second World War. He had been in contact with an Austrian historian who assisted him in tracking down details about where his grandparents lived, the locations of their shops, and the schools their children attended.

At the time, I was organising a visit to Austria with two of my children, Benjamin and Natalie. I wrote to Yuval and asked him to put me in touch with the historian, whom I then contacted for assistance. She informed me that she had discovered a file bearing the Salamon name in the Burgenland state archives in Mattersberg, in a section chillingly named "Aryanisation of the Jews of South Burgenland". I arranged to view the file during our visit that February.

I had always wanted to visit Austria. We stayed in Leopoldstadt, the district in Vienna where Jews had lived for centuries, and we visited the many addresses related to our family. We also attended a Friday night service at the Stadttempel, the only synagogue in Vienna that survived Kristallnacht – the Nazi pogrom of November 1938 – and we made our way to Rohrbach.

We also went to Mattersburg and visited the archives there. It was incredible to open a file related to my grandparents that hadn't been touched for 84 years, and we handled the papers delicately. The archivists were extremely helpful and allowed us to take photos and copies of the documents. We examined handwritten letters from Frieda to the Viennese authorities, official forms, and other documents she had to complete relating to her emigration, as well as receipts for expenses incurred in preparation for her departure and unpaid tax demands. This file offered an incredible insight into the five months between April and August 1939, during which my grandmother was alone in Vienna with her three sons after my grandfather had left for the UK, and the demanding and demeaning process of emigration she endured.

In June 2023, I travelled to New York for the bar mitzvah of Sigi's grandson. I visited my favourite New York deli, Zabar's, on the Upper West Side. Perusing the shelves, I came upon a book, *Zabar's: A Family Story*, written by a member of the family. Reading it, I realised that their story was a similar story to that of my family.

That was the spark that ignited the idea for this book.

In 2023, I turned 60, and it also marked 30 years since I started working in the family store – originally called Bridge Street Stores by my grandparents, and now known as Wally's Delicatessen. The shop was founded in Cardiff by my grandparents in 1949 and has been run by my father and uncle, and then me, since. As I became increasingly aware that I might be the last family member running the shop, I realised how sad it would be if all trace of the Salamon family's retail history in Cardiff were lost. Therefore, I wanted to preserve our heritage forever, put it "on the record" for my children and grandchildren to come, and for current and future generations of customers and employees, many of whom have been loyal to the family store for decades.

In the changing and challenging times in which we live, recording Holocaust survivors' stories is vital for preserving cultural identity, passing down knowledge across generations, and ensuring that people's experiences are documented and remembered so that nothing like this can ever happen again. To this end, I decided to explore the story of the shop: its origins, heritage, culture, and the people involved – both customers and employees – and its role in the refugee community and the broader business community in South Wales. In doing so, I have gained a deeper understanding of, and illuminated, wider historical events during this period, and addressed issues that remain highly relevant today. My family's story provides a glimpse into what it was like to be a newly-arrived immigrant in the UK in the 1930s, the tumultuous times they experienced, and the challenges of integration. I hope to offer valuable insights on how we should approach today's immigration issues.

Due to my lack of writing experience, I first reached out to a local journalist, Jenny White, who was passionate about food journalism and displayed true enthusiasm for the project.

Jenny interviewed family members and former staff of Wally's, assisting me in writing the first draft of this book. Concurrently, I began conducting further historical research and reached out to several organisations for archival documents. I also sifted through family records for information relevant to the book. I soon realised that, between my immediate and extended family, we possessed a wealth of vital information about our family history; however, it was scattered and disjointed; none of us had the complete picture. All these documents, photographs, and personal memories needed to be woven together to create a cohesive narrative of our family history.

I have kept this account as factual as possible, using only primary and other historical sources to describe the horrors into which my family was plunged before and during the Second World War. I have not imagined conversations or fictionalised the story for dramatic effect; I believe it stands well on its own. I may have strayed into narrating my thoughts on how difficult certain times, actions, or decisions must have been for family members, or I might have assumed a probable course of action based on known historical events. For that, you shall have to forgive me.

In August 2023, during an emotional visit to Kent, I went to Sandwich, near the site of the Kitchener Camp, where Kitchener men spent time at the cinema and pubs. I walked over the bridge into the town and through the toll gate my grandfather and his fellow Kitchener men would have passed on their way to Sandwich. I also visited the homes where my grandmother had worked in domestic service and where my father and his brothers lived after arriving in the UK.

This book began as an account of Wally's history. However, I quickly realised that there was a much larger story to tell – one of persecution and escape, survival and rebirth, and being part of a community of refugees and a food community in Cardiff for over 76 years. It starts sombrely, detailing the family's persecution and attempts to flee Nazi Europe, but it also includes uplifting and warm descriptions of family life, alongside the founding and evolution of the family store.

This is the story of three generations of men and their family business, whose lives were entwined with the most seismic events of the 20th century.

Salamon Family Tree

		Izak m.	Rechel
		Salamon	Flock
		1824-1889	1828-1900
		Jozef m.	Karoliny
		Salamon	Reichenbaum
		1866-1942	1873-1940
Ruzia	Maks	Ignatz m.	Frieda
Salamon	Salamon	Salamon	Stein
1902-1974	1904-1991	1898-1963	1902-1967
Sigi	Otto	Wally m.	Laraine
Salamon	Salamon	Salamon	Bassett
1929-2010	1931-2003	1936-2008	1941-living
Rochelle	Belinda	Steven	
Salamon	Salamon	Salamon	
1967-living	1961-living	1963-living	

Map of Europe – 1939

Map of Europe showing key locations where events happened in this book: Suchej, Poland; Sereth, Romania; Vienna and Rohrbach an der Teich, Austria; Sandwich, England; and Cardiff, Wales.

Introduction

Historians have extensively debated the causes of the Second World War. The event that ultimately ignited it was Germany's invasion of Poland on September 1, 1939, followed by Britain and France's declarations of war on Germany. However, its root cause was likely the result of prior events across Europe.

The Austro-Hungarian Empire dominated Central Europe from 1867 to 1918. It was a military and diplomatic alliance, comprising two sovereign states under a single monarch who held the titles of Emperor of Austria and King of Hungary. The Austrian government, which had ruled the monarchy until 1867, became the government of the Austrian part, while a separate Hungarian government was established for the other part.

Austria-Hungary was geographically the second-largest country in Europe and the third-most populous (after Russia and the German Empire). It encompassed the region of Galicia in southern Poland, which had been annexed in 1804, and which was home to almost one million Jews at the turn of the 20th century, making up 10 percent of the total population.

The two countries had joint diplomatic and defence policies, and common foreign policy and defence ministries were maintained under the emperor's direct control. All other state functions were managed separately, as no common citizenship existed.

This led to several disputes, including which language would be customary. The Germans, the most influential ethnic group, demanded the recognition of their language as the dominant language in every part of the empire.

By 1900, Jews numbered about two million in the whole territory of the Austro-Hungarian Empire. Antisemitic parties and movements existed, but the governments in Vienna and Budapest didn't initiate pogroms or implement official antisemitic policies. They feared that such ethnic violence could ignite other ethnic minorities and escalate out of control.

In that period, most Jews in Austria-Hungary lived in small *shtetls* (villages); however, large communities also existed in some cities, including Vienna and Kraków. Thanks to the modernity of the constitution and the benevolence of Emperor Franz Joseph, Jews came to regard the Austro-Hungarian period as a golden era of their history.

Tensions, however, were simmering within the empire's regions, with each realm having expansionist ambitions.

In 1914, Slavic militants rejected Austria's plan to absorb their region fully. On June 28, 1914, they assassinated the Austrian heir, Archduke Franz Ferdinand, in the Bosnian capital, Sarajevo, triggering a sequence of events that led to the First World War.

The Austro-Hungarian Empire played a relatively passive role in the war, as Germany increasingly dominated and controlled it. Towards the war's end, the army lost all ability to act independently of Germany. Its operational capability was seriously affected by supply shortages, low morale, and a high casualty rate, and the army's composition of multiple ethnicities with different languages and customs.

On September 7, 1916, the German Emperor was given complete control of all the armed forces, and Austria-Hungary effectively became a puppet state of Germany. The Austrians viewed the German Army favourably; however, the Germans believed that Germany could do better.

By 1918, the economic situation had deteriorated, and governmental failure on the home front ended popular support for the war. The Austro-Hungarian monarchy collapsed with dramatic speed in the autumn of 1918. Nationalist movements seized the opportunity to erode social unity.

By the end of October, there was nothing left of the empire. On November 12, the German-Austrian National Council proclaimed the independent Republic of Austria, and Hungary followed suit.

By the end of the First World War in late 1918, Europe's social, political, and economic circumstances had fundamentally and irrevocably changed. The Allies had been victorious, but many of Europe's economies and infrastructures had been devastated, including those of the victors. These concerns were addressed in 1919 by a series of treaties between the victor countries and the defeated: the Treaty of Versailles with the Weimar Republic; the Treaty of Saint-Germain-en-Laye with Austria; and the Treaty of Trianon with Hungary, where demands such as reparations and a demilitarised Rhineland were laid out. These treaties regulated the new borders of Austria and Hungary, reducing them to small-sized and landlocked states. The Republic of Austria lost roughly 60 percent of the old Austrian Empire's territory. It also had to drop its plans for union with Germany, as it was not allowed to unite with Germany without League of Nations' approval.

The Second Polish Republic was also established as an independent sovereign state by the treaties, which included mutual recognition of the rights of citizens and rights of residence. Poland further solidified its independence in a series of border wars between 1918 and 1921 with Ukraine and Russia.

The German (Weimar Republic) government printed trillions of marks to pay reparations and compensate for the lack of funds, which created hyperinflation. The Germans largely viewed the massive reparations and the principle of a demilitarised Rhineland as insulting and unreasonable, and, during the interwar period, deep anger arose in the Weimar Republic over the conditions of the treaty.

During the worldwide economic crisis of the Great Depression in the 1930s, many people lost faith in liberal democracy, and countries turned to authoritarian regimes. The German people largely viewed the treaty as placing the blame, or war guilt, on Germany and Austria-Hungary and punishing them for their responsibility, rather than working out an agreement to assure long-term peace. Resentment over the treaty's terms was intensified by the instability of internal politics in Germany, as people on all sides of the political spectrum rejected the Weimar Republic and supported anyone who stood up to it.

The most extreme political aspirant to emerge from that situation was Austrian-born Adolf Hitler, who in 1921 became the leader of the Nazi Party. Hitler attempted a coup d'état in Munich in 1923 in what became known as the "Beer Hall Putsch", intending to establish a Greater Germanic Reich. Although he failed, Hitler was seen as a national hero among the German population. He was sentenced to five years in prison, serving just over a year. While there, he wrote his political manifesto, *Mein Kampf* (My Struggle), claiming a Jewish conspiracy to gain world leadership. This world view later became a central theme in Nazi propaganda to justify persecution and annihilation of the Jews.

The Nazis assumed full power in Germany on January 30, 1933, when Hitler became chancellor, demanding the undoing of the Versailles provisions and promoting pan-German unity and antisemitism. Their ambitious and aggressive domestic and foreign policies reflected their ideologies of antisemitism, unification of all Germans, the acquisition of *lebensraum* (living space), the elimination of Bolshevism, and the establishment of an Aryan master race over *untermenschen* (subhumans), such as Jews.

Austrian Jews knew what was unfolding in Germany. They followed Hitler's rallies and propaganda but mostly felt secure in their home country, where the growing National Socialist movement had little impact on their day-to-day lives, and which was banned by Chancellor Dollfuss, who supported Austrian independence.

Before the collapse of the Austro-Hungarian Empire, Jews there had lived relatively free and secure lives, supported by the liberal policies of Emperor Franz Jozef I. They flourished in the arts, sports, professional, academic, and business worlds. However, following the end of the First World War, anti-Jewish sentiment in Austria increased as antisemites began blaming Jews for the downfall of the empire. During the 1920s and early 1930s, antisemitic parades were frequent, and occasional mob violence erupted, although this was primarily contained to Vienna where the majority of Austrian Jews lived. For Jews living in Lower Austria's provincial territories, life continued largely unaffected by the shifting political landscape elsewhere.

From 1933, the Nazi Party immediately passed legislation that discriminated against German Jews. With these laws, they removed Jews from government positions and prevented them from engaging in social and cultural activities. Jewish businesses were boycotted, and members of professions like doctors and lawyers were prohibited from practising.

Austrian Nazi revolutionaries were emboldened by the events in Germany and assassinated Chancellor Dollfuss in a failed coup in July 1934.

The Nazis passed the Nuremburg Laws in 1935, which further eased the way for the persecution of Jews in Germany. These laws systematically detailed whether a person was a Jew based on their lineage, and barred Jews from marrying non-Jews.

German anti-Jewish legislation continued in the following years. Jews weren't allowed to work, and a curfew was enforced; Jewish assets were confiscated, and Jews were made to identify themselves as Jewish on their identification documents.

Meanwhile, Hitler was making increasingly aggressive territorial demands, threatening war if they weren't met. In 1936, the Austrian Chancellor, Schuschnigg, hoping to appease Hitler, signed the German-Austrian Agreement. This pact recognised Austria's independence, but the price was that Austria's foreign policy had to be consistent with Germany's. The agreement also allowed Nazis to hold official posts in Austria.

Nazi influence over Austrian politics spread to all areas of government, particularly the police, where Nazi sympathiser Seyss-Inquart was given total control. Nazis imprisoned in Austrian jails were released, and antisemitic violence escalated. And yet, few Austrian Jews realised the importance of fleeing to safety.

Schuschnigg could not hold Hitler off any longer, and in March 1938, Germany seized Austria and demanded the Sudetenland from Czechoslovakia.

Following the annexation of Austria, anti-Jewish decrees were swiftly enacted to suppress Jewish communities, and power was transferred to Berlin. The Nuremberg Race Laws were applied to Austria, and the systematic persecution and expulsion of Austrian Jews began.

At first, Hitler's aggressive moves met only with appeasement from the other major world powers. The League of Nations proved helpless. A decisive event was the 1938 Munich Conference, which formally approved Germany's annexation of the Sudetenland. Hitler promised it was his last territorial claim; nevertheless, he gradually became even more aggressive, and European governments finally realised that appeasement would not guarantee peace. By then, it was too late.

On September 1, 1939, Germany invaded Poland, triggering the Second World War. For Jews trapped in the Reich, there was nowhere to turn.

Part One
The Grandfather

Ignatz Salamon 1898-1963

1

Where it all Began

Burgenland 1925-1938

In April 1938, nine-year-old Sigi Salamon was walking home in the Austrian village of Rohrbach an der Teich. His surroundings were, as always, tranquil. This was a typical, sleepy Burgenland village, surrounded by fields and a lazy ripple of wooded hills. Then came a sound that startled him. It was faint at first, just the distant rumble of an engine, but as the source of the sound became visible, his chest tightened. It was a large black car full of officials, likely a Mercedes 260D, nicknamed the "Gestapo Gangster". When it pulled up beside him, a uniformed man peered out and barked: *"Hey, junge. Wo ist der Juden geschäft?"* (Hey, boy. Where's the Jew shop?)

Heart pounding, Sigi thought quickly and pointed in a random direction. As soon as the car was out of sight, he raced across the fields to his family home – a *gemischwarenhandlung*, or general store, the village's only shop – to warn his family that the Germans were coming. Sigi sensed danger.

For the Salamon family, as for most Jews, there was nowhere to hide. The men, who Sigi later remembered as being *Schutzstaffel* (SS), but who were likely officials from the Oberwart District Administration working in cooperation with the *Geheime Staatspolizei* (Gestapo), arrived shortly after he did. Thanks to Sigi's quick thinking, the family was expecting them, and this gave his father, Ignatz, just enough time to prepare what he would say to them. He hoped he would be able to talk their way to safety.

The officers stormed into the store, bringing a prickling atmosphere of contempt, fear, and outright threat. With no explanation, they gave the family 48 hours to leave. Ignatz stood his ground, protesting that he had residence rights as a Polish citizen, and that he and his family could not be treated like this. But it made no difference. With the Anschluss, everyone in Austria had become citizens of the Greater German Reich.

Amidst all the shouting and confusion, Sigi and his two brothers were bewildered and didn't fully understand what was happening.

The Salamon family's happy life in Rohrbach was over all at once. The growing sense of dread, which they had all experienced over the preceding months, fostered by the unfolding events in Nazi Germany and the increasing support for Austrian Nationalist movements, now manifested in the form of the officers who coldly stripped them not only of their home and business but most of their possessions.

The family was instructed to take with them only what they could carry. The rest, everything they owned, was forcibly signed over to the authorities, although the officials contemptuously demanded they sign a declaration saying that their departure was voluntary. This couldn't have been further from the truth.

With guns in their faces, they had no choice but to comply. In despair, they realised that the age-old narrative of persecution and displacement of Jews, which always carried with it the real threat of violence and murder, was starting to play out again, in the one place where Ignatz and Frieda had thought their boys would be safe to grow up.

The Salamon family consisted of my grandfather, Ignatz, aged 40, who was slightly built, with a receding hairline and a fashionable "toothbrush" moustache; my grandmother, Frieda, aged 36, short and well-rounded, with curly hair cut in a bob; and their three sons: my father Wally, aged two, stockily built with a mass of unkempt hair; and my uncles Otto, aged seven, blond with a straight fringe in a bowl-cut style; and Sigi, aged nine, with darker hair and deep-set eyes.

They had lived in Rohrbach an der Teich since 1933, and initially, it had seemed the perfect place to settle. They couldn't have known then that this day would be the start of an incredible journey of survival, escape, and rebirth, which would see them within just a few years settled in a foreign land where they would go on to reopen the family store and lay the foundations for the thriving business known today as Wally's Delicatessen.

For centuries, Burgenland was a place where Jews had lived free from persecution, under the protection of the Esterházy princes – a noble family with origins in the Middle Ages and the greatest landowner magnates in the Habsburg monarchy, to whom they were consistently loyal. In the later Austro-Hungarian Empire under Emperor Franz Josef, Jews enjoyed a period of prosperity, after being granted full equal rights under the emperor's liberalisation laws. The emperor also supported and financed the establishment of Jewish institutions and encouraged religious study. Jews contributed hugely to Austrian culture, flourishing in the arts, business, and academic worlds.

Jews happily coexisted alongside their non-Jewish neighbours, and in 1934, the Jewish population in Burgenland numbered around 4,000. Neither Ignatz nor Frieda were native to the area, but settling there made sense because they were Jewish and came from small rural communities in their respective countries of birth.

*

Ignatz's story began in southern Poland. He was born in Suchej (now called Sucha Beskidzka) in 1898, the son of Jozefa (Jozef) Salamon and Karoliny (Karolina) Fani Reichenbaum. His given Polish name was Ignacy, a shortened form of Ignatius. The name Ignatz, which he and his family used, is the German form of the name. Official Polish documents, however, refer to him as Ignacy.

Jozef and Karolina's families had lived contentedly in this part of Poland for several generations, benefiting from a prolonged period of statutory religious tolerance and social autonomy up to the turn of the 18th century. Following the Partition of Poland in 1795, the region fell under Austrian command and later became a province of the Austro-Hungarian Empire, known as Galicia. Jews in Galicia enjoyed the freedom to trade, educate, and follow their religious practices.

Before the Second World War, Poland was the heart of the European Jewish world, home to around three million Jews, the most significant minority in Poland. Jews and Poles spoke each other's languages (Yiddish was the common language among Jews in Galicia) and interacted in the markets and on the streets. Growing antisemitism did affect their lives, but Jews were still very much part of Poland, and Polish culture was, in part, Jewish.

Suchej was a small valley town on the Skawa River, near Kraków and close to the borders of Slovakia and Czechoslovakia. Before the Second World War, it had around 6,000 inhabitants, including about 500 Jews. With its 16th-century Renaissance castle and 17th-century parish church, Suchej was an attractive town to visit and where the Jewish community flourished.

Whilst Jozef was not religious, his wife, in common with so many in her community, was fervently so. She would fastidiously observe all the rituals of Jewish life, including keeping *kashrut* (Jewish dietary laws), and tried to instil this *yiddishkeit* (living by Jewish customs) into her children and grandchildren, although with limited success.

Jozef was one of seven children born to Izak Salamon and Rechel Flock in the nearby town of Tarnow in 1866, but four of his siblings had died as infants, probably due to typhoid or tuberculosis, which were prevalent at the time. It was common for families to have lots of children, but there was a high infant mortality rate due to a lack of medicines and immunisations. Jozef became a policeman, then a businessman, owning a general store and later a freight forwarding business. He was also conscripted into the Polish Army on more than one occasion.

Karolina, the daughter of Jakob Reichenbaum and Hani Flach, was born in 1873. Her only sibling, her brother Heinrich (Joachim), born in 1880, was an innkeeper.

Karolina and Jozef produced a large family: Ignatz had six younger siblings, five sisters and a brother, all born and raised in Suchej. They were always known in their families by their shortened names. The eldest was Rosalia (Ruzia), born in 1902, followed by Maksymillian (Maks) in 1904, Manya (Mina) in 1905, Josefina (Pepka) in 1907, Anna (Anda) in 1909, and Sabena (Sabka) in 1911. They were a close-knit family, so as the children grew up, they continued to stay in touch and meet regularly.

Ignatz left home in 1916, aged 17, when his conscription into the Polish Legion suspended his apprenticeship to Jozef as a trade merchant. He had worked in his father's companies since 1913, first as an intern and then from 1915 as independent head of the business following his father's conscription into the military.

His dreams and aspirations of following in his father's footsteps were instantly dashed. He fought for Polish independence in the Polish-Ukrainian War of 1918-1919, successfully resisting efforts to set up a West Ukrainian People's Republic following the Ukrainian Army's incursion into western Galicia.

He then served in the Polish Army during the Polish-Soviet War of 1919-1921, reaching the rank of regimental sergeant major with the 76th Lidski Rifles Regiment. Following the collapse of the Austro-Hungarian Empire and the establishment of an independent Polish state in 1919, the Soviets under Lenin wanted to take advantage of the chaos to spread communism into Europe. Poland's leaders, however, were keen to re-establish Poland's historic borders, secure their position within the region, and bolster their newly-gained independence.

Living conditions for the soldiers were terrible, with little food and warmth. At the front, things were particularly atrocious, where the muddy terrain made passage hard going. A photo of Ignatz at this time, aged about 20, in his army trench coat, peaked cap, and mud-encased boots, sums up the conditions. The regiment engaged in several key battles, including the Battle of Warsaw, which delivered Poland a decisive victory.

Ignatz in the Polish Army, circa 1918.

Ignatz performed well in the army. He oversaw the battalion's office for five months in Ciechanów, Poland, and on February 3, 1921, he was allowed to wear the Decoration of Honour for service. His discharge documents, dated April 20, 1921, read:

"During this time, he distinguished himself, besides of an exact knowledge of the office work, by an excellent spirit of work, exactness in carrying out the orders, orientation, and sense for organisation. He worked at the entire satisfaction of his superiors and his behaviour was always an exemplary one."

These qualities were to stand Ignatz in good stead in later life.

Ignatz (front row, far left) in the Polish Army, circa 1916.

*

Frieda's story began in a different country, but Ignatz's army career was to bring them together. She was born in Sereth, Bukovina,[1] in 1902, to Moses Stein, a merchant, and his wife, Rosa Kohlreiter. Frieda's family had lived in this area for generations, benefiting from the liberal attitude of the emperor towards Jews. She had an older brother, Yaakov, born in 1894, and they enjoyed a happy and close family life in Sereth, with many friends. Frieda loved dressing in her best clothes and posing for the camera and developed considerable talents as a seamstress.

---

[1] Bukovina was then part of the Austro-Hungarian province of Galicia but is now in Romania.

Frieda Stein, circa 1918.

Ignatz came into her life when he was billeted in Sereth at the home of Frieda's parents. While their native tongues differed, the young army recruit spoke German – the dominant language in the Austro-Hungarian Empire – as did Frieda, so communication was easy. The attraction was instant; by late 1918, romance had blossomed, and Ignatz was sending postcards to Frieda as his perilous military career continued.

By June 1922, Ignatz had been discharged from the army and had settled in Vienna, where he was preparing to marry Frieda. By the following June, she had joined him there. At the time, Austria was a far safer prospect for them than Poland, where the

Polish-Ukrainian War and the Polish-Soviet War had led to a rise in antisemitism. In the years leading up to their wedding, hundreds of Jews had been murdered in pogroms on Polish territories. Jewish army veterans, despite their service, were now viewed with suspicion and many were interned by the authorities. Against this backdrop, Ignatz and Frieda were eager to find a place to settle and raise a family without being in constant danger.

Other countries also offered better economic prospects for Jews. Wladyslaw Grabski, the Polish prime minister in 1920 and again from 1923 to 1925, introduced tax reforms that placed many Jewish businesses on the brink of ruin. The taxation policy, which was viewed as anti-Jewish, prompted many Jews to make *aliyah* (emigration to Palestine)—a mass migration that would go down in history as "Grabski's Aliyah".

For Ignatz and Frieda, Austria offered a suitable neutral territory for a Pole and a Romanian to settle, with German as their common language. They would not be lonely either: Frieda's brother Yaakov and his wife Zila also relocated to Vienna, where Zila had secured a position at Marmor Bank.

Ignatz and Fritzi (as she was affectionately known) married on July 24, 1923, in the Pazmanitentempel – a grand synagogue built in 1913, also known as the Kaiser Franz Josef Huldigungs Tempel. Arguably the most beautiful synagogue in Vienna, it was destroyed just 15 years after Ignatz and Frieda's marriage on Kristallnacht, the devastating pogrom of November 1938.

But on the day of Ignatz and Frieda's wedding, it was a place of joy and celebration, and nobody could imagine what lay ahead. They were married under a *chuppah* (wedding canopy) by Rabbi Dr Salomon Funk, with Moses Stein, Frieda's father, and Hermann Geffner, one of her relatives, as witnesses. The couple's proud parents looked on as Ignatz smashed a glass under his feet – an age-old ceremony which for many Jews symbolises the destruction of the Temple in Jerusalem. Another interpretation of this custom is that it will protect the marriage, with the implied prayer: "As this glass shatters, so may your marriage never break." Everyone in attendance would then have yelled *"mazel tov!"* (good luck). A flurry of congratulatory telegrams was received from family members who could not attend, including one from Ignatz's uncle, Heinrich (Joachim) Reichenbaum, who would be brutally murdered in Auschwitz just 19 years later. No photographs survive of the day, so I can only imagine how beautiful and happy the newly married couple must have looked.

For all the beauty and vibrancy of Vienna, the newlyweds longed for a more rural setting; by February 1925, they had moved south to the tiny hamlet of Kukmirn, in the Güssing district, southeast Burgenland, close to the Hungarian border. Yaakov and Zila kept pace, settling in a nearby village, Neuberg, in 1925, where they opened two shops, one run by Yaakov and the other by Zila.

Meanwhile, Ignatz and Frieda opened a general store in nearby Eisenhüttl. Ignatz is listed in documents from the time as a *kaufmann* (merchant) and a driver. He had a pick-up truck, possibly a Ford Model T Roadster, with a low-sided flatbed rear end, running boards, a starting handle at the front to crank up the engine, and a canvas roof, effectively making it a convertible pickup. It was his pride and joy, and he enjoyed maintaining it, a hobby that lasted well into his later years. He would drive around local villages selling wares from the store, including fruit and vegetables, poultry, basic hardware items, and clothing sewn by Frieda, and he looked both proud and stylish in a photograph taken at the time with his driver's cap and goggles. Frieda was also a key part of the business and was certified by Burgenland Merchant Associations on four occasions as a commercial assistant to Ignatz. This was a good grounding for the later business they would open together.

Ignatz, Frieda, Yaakov, and Zila were probably the only Jews in their respective villages, and the couples met up regularly. However, the broader area of Burgenland was home to seven thriving Jewish communities following several centuries during which Jews could live, work, and practise their religion freely in the region. They felt safe here.

Ignatz in his pick-up truck, Eisenhüttl, circa 1926.

Family photo. Left to right: Frieda, Ignatz,
Zila, Yaakov, circa 1923.

However, not everything was going according to plan. According to an announcement in a local newspaper, Ignatz's business went bankrupt in February 1932, and settlement proceedings over the assets were opened in Vienna at the Regional Courts of the Palace of Justice on April 18, 1932. It's unclear why their business failed or what the outcome of these proceedings was, but probably, after settling their debt, they moved on from Eisenhüttl.

The move, in 1933, brought them to Rohrbach an der Teich, a tiny village of just a few hundred people set on the banks of the Teichbach, a tributary of the Pinka. Located 20 kilometres from the Hungarian border, it was charmingly picturesque, with a pretty village square and the white steeple of the Church of the Ascension of Christ dominating the otherwise flat skyline. However, it lacked modern amenities such as proper pavements, running water, and electricity. Sigi later recalled that water had to be carried into the house and poured into a large metal tub for bathing.

Photographs from the time show a stream, possibly a sewer, running along an open ditch in a rough road. It was predominantly a farming community, and many houses had large, shuttered doorways, designed to enable the householders to bring cows in from the fields into their backyards. While it was, in some ways, a more complicated life than the city, it was a beautiful and peaceful setting, as it still is today. The Teichbach still traces its sparkling path through the village, the air is fresh and clean, and beyond the small collection of houses, green fields unfurl under big skies dotted with rolling clouds.

When Ignatz and Frieda moved there, they already had Sigi (Sigmund, born January 1929) and Otto (born January 1931), aged four and two, respectively. My father, Wally (Walter), followed on August 30, 1936. A swastika is stamped on my father's birth certificate, placed there in February 1939 when the family had to later register with the German authorities in Vienna. The swastika was a symbol long used in various Eurasian and native American cultures which the Nazis appropriated as their party insignia at the start of the 20th century. Was this Nazi symbol placed there to show who was in control, or to strike fear into the hearts of Jews? It certainly would have worked on both accounts. Ignatz and Frieda would have been under no illusions that they were now at their mercy.

Today's generations might think about the Holocaust merely as a dark period in human history. But this document has always been a chilling reminder of how closely my family was entwined with it. This document, more than any other I have seen, makes me realise that my father, his parents and brothers, were all survivors of the Holocaust. The term survivor is often misunderstood as applying solely to those Jews who survived the concentration camps. However, in the wider sense, anyone who lived after being persecuted by the Nazis was a survivor. Survivors are classified as first-generation, second-generation, third-generation, and so on. I have often wondered if I should be considered second-generation or third-generation. I guess my father was a first-generation survivor, so I'm second-generation. Indeed, my generation was the first to be born in the UK.

Wally's birth certificate, with swastika.

My father's Hebrew name was given after a relative, Hersch Salamon, his grandfather Izak's brother. His Hebrew name was Zvi, meaning gazelle (although I was always told it meant wolf), or Hersch in Polish. He always used to say it as Hersch-Zvi.

The family likely moved to Rohrbach an der Teich because a shop became available there. Located at 30 Vordergasse on the main road through the village, it was a small, single-storey unit with shuttered windows and a few short wooden steps leading from the road to the threshold. Here, they sold poultry, fruit, vegetables, other foodstuffs, and hardware. A sign outside the store advertised Sphinx Benzin, a motor engine lubricating oil. The family kept chickens in the backyard for eggs, which were put to practical use in the business, as shown by an advertisement in a local newspaper for *striezel* (a traditional kind of milk bread) made with country butter and mushrooms, known as *waldschwamme* (forest sponges).

Wally and Frieda with chickens, Rohrbach an der Teich, circa 1937.

The Salamon family store in Rohrbach an der Teich, circa 1938.

Before 1938, life was good, if not financially abundant. Frieda continued sewing; she loved to make clothes, especially shirts, which she sold around the local villages on the weekends. Family legend has it that the three small boys were sometimes put to sit in herring barrels to keep them out of trouble while my grandmother worked. They integrated well into the local community. Ignatz was listed in *Die Vereinszeitung*, a local club newspaper, as one of several donors yearly to the much-admired fire brigade, in which their neighbour, Leopold Lackinger, held a prominent position.

They stayed close to their families back home but only visited occasionally. A photograph, taken around 1930, shows a family gathering in front of a wooden picket fence outside a dwelling, possibly the family home in Suchej. A baby Sigi is sitting on Frieda's lap, with Ignatz standing behind them, smartly dressed in his trilby and suit. Next to him is Romek, his brother-in-law, resplendent in his Polish Army uniform, with Ruzia, his wife and Ignatz's sister, sitting in front of him holding her first-born, Nusia, on her lap.

Ignatz's other sisters are also in the photograph, and one of their husbands and a child, probably Manya's. In the centre of the picture are Ignatz's parents, Jozef and Karolina, looking proud, surrounded by their family, if a little unsure of themselves.

Family gathering, circa 1930 – front row, left to right:
Manya, Karolina, Jozef, Ruzia with Nusia on her lap,
Frieda with Sigi on her lap. Back row, left to right: brother-in-law
and child, Anna, Sabena, Romek, Ignatz.

Another photograph taken a few years later shows Frieda, Sigi, Otto, and two of her sisters-in-law dressed up in their best outfits, including hats for the women and caps for the boys, outside a large brick building. This was probably a trip to synagogue for *Yom-Tov* (a Jewish holiday), when it's traditional for Jews to gather with their families to celebrate.

But there was a growing sense of unease behind the reassuring rhythms of daily life. The family had made friends in the village, and the boys often played with the village kids, but Sigi was hurt

Synagogue visit, Suchej, circa 1934. Left to right:
Sigi, Anna, Manya, Frieda, Otto.

when they made up a song about him and taunted him for being Jewish. When the other boys joined the *Hitlerjugend* (Hitler Youth) – the youth wing of the Nazi party – not knowing any better Sigi wanted to join too, but found himself excluded on account of being Jewish. These cruelties would seem small in the light of what lay ahead.

The family would have been aware of what was going on in Nazi Germany, and the increased support for nationalist movements at home would not have gone unnoticed. However, they were happy in Rohrbach, and the troubles seemed far off. Did they believe they would be immune, living as they were in a backwater in southern Austria? I wonder what conversations, if any, they had about this. Did they discuss it with Frieda's brother, Yaakov?

Maybe they thought that, as Hitler was Austrian himself, no harm would come to them. They may have surmised that other Jews in the region weren't uprooting in droves, so why should they? Ultimately, they followed their instincts and remained. Later, their intuition would prove their salvation, but they could not have been more wrong.

2

Nazi Persecution

The Anschluss 1938

In the 1930s, the Republic of Austria was still a relatively new state, created by treaties signed after the First World War. Now less than half the size of the former Austro-Hungarian Empire, Austria was weak and potentially volatile. Much of its population believed their future would be more secure and prosperous if Austria united with Germany. Post-war treaties forbade this, but it didn't stop many people from viewing unification as the way forward.

The führer, Adolf Hitler, railed against the new post-war borders. He became the German chancellor in 1933 and gradually introduced more anti-Jewish measures. His vision for a Nazi German empire, outlined in his political manifesto published in 1925, *Mein Kampf*, included the union of Austria and Germany to make a Greater Germany (the Reich). His plans also included the removal of Jews, and as his power grew, he did all he could to make this happen by encouraging antisemitism.

In May 1933, Austrian Nazis launched a campaign of protests and physical attacks on Jewish businesses. The following year there was a failed Nazi coup, in which the Austrian chancellor, Engelbert Dollfuss, was assassinated. In the aftermath, the replacement chancellor, Kurt von Schuschnigg, came under growing pressure to cooperate with the Germans. In July 1936 he signed the

Austro-German Agreement with Hitler. While this was seemingly a pact of cooperation, it was a calculated move by Hitler to gain influence and control over Austria, and which paved the way for increased Nazi influence. This came to fruition at a meeting with Hitler in February 1938, at the Berghof – the chancellor's primary residence above the town of Berchtesgaden – when von Schuschnigg was intimidated into appointing Nazis to his cabinet and granting the Nazi Party full political rights, seriously compromising Austrian independence from Germany.

In a final effort to preserve Austrian independence, Schuschnigg called a plebiscite, confident that most of the population would vote in support. This infuriated Hitler. He demanded that Schuschnigg call off the vote and resign as chancellor, threatening invasion if he didn't comply. He also demanded that the Austrian Nazi, Arthur Seyss-Inquart, be made the new Austrian chancellor.

Schuschnigg caved in and resigned, concluding his resignation speech with the prophetic words: *"Gott beschütze Österreich"* (God protect Austria). Shortly after midnight on March 12, the Austrian president Wilhelm Miklas appointed Seyss-Inquart as Austria's new chancellor, opening the way for a German invasion. Unlike most invasions, however, many Austrians celebrated, seeing it as the only workable solution to the country's economic challenges, military weakness, and social problems. Thousands paraded in support of the new regime, and violence against Jews soared.

On March 15, Hitler gave a triumphal address to 200,000 cheering Austrians gathered at the Heldenplatz, a public square in front of the town hall in the heart of Vienna. This was a terrifying moment for Jews now trapped in the country.

It is hard to imagine what it was like to be there at that time. Overnight, worlds were shattered, dreams and aspirations smashed, and families torn apart. Attacking Jews quickly became the norm; former neighbours turned tormenters and informants.

Jubilant crowds welcoming Hitler to Vienna, 1938.

Genia Shuerman was a Jew who lived in the same building in Vienna as my grandparents in 1939 and later, like them, ended up living in Cardiff. She summed up the feeling of terror felt by the Jewish community in an interview recorded in 1988 by my mother for The National Sound Archive project, The National Life Story Collection – The Living Memory of the Jewish Community:

"I remember the morning Hitler's troops marched into Vienna. It was all so quiet. All the shops were shut, yet we knew something was about to happen. People stood around in groups on the streets, talking and waiting. Before long we heard the ominous sounds of hundreds of Nazi voices chanting the Horst Wessel song and Heil Hitler over and over again. That same night many families were arrested, including myself and my daughter, dressed only in our nightclothes. We were released three days later as I was still a Polish citizen, although that was revoked soon afterwards.

"We all were ordered to assemble in Prater Strasse centre to listen to Hitler. He had ordered all the prisons to be opened, and the criminals were let loose, beating and robbing Jews and looting shops and houses. We heard the sounds of terrible screaming every night but were too frightened to venture out to investigate, as we heard that anyone who did so was beaten up, or even killed, by Nazis.

"The Gestapo were knocking on doors and ordering the residents to leave their homes at once, whereupon they were taken to prison. They had to sign a form that they were handing over their entire possessions to them. My husband and my two brothers were arrested. Conditions in the prisons were terrible; prisoners were cold, hungry, and had to do hard manual labour.

"Every night was full of terror, with the sounds of screaming and knocking on doors. We had to listen to the crowds chanting Heil Hitler continuously."

The events in Austria of March 11-13, 1938, are known as the Anschluss, literally meaning a joining or unification. But this was, in every aspect, an annexation of Austria by Nazi Germany, and it had a devastating effect. From this point on, the Nazis transferred power to Berlin, from where they directed persecution against Austrian Jews and engineered their eventual forced emigration. As antisemitic violence steadily increased, Jews were regularly assaulted, humiliated, and forced to carry out demeaning tasks, such as cleaning the streets and public toilets with toothbrushes while circled by baying hordes of locals.

Gradually, new laws removed further freedoms. Jews were barred from public transport and public places. Thousands were arrested. Nobody knew what would happen next or how to escape it. Desperate and without hope, many took their own lives.

By the time the officials arrived in Rohrbach an der Teich and asked Sigi for directions to "the Jew store", the Nazis were energetically advancing their mission to make Austria *Judenfrei* – Jew-free – a policy that would eventually be applied to the whole Reich.

The precise details of how they would achieve this were a work in progress. The ongoing practice of persecuting Jews and depriving them of their livelihoods and liberties was designed to encourage Jews to leave of their own accord, and many thousands had already done so. But most Jews couldn't go, and indeed many didn't want to; after all, they were proud Austrians, and it was their home. Jews, therefore, had to be forced to leave.

Burgenland was a prime target, as it was known to be a place where there was a flourishing Jewish community. The new *gauleiter* (governor) of the region, Tobias Portschy, was a committed Nazi Party official with an obsessive allegiance to Hitler. He devised a plan to remove all Jews from the area quickly. An ultimatum to leave Burgenland by April 19, 1938, or face immediate arrest and deportation to a concentration camp, was followed soon by more draconian measures, including the forced closure of Jewish businesses, the confiscation of Jewish money and possessions, and a ban on trading with Jews.

This was a localised policy, the first of its kind in the Reich, and a model so successfully applied that it would be followed elsewhere. What would happen to the Jews who were forced from the region, or where they would go, was not of Portschy's concern. It was for the Nazis in Vienna to get the Jews out of the country altogether.

By April 1938, this devastating tide had fully hit the Salamon family. After filling out a questionnaire at the police station giving full details of all their assets, Ignatz was given a meagre 3,000 reichsmarks in compensation (equivalent to about £1,000 at the time, or £15,000 today), which they would have to rely on for subsistence in Vienna. The confiscated assets – the store, their money and possessions, and Ignatz's treasured truck – were passed to a newly established body set up by the Nazis to control the expropriation of confiscated assets, the *Vermögensverkehrsstelle* (Government Property Transaction Office), which used them to fund the emigration of Jews from Austria. I am somewhat surprised that they received any compensation at all, however meagre.

However, this was at the very start of the Nazi process of ethnic cleansing, which would be repeated throughout the Reich with ever more horrific intent, and I suppose there was still a modicum of due process around the evictions.

This pattern was repeated throughout the region, and before long the ethnic cleansing of Burgenland was complete. The family were loaded into crowded trucks, along with many other Burgenland Jews, taking with them only what they could carry. They were transported to Vienna, where the Nazis were implementing a forced emigration policy at pace.

I have tried to picture this scene many times to grasp the enormity of it: my grandparents being forcibly uprooted at gunpoint, with three young children, aged only nine, seven, and two. I wonder if they went quietly, whether they were tearful or kept their composure for their boys' sake. Knowing what I now know about my grandparents, I sense it was the latter. And how did my father and his brothers react? Did they understand what was happening?

At this time, forced emigration was the Nazi's primary method of removing the Jews. Persecution was the main tool to encourage people to leave, together with the threat of arrest and imprisonment in concentration camps, from which few emerged. It mattered little to them whether people left by legal or illegal means. This was a practical plan for as long as the borders were open, but it ended abruptly once the war started. More sinister methods would be developed later, but for now the Nazis wanted – and forced – the Jews who could leave to do so.

The Nazis also cynically manipulated members of Vienna's Jewish community to organise the expulsion, convincing them that by co-operating they would best protect their community. Rabbi Benjamin Murmelstein of the *Israelitische Kultusgemeinde Wien* (IKG), the representative body for the Jewish community of Vienna, was a key facilitator of the deportation plan, reporting to *Untersturmführer* (second lieutenant) Adolf Eichmann, the SS officer who oversaw Jewish emigration. Eichmann was keenly aware of the advantages of using Jewish community leaders to persuade Jews to leave, but the strategy caused recriminations within the Jewish community and an enduring sense of betrayal.

Amidst all this, Ignatz and his family lived in Vienna in virtual destitution. The city was a frightening place for Jews: Nazi insignia adorned the buildings, and hostile soldiers patrolled the streets, giving the Nazi salute as they went by. Ignatz knew they could not remain there for long; they would have to get out of Austria, but the doors to freedom slammed shut one by one. At first, Ignatz had his eyes set on Poland; after all, he was a proud Polish citizen. Increasingly desperate to find a way out of the country, even if Poland was far from a haven, he pleaded his case, placing his hopes for saving his family in the hands of soul-crushing bureaucracy.

But Poland refused to accept them, and on August 21, 1938, Ignatz was deprived of his Polish nationality, rendering him stateless. This followed a decree by the Polish government denaturalising all Poles who had lived abroad for five years or more – a move designed to stop Polish Jews from being able to return to their homeland.

It was a massive blow at the time. Still, it helped to save their lives, because in October that same year, Adolf Eichmann ordered that all Polish Jews in Austria must be deported to Poland, where the family would almost certainly have been murdered in the Holocaust.

Ironically, by an extraordinary twist of fate, my grandfather's life may previously have been saved by the fact that he was still a Polish citizen in May 1938, when thousands of Austrian, German, and stateless Jewish men (but not Poles) were arrested and sent to Dachau concentration camp.

Dachau was a spectre all Jews feared. The few people released from the camp were forbidden to discuss conditions inside. However, word still got around of torture and beatings, of people being frozen and starved to death, and of inmates being forced to stand on parade outdoors for hours at a time until some dropped down dead. There were tales of desperate men throwing themselves onto the electric fence – something that always led to further torture for those who remained.

Ignatz's submission to the IKG's *Auswanderungsabteilung* (emigration department), stating that he had no monthly income, shows how dire the family's situation was.

At this time, they were living at 20 Zirkusgasse in Vienna's Second District (known as Leopoldstadt), likely with Frieda's brother Yaakov and his wife Zila, who had been ordered to leave their village of Neuberg, and probably with others too, forced together in cold and cramped conditions.

Leopoldstadt, named after the holy Roman Emperor, Leopold I, who had forcibly expelled Jews from the area in 1670, is in the city's heart, edged by the Danube Canal and the Danube River. During the Austro-Hungarian Empire, many Jewish immigrants again flocked to Leopoldstadt, leading to it being called *Mazzesinsel* (Island of Matzo, referring to the unleavened bread eaten during Passover). It was a maze of tightly packed streets, with many synagogues for its 60,000 Jews, cafes, theatres, and shops. The picturesque Prater Park, with its famous giant Ferris wheel, was a focal point for family gatherings.

They were probably helped to find accommodation by the IKG, which Eichmann allowed to offer charitable aid to incoming Jews in the full expectation that they would later, more easily, go along with his forced emigration plan, and which he would use the IKG to implement.

Destitute, hungry, and despairing of how they could protect their children, Ignatz and Frieda lived from hand to mouth, accepting charity where it was offered. I can only imagine how humiliating this must have been for such a proud, previously self-sufficient couple.

Like most of Austria's remaining Jews, who were now almost all living in poverty in Vienna, they had to rely on the charitable support of the IKG, which provided cash, housing, and some basic furnishings with the help of local volunteers. For food, charity-run soup kitchens, funded partly by donations from the Central British Fund for German Jewry (a forerunner of World Jewish Relief), were a much-needed lifeline. To further assuage the fears of the Jewish community, the IKG was allowed to run a small number of Jewish schools and limited medical facilities. Sigi and Otto were enrolled in school, which would have given them some sense of normality amidst the upheaval they had experienced, but my father, Wally, was too young and stayed by his parents' side.

As the pressure on the family intensified, so did Ignatz's efforts to find a way to get them all out of the country. On May 12, 1938, and again on June 1, 1938, he submitted questionnaires to the Welfare Centre of the IKG's emigration department, saying he wanted to take Frieda and the three children to America. He listed relatives in the US: three cousins, an aunt, and two uncles. He completed a questionnaire for the US Consulate and was put on a waiting list pending submission of further documentation, particularly an affidavit of support.

Ignatz's US emigration application to the IKG, 1938.

29

However, getting a visa wasn't easy. The US opposed large-scale immigration, and only 20,000 visas were granted in 1938 out of 300,000 applications from Germany and Austria.

Ignatz knew that the clock was ticking. Just walking out on the street was now dangerous for him and his family, with Jews taunted and beaten, seemingly at every opportunity. Jewish shops were looted and scrawled with the word *Jude* (Jew) in dripping red paint, cafes and shops displayed signs reading "*Juden verboten*" (Jews forbidden), and signs everywhere encouraged people "*kauf nicht bei Juden*" (don't buy from Jews).

There was to be no justice; my family knew that by now, and by October 1938, the situation had approached boiling point. The violence against Jews became more savage and frequent, and in Leopoldstadt, attacks on synagogues surged. Now, more than ever, they feared even to leave their cold and cramped home, yet they also longed to be as far away from it as possible, in another country, free from persecution.

Then, on November 7, 1938, an event occurred that would make things much worse.

3

The End Game

Kristallnacht 1938

Life in Vienna was perilous, and the family had to plan every move cautiously. Abuse and torment from both the Nazis and the Viennese public were commonplace. In later years, Sigi recounted that he and his brothers were afraid to go to sleep at night. During the day, he would take circuitous routes home from school to avoid abuse – or worse – from the locals.

As the Nazis stoked aggression against Jews, the atmosphere in Vienna resembled a tinderbox, and eventually it transformed from smouldering to fully ablaze. The catalyst was an act by a 17-year-old Polish Jew living in Paris, named Herschel Grynszpan. His parents had been brutally expelled from Germany, supposedly to return to Poland, but had ended up being held in a refugee camp at the border.

Grynszpan was already under intense pressure; he was living in Paris illegally, making his situation precarious, and it seemed there was no way to help his parents. On November 7, 1938, Grynszpan visited the German Embassy to confront the ambassador. In the ensuing melee, Grynszpan fired five bullets into Ernst vom Rath, a junior embassy official, who died two days later.

When news of Rath's death reached Hitler, he was in Munich at a Nazi Party celebration. The assassination provided a welcome pretext to strike out against the Jewish population with unprecedented brutality. With Hitler's backing, Nazi propaganda minister Joseph Goebbels urged violent reprisals, labelling Rath's murder as a calculated act by Jews. The Nazi Party not only condoned retaliatory action but also orchestrated it, with Nazi officials calling their home districts and communicating Goebbel's instructions.

On November 9, Gestapo chief Heinrich Müller ordered a series of actions throughout the Reich against Jews, and especially their synagogues, which sparked violence in the streets. About 7,500 Jewish businesses and more than 1,000 synagogues, cemeteries, and Jewish institutions were attacked, desecrated, and destroyed. Looting and arson were rife; holy Torah scrolls were burned in the streets, and Jewish families were terrorised and beaten inside and outside their homes. Following orders given by Nazi leaders, police forces and fire brigades didn't intervene to stop the destruction.

Contrary to what the Nazis claimed at the time, it's now believed that hundreds of Jews died, by suicide, murdered on the night of the riots, or in the aftermath because of their injuries.

A ruined synagogue after Kristallnacht, November 1938.

The pogrom of November 9-10 became known as Kristallnacht, or the Night of Broken Glass, due to the sheer volume of shattered glass that littered the streets in the aftermath of the destruction. It spanned Nazi Germany and Austria, reaching occupied areas in the Sudetenland, but the violence was particularly severe in Vienna.

Damaged shop after Kristallnacht, November 1938.

When recounting her memories in 1988, Genia Shuerman recalled the events in Vienna during those fateful days:

"We felt something in the air; there was a mounting tension. We stayed indoors and heard Nazi groups going from house to house searching for food and carrying away goods and furniture. We were ordered to stand in the centre of Prater in the middle of the night, so we could see and hear 'what you Jews deserve', and we saw houses and shops being ransacked. Suddenly, the whole town was ablaze with our beautiful synagogues burning. Thugs carried the torn and burning fragments of our holy Torah scrolls aloft. Then we were violently pushed aside to make way for Hitler to come through and address the crowds.

"In the next days, you didn't dare go outside. Those who did
were beaten up, arrested, and carted off to prison or the camps."

This first-hand account of that fateful night evokes outrage,
anger, and sadness, even after all this time. No matter how often
I have seen depictions of these events in films or read about them
in books, to read a first-hand account from a witness to the events,
someone I knew, really brings home the terror they experienced.

While the Nazis later claimed the violence was disorganised
and perpetrated by locals, it was carefully orchestrated, with Nazi
Stormtroopers and the Hitler Youth leading the attacks while
disguised in civilian clothing. Special efforts were made to protect
non-Jewish homes, businesses, and official premises involved in
Eichmann's programme of Jewish expulsion. It was later reported,
ironically, that he was angry at the amount of valuable Jewish assets
that were destroyed – estimated to be worth more than 225 million
reichsmarks – as they could have been helpful to the Nazis.

In the following days, some 30,000 Jews were rounded up and
transported to Buchenwald or Dachau concentration camps,
although there is no evidence to suggest Ignatz was sent there.
These men hadn't committed any crime; the police arrested them
simply for being Jewish. In the concentration camps, the men were
humiliated and subjected to violent attacks, and many hundreds
were murdered or died from their treatment.

The pogrom and the arrests terrified and shocked Jewish
families and communities. For many, this was the final straw, as they
realised there was no future for Jews in the German Reich. Many
historians regard that night of vandalism, violence, and persecution
as the beginning of the Holocaust, marking the transition from the
discrimination against Jews that had persisted since 1933 to their
later systematic persecution.

The Salamon family found themselves in grave danger as the
events unfolded. At 20 Zirkusgasse, they lived next door to a grand
Turkish synagogue, built in 1885 for the Sephardic community in
Vienna (descendants of families expelled from Spain and Portugal

under the Inquisition in the 15th century). Sigi later recollected his fear as he listened to German guards arguing while they pulled the books from the synagogue and broke all the windows. Then he saw everything go up in flames as the synagogue burned down. Today, a plaque at the site commemorates these events.

Precisely what happened to the family on Kristallnacht has not been recorded: the rioters may have forcibly evicted them, or their building may also have burned down or been irrevocably damaged. Whatever the cause, records show that by December 27, 1938, they had moved to a different address: Apartment 10, 7 Kleine Pfarrgasse, Leopoldstadt – a five-storey block built in 1903 in the Secessionist style. The building was adorned with four mascarons[2] on the fifth floor. It is possible that the IKG helped them find this new accommodation, probably in an apartment vacated by other Jews who had already emigrated.

Steven outside 7 Kleine Pfarrgasse, Leopoldstadt, Wien II, in 2023.

---

[2] Ornamental elements depicting a frightening human face, originally intended to frighten away evil spirits so they would not enter the building

Today, 7 Kleine Pfarrgasse has a *Stolperstein* in the pavement outside. A *Stolperstein* – meaning "stumbling block" – is a small brass plate inscribed with the names and life dates of victims of Nazi extermination or persecution. It is positioned at the last place a person freely chose to live before they fell victim to Nazi terror. The *Stolperstein* outside 7 Kleine Pfarrgasse reads:

"Hier Wohnten (Here Lived)"

"Ernst (Elio) Gottfried 24.8.1889
Am 12.8.1942 *Nach Auschwitz Deportiert* (Deported to Auschwitz)
Im Holocaust Ermordet (Murdered in the Holocaust)"

"Anna Gottfried 15.3.1899
Am 6.9.1943 *Nach Auschwitz Deportiert* (Deported to Auschwitz)
Im Holocaust Ermordet (Murdered in the Holocaust)"

"Paula Kohn *geb.* (born) Gottfried 10.8.1914
Am 31.7.1943 Nach Auschwitz *Deportiert* (Deported to Auschwitz)
Im Holocaust Ermordet (Murdered in the Holocaust)"

"Lilly (Lucy) Weiner *geb.* (born) Fuchs 15.9.1920
Am 6.10.1944 *Gemeinsam Mit Säugling Dan Nach Auschwitz Deportiert* (Deported to Auschwitz together with infant Dan)
Im Holocaust Ermordet (Murdered in the Holocaust)"

These people, including three from one family, were possibly my grandparents' neighbours, and perhaps even friends, in those last days before they left Vienna. Their fate, being murdered at Auschwitz, was the same fate facing Ignatz and Frieda if they were not able to escape. They didn't yet know it, but on January 20,

1942, at the Wannsee Conference, SS Officer Reinhard Heydrich would present his plan for the eradication, by extermination, of all Jews in Europe. This would become known as "the Final Solution to the Jewish Question" and lead to the murder of six million Jews across Europe.

4

A Break for Freedom

Kitchener Camp 1939

While the Nazis wanted rid of the Jews, managing to emigrate was, in fact, agonisingly difficult. The Nazis wanted their methods of making Austria Jew-free to be copied across all areas of the Reich, but the sticking point was that other countries were unwilling to accept them.

Torn between a sense of moral responsibility to help the Jews and fear that an influx of immigrants would upset their economies, many countries were at an impasse. In July 1938, a conference was organised at Evian in France to discuss the refugee crisis. Delegates from 32 countries attended, but the results did little to alleviate the situation. Most of the speakers at best offered excuses rather than help; at worst, they displayed indifference or outright distaste for Jews. Potential issues such as competition for jobs and social support were expounded, and this only served to embolden Hitler further.

Eventually, it was agreed that each country would set its immigration quotas and rules. The US required immigrants to have a sworn statement from a citizen promising employment and accommodation. Palestine, then governed by Britain under mandate, was turning away boatloads of refugees, with many drowning at sea or being sent to camps. However, a small proportion made it to Palestine illegally. In the UK, immigrants faced tight admission rules based on financial means and the ability to take on agricultural or domestic service jobs.

Proving financial means was near impossible, however, for most Jews. They had been stripped of all their money and belongings by the Nazis, who then used those assets to fund their expulsion. Things worsened further after Kristallnacht, when Reichsmarschall Hermann Göring pinned the blame for the damage on the Jews and issued them with a bill equivalent to about £5billion in today's money – a ploy to enable the Nazis to confiscate any insurance payments made to Jews to repair the damage done during Kristallnacht. The Nazis may have been happy to be rid of Jews, but they ensured that any remaining money the Jews had was left behind.

This devastating pogrom also served as an excuse to rob Jews of most of their last remaining rights and freedoms. To shame them and to make them instantly identifiable, Jews were forced to add the name Sara (for women) or Israel (for men) to their names — I have seen identification cards for all five members of my family attesting to this.

Desperate and even more determined after these events, Ignatz wrote letter after letter to the US, including his cousin Harry Salamon, seeking someone to provide an affidavit to support the family's emigration. Some families managed to get their children out of Austria via the Kindertransport (child transport) rescue effort, which brought 10,000 children, frightened and alone, from Europe to the UK. For reasons unknown, this wasn't the case for my family.

While their efforts to find an escape route continued, they had to focus on survival and keeping what little freedom remained. In 1939, Frieda's beloved brother Yaakov, his wife Zila and their two children, Yitzhak and Ruthi, were imprisoned after a Gestapo mass arrest. The Gestapo was effectively the Nazi secret police, working without any institutional supervision and endowed with special rights. It monitored and persecuted those individuals the Nazi state had declared "enemies of the state and the people", although the criteria they used to determine this was entirely at the mercy of their whims. Mass arrests were used as a tool to frighten people and keep them suppressed and obedient. Tales circulated of the torture endured in Gestapo headquarters, although few who went inside ever emerged.

It is not clear why Yaakov and Zila were arrested – quite possibly it was for no reason other than being Jewish. It was a grim and terrifying experience, but the inmates supported each other in whatever way they could. Yitzhak later remembered some of the other prisoners throwing them candies. They were eventually released from prison after a fortuitous visit from the Red Cross, but by now it was starkly evident to Ignatz and Frieda that to be truly safe, they must escape the country.

At the behest of Adolf Eichmann, the IKG was hard at work trying to make this happen. Representatives travelled widely to consult with Jewish organisations and secure money for essentials such as transport, visas, and passports. Eichmann, known by Jews in Vienna as *"Das Teufels Stellverterer"* (the Devil's Deputy), creamed off much of the money the IKG managed to generate. But he became increasingly frustrated by the number of Jews remaining in Vienna. Feeling the process wasn't progressing fast enough, he became more amenable to mass emigration schemes to resolve "the Jewish Question" – a term that predated Nazi rule, but which took on far more sinister connotations as it became central to Nazi policy.

One was a plan to grant 4,000 adult Jewish men – half from Vienna and the other half from Berlin – entry to the UK. They would live at Kitchener Camp, a disused camp in a former First World War military barracks at Richborough Port, in Sandwich, Kent. The plan took root after the horrors of Kristallnacht sparked a sense of moral duty among several key decision-makers in the UK government.

Professor Sir Norman Bentwich of the Central British Fund for German Jewry (CBF) persuaded the British government to admit this small number of refugees. However, they added some tight stipulations, including that the CBF must financially support the men and, crucially, that they would not make the UK their permanent home.

The plan, which was named the Richborough Transit Camp Scheme, had to be executed quickly; the situation in Europe was becoming ever more desperate and war was looming. Kitchener Camp, long since abandoned, was in a poor state of repair, so local tradesmen were initially tasked with making it habitable. That job was then continued by the first waves of refugees, who started to arrive from the beginning of 1939 and were selected on account of their valuable skills.

Brothers Phineas and Jonas May, both members of the Jewish Lads' Brigade who had previously run teenagers' summer camps, were given responsibility for managing the camp. This was to be an exceedingly difficult undertaking, but they rose to the task, with Jonas taking the role of camp director and Phineas becoming its quartermaster, responsible for the day-to-day running of the camp.

The facility was big: it included 48 huts, each of which could accommodate 72 men in double bunks; two large dining rooms; a library; an orchestra; a cinema; a hospital; and a Post Office.

The men were encouraged to bring personal items, such as books and musical instruments, and camp life included cultural activities such as concerts and art lessons, as well as practical tuition in English and skilled trades. The men also conducted renovation work to make the run-down camp more habitable.

Some of them served as camp guards, but this was not a prison: the men were free to come and go, make social visits, explore the local area, and, of course, visit overseas consulates to make essential arrangements for onward emigration or the arrival of their relatives.

In Vienna, the IKG decided which men could go to Kitchener Camp. The decision to send men, rather than women and children, was contentious but was probably based on the belief that men were at higher risk of being sent to concentration camps or being murdered in other ways. It was also hoped that their wives and children could follow once the men were in the UK.

The plan may have appealed to Eichmann, who had to approve the visas, because he would save money on imprisoning men. This is borne out by the fact that men who had been interned in Dachau and

Buchenwald after Kristallnacht were prioritised for the scheme, as part of an agreement with Eichmann that they would emigrate upon their release. If they didn't comply, they faced immediate re-arrest.

From the UK's point of view, it was an opportunity to gain men with valuable skills. With the coming conflict and the interrogation of prisoners of war in mind, it discreetly encouraged the selection of men who could function as translators. The rescue effort was restricted to adult men under 40. Ignatz was at the upper end of this bracket, but it was beginning to look like this scheme might be the only way to save his family.

So far, his hopes had been pinned on the US, where he had several cousins who had previously emigrated and now lived in Brooklyn. Ignatz had applied for an American Entry Visa and was on a waiting list at the US Consulate, pending additional documentation.

He had been in correspondence since January 1939 with an old school friend and neighbour from Poland, Yetti Löwenstein, who had emigrated to the US with her family just six months earlier. It is unclear how he knew where to contact her, but she expressed astonishment to hear from him. In one of her letters, which my father had translated by a customer, she said, "Life is difficult, but we are free."

She and her husband worked for a shirt manufacturer, I. Jablow & Co. in Philadelphia, and earned just enough to live on. When she received his letter, she tried to contact Harry Salamon, Ignatz's cousin. However, she couldn't speak with him, as he spoke no German and her English was not particularly good, so she gave Ignatz's letter to her boss Alex Jablow, whom she described as a "fine, good man", who then contacted Harry.

Yetti explained to Ignatz that Harry wasn't in a financial position to provide an affidavit but was prepared to put the family up and give them money, should they manage to get to the US. However, Alex Jablow, a descendant of Russian Jews, and his wife Kitty, a descendant of Hungarian Jews, were more sympathetic to the family's plight. Yetti persuaded Jablow to provide an affidavit which promised the family "board and lodgings, medical attention, hospitalisation when required, an allowance of $30 per week for incidentals, and a guarantee that they would not become a public charge". To achieve this, Jablow had to supply three years of tax returns.

The affidavit was sworn before a public notary on March 24, 1939. It was supported by a letter to the American Consul in Vienna from the Corn Exchange National Bank in Philadelphia on February 7, 1939, in which they vouched for Mr Jablow, saying he had been "well and favourably known to us for a number of years" and was "one of our valued depositors". They added that they had loaned him five-figure amounts from time to time, and that he had taken care of the obligations satisfactorily. He also maintained a satisfactory personal checking account with them.

Addendum to Alex Jablow's Affidavit of Support, 1939.

While Ignatz had not yet been able to get through the bureaucratic process that would enable his family to get directly to the US, the Kitchener Camp scheme now offered another route. The US visa application, supported by an affidavit, would prove that he did not intend to remain in the UK and become a drain on the country's resources. Additionally, his onward passage, and that of his family should they follow him, was assured or at least reasonably likely. This made him a possible candidate for the Kitchener Camp rescue.

Ignatz didn't fulfil many other criteria, however. He had not been interned in a camp, he wasn't a skilled tradesman who could help build and renovate the camp, and he had no skills or qualifications that would be of use to British Intelligence other than his fluency in both Polish and German, which would qualify him as a translator. The only other criterion he fulfilled was that nobody could help finance his emigration.

The most likely explanation for how Ignatz was accepted for the Kitchener Camp scheme was that he was in the right place at the right time. He frequently visited the IKG in his plight for charity and assistance in leaving Austria. In early 1939, the Kitchener Camp scheme was getting going; it had not yet been widely advertised in the Jewish press, and places weren't yet being prioritised for men released from the camps.

The focus at the start was on men with a good chance of early onward emigration, including Ignatz. The provision of the affidavit by Alex Jablow – a sympathetic fellow Jew living thousands of miles away, but a stranger to Ignatz – was the most critical act by which my family were saved from the Nazis.

Ironically, it was Eichmann who paved the path to escape and safety. Even so, it's incredible that Ignatz made it through the highly competitive and opaque selection process, which sparked so much outrage over who was and was not selected that the British Commission eventually had to get involved.

Against all odds, in April 1939, my grandfather received his *Fremdenpass* (alien passport), allowing him to leave Austria and travel to Kitchener Camp. He held a ticket to freedom in his hand, but not for his beloved family, whom he had fought so hard to protect. He now faced an agonising decision: save himself and then work to bring them to the UK, or remain trapped with them in Vienna and face an uncertain fate. It was an unimaginable "Hobson's choice": leave and risk losing his family, or stay and risk losing everything.

Ignatz's Fremdenpass, 1939.

He would not have known then that war was just a few months away, and that following Germany's invasion of Poland on September 1, 1939, the borders would close and all hopes of getting his family out of Vienna would be dashed. He knew that the danger to his family was increasing daily and that Kitchener Camp offered a potential route out for all of them. He had likely been told by the IKG, perhaps inadvisably, that once he was in the UK, his wife could apply for a domestic service visa, which were only available to married women whose husbands were already in the UK. However, he had to get there first to open the way for Frieda and the children to follow.

The terrifying first step was to set off for the UK alone, with no guarantee of whether or when he would see his family again. Frieda would be on her own with the children, in danger, and in dire poverty, and he would be many hundreds of miles away, with no way to protect or provide for them.

Ignatz might have justified his choices to himself, but there is no way of knowing how Frieda reacted. Was she fully supportive of her husband, confident that he was making the right decision for the family? Or did she push back, terrified of the consequences for her and the boys? We will never know.

A poignant family photograph, taken on the banks of the Danube just before Ignatz's departure, evokes the anguish they all must have felt. In the picture, all five family members are connected through touching hands: Frieda rests her left hand on Ignatz's shoulder; both my grandparents have their hands on the shoulders of Sigi and Otto in front of them, whilst in turn Sigi and Otto's hands are on Wally's shoulders. They didn't know their fate or whether this was the last time they would be together.

Last photo in Vienna on the banks of the Danube, 1939.
Back row: Frieda, Ignatz. Middle row: Sigi, Otto. Front row: Wally.

It must have been an agonising decision, but there was no other choice, and Ignatz trusted his instincts. It was a miracle that he had been accepted on the scheme; their world had been turned upside down, and something had to change.

The opportunity would not come again, so he took it, departing with a teary farewell from the Nordbahnof railway station on May 11, 1939, with 119 other nervous refugees. Arriving in Kent a day later, he was determined that his family would follow as soon as possible.

5

Safety at Last

Domestic Service 1939-1940

Kitchener Camp was cold, utilitarian, and still rough around the edges while the renovation continued. The refugees quickly immersed themselves in the cycle of manual work, skills training, and compulsory English lessons. These were vital, because speaking German was forbidden and English was needed to write the letters to secure the men's onward emigration.

Ignatz was focused on getting his family out of Austria, but much of this now depended on Frieda's efforts. It was becoming a race against time as the news from Europe worsened. To the family's immense relief, she applied and was accepted for a domestic service visa covering herself and the three boys. The Central Office for Refugees (Domestic Bureau) issued this on July 10, 1939, and it restricted her from taking any form of employment other than as a resident domestic servant for a private household.

Domestic service visas, which were available to selected women aged 18 to 55, became a key escape route for Jewish women trapped in the Reich. Between 1938 and 1939, 20,000 women, mainly from Austria, were granted this lifeline. The UK Home Office saw it as a way to save lives while addressing labour shortages, and with the CBF promising to cover the costs of caring for the refugees, the scheme posed no financial risk to the UK.

Frieda's domestic service visa, 1939.

To gain her visa, Frieda had to apply to the British Consulate Office in Vienna, lining up in endless queues, at the mercy of the Viennese public hurling insults and worse. She had to provide references and fill in forms that detailed her life and medical history. In May 1939, she obtained a character reference from Rabbi Benjamin Murmelstein of the IKG, who stated: "She enjoys a good reputation, and nothing detrimental is known about her."

She also submitted a medical certificate to the British Consulate which stated that she was not mentally or physically defective in any way, was not afflicted with "tuberculosis or any infectious, loathsome or contagious disease", and was "not suffering from favus, leprosy, framoesia or yaws, trachoma, syphilis or scabies". It also certified that she had never been in a mental hospital or prison. She was in good health for her journey to follow, but there were further hurdles to overcome.

Day-to-day living was extremely difficult for Frieda, with three young boys to care for on her own now that her husband had left for England. The Nazis were tightening their grip on the Jewish population in Vienna, with more anti-Jewish laws and decrees emanating from Berlin. Under the Nuremberg Race Laws, Jews were barred from public places such as cinemas, theatres, and sports facilities, and "Aryan-only" zones were established. Antisemitic abuse and attacks were now normal behaviour to be endured. Perversely, while the Nazis wanted Jews to emigrate, they increasingly made the entire process excruciatingly difficult to navigate.

Everyone was frantically trying to find an escape route while trying to avoid the worst of the daily torment and abuse. These three months my grandmother spent in Vienna with her children have always intrigued me. I cannot imagine the difficulties she faced and the resilience she would have needed to arrange everything for her escape. I am not sure how she managed.

What little money the family had been given in return for confiscating their business and possessions was long gone. Frieda had been supporting her children on charity handouts. She could not cover her visa fees and unpaid taxes, including an emigration tax (known as a "defection levy") charged by the authorities.

With nowhere else to turn, she appealed to the Property Transaction Office (*Vermögensverkehrsstelle*) in July 1939, which the Nazis had set up to deal with the expropriation of Jewish-owned assets (ironically, including their own) for financial assistance with her visa fees, and to the Ministry for Commerce and Work to pay her unpaid taxes. In her letter, she wrote that she was *"ganz mittellos"* (completely penniless).

She had to prove where the compensation payment they received for the shop had been spent, by showing bills for the clothing and other things she needed to leave the country, including paying for the transportation of her possessions to the UK. A receipt submitted by Frieda shows she spent 219 reichsmarks on July 26 at Alligatoy *Lederwaren* (leather goods) on one ship's suitcase, as well as two other suitcases, one briefcase, one handbag, one hat case, and one belt. Other items bought included a camisole, woollen vests, children's trousers, and hygiene products.

She managed to arrange payment of 1,354.66 reichsmarks to cover her transport costs, spending, shipping costs for equipment, and tax arrears.

Frieda's letter to the Property Transaction Office, June 1939.

She then arranged with a freight forwarding company to ship her belongings to London, amounting to 350 kilos, including her beloved sewing machine. However, it is unclear whether any of these items ever arrived.

Finally, in mid-August 1939, she was able to leave with the children on a third-class train to Dover, via Ostend, arriving on August 21, 1939. Frieda bought two-and-a-half third-class tickets for her and the three boys, the most she could afford; since Wally was still a baby, he could sit on her lap. They travelled for two days by train in stuffy, crowded conditions, and had little to eat or drink until they boarded the boat for the sea crossing.

Ignatz and Frieda had left their adopted homeland but feared for their family members who had been left behind. They had escaped with no small measure of luck, but scattered all over Europe were their parents, sisters, brothers, aunts, and uncles, many of whom they would never see again. Maybe they thought they could send for their families once they were safe. By then, however, it was too late.

Frieda and the boys arrived in Kent with only what they were wearing or could carry. Dad had a story, often told, that his mother had made each boy put on two pairs of trousers and hung a spare pair of shoes around their necks – the epitome of starting with nothing.

While the family remember my grandmother as a quiet woman, it's clear she also had enormous grit and determination, which got her, Sigi, Otto, and Wally safely out of the Reich on the very eve of the Second World War. Had their departure been just a few days later, the borders would have been closed and they would all have been trapped in Vienna, facing deportation to concentration camps and almost certain death, all without Ignatz by their side. Tragically, this was to be the fate of many of the Kitchener Camp men's families, who failed to escape as the war closed in.

*

There was no immediate reunion when they arrived in Kent; the family was further divided. My grandmother was allocated a domestic service position to Mrs Marchant at an isolated farm, Little Robhurst, in Woodchurch, Kent, where she lived in the maid's quarters next to the magnificent homestead.

Wally, Otto, and Sigi were taken in by Mr and Mrs Keen, a blacksmith and his wife living 10 miles away in Ashford. The Keens lived in a modest terraced house, and provided them with a home, food, and schooling. They were paid for taking the boys in: Frieda received 19 shillings weekly from the German Jewish Aid Committee towards the maintenance of two boys, which was passed on to the host family.

It was a tough, lonely time for all of them. The boys were just ten, eight, and three years old. None spoke English, and communication with their hosts was difficult and frustrating. Frieda rarely saw her children, as the nature of her work and the limitations of the visa programme prevented visits. When she did visit, Sigi recalled, she was forbidden from seeing them other than through the kitchen window. In any case, with little money or transport options, reaching Ashford was difficult for Frieda.

Like most women who had escaped Europe on domestic service visas, Frieda had been given a job as a maid in a middle-class family. There was a good reason the UK had a shortage of domestic workers: it was a tough job, barely regulated, with extended hours and little freedom, so many local women had moved on to factory jobs and work supporting the approaching war. This meant that, at first, the refugees were welcomed with open arms, helped by the fact that the Kitchener Camp men had been warmly accepted as part of the community.

Frieda did her best to settle into her role of cooking, cleaning, and domestic chores. Before she departed from Vienna, she had been provided with a booklet by the IKG outlining the basic requirements for domestic service, including some useful English expressions and information on traditional English foods, which were foreign to her but which she did her best to make. But, as time passed, her mistress, the local Ladies' Guild president, took every opportunity to make her life miserable. This behaviour change coincided with a growing national distrust of German-speaking foreigners. Fears of a "fifth column" (a group of people embedded in society who covertly sabotage the nation's interests) were prevalent.

It must have been awful for Frieda. She had escaped hell only to end up in these wretched circumstances, and she must have longed for some normality.

Meanwhile, the boys, who were already traumatised by what they had gone through in Austria, were also having a tough time. They didn't speak English, and their host family shouting at them in a strange tongue was frightening and confusing. Many years later, while chatting at Dad's 70th birthday celebrations in Spain, Sigi recounted with undisguised fury that their host treated them like zoo exhibits, on one occasion getting them to parade naked in front of her friends so they could see "what a Jewish boy looked like".

She also instilled a lifelong dislike of dogs into my father, by getting her Alsatian to sit on his pram while he was in it. Sigi remembered that she also enjoyed setting the dog on the boys:

"She would only have to say to it, 'Seize them, seize them,' which she did very often, and the dog would bark at us, come at us. To this day, I'm afraid of dogs."

Sigi also spoke of the rare occasions that his mother was allowed to see him and his brothers, when their host insisted she keep her distance, saying: "She couldn't touch us because this woman would get mad and have a tantrum."

She was also violent towards the boys: on one occasion, Sigi remembered seeing her pick Wally up and throw him against the wall. Yet, recalling all this, he added philosophically: "Anyway, listen, whatever hardship we had there, they saved our lives.

Because without the papers they gave us, we wouldn't have been able to come into the country."

Ignatz had informed Yetti Löwenstein by letter in October 1939 that he had "luckily succeeded in having my wife and family with me in England", although whether he had managed to see Frieda and the boys by then is unknown. If they had reunited, it was likely at Kitchener Camp, without the children. They probably communicated by letter, although none survive. Regardless, Ignatz would have been overjoyed that they were all safe.

While Frieda and the boys struggled to feel at home in the UK, Ignatz was on the move again. The outbreak of war had brought some momentous changes to his situation.

6

I Understand the Risks

Military Service 1939-1942

Life assumed a semblance of routine for several months after Ignatz arrived at Kitchener Camp. He was based in Camp 1370, Hut 2/1, and from May 5 until November 29, 1939, he worked as a day guard for the camp police. "A role that would have suited him very well, having been a sergeant major in the Polish Army," says my sister Rochelle.

Ignatz wearing the armband of the Kitchener Camp Day Guard, 1939. Front row, fifth from left.

The camp was self-policing and the inmates weren't prisoners; it wasn't an internment camp (despite being referred to as such by my family when I was growing up). The men made friends in Sandwich and regularly walked the short distance across the bridge and through the tollgate. A plaque on the toll gate today reads:

"This plaque is to commemorate the RICHBOROUGH TRANSIT CAMP 1939-1940 where 5,000 men found refuge from Nazi persecution on the Continent. During the Second World War, most of them volunteered to fight for the Allied cause.

"Erected in gratitude to the citizens of Sandwich and East Kent who, as in the past, welcomed the refugees."

The men used the local Post Office to send letters (letter writing was a constant activity for most, desperately seeking ways out for them and their families), and frequented local establishments, including the Odeon cinema.

The Odeon chain was founded by Oscar Deutsch, the son of Hungarian Jews, who funded a 1,000-seat cinema within Kitchener Camp. It is sometimes said that Odeon stood for "Oscar Deutsch Entertains Our Nation", but more likely this was a publicity gimmick, with the word's origin stemming from the original Odeons of ancient Greece.

Another favourite haunt of the men was The Bell Hotel. Today, the hotel has a Blue Plaque, commissioned by the Association of Jewish Refugees, which reads:

"A meeting place for Jewish refugees from The Kitchener Camp, Richborough, Sandwich 1939-40."

With the outbreak of war, everything changed, and Ignatz was allowed to enlist with the Auxiliary Military Pioneer Corps (AMPC). To be accepted, he had to go before a military tribunal at the camp so they could assess his security risk and see if he was a "friendly alien" or a threat to national security. Naturally, he was classified in category "C" (no threat), and he received his Exemption from Internment Certificate on November 10, allowing him to join the AMPC. Joining the AMPC was, overall, a wise decision, and many of the men at Kitchener Camp followed the same route. Frieda received her certificate a month later, on December 10, from a tribunal in Woodchurch.

Ignatz's Exemption from Internment certificate, 1939.

With the outbreak of war, uneasiness about having German speakers on British soil grew, and the days of Kitchener Camp were numbered. It was feared that its men might be secret Nazi sympathisers or spies, primarily as they were based so near the coast. The threat of internment or deportation loomed once again. Kitchener Camp men who didn't sign up went on to be interned on the Isle of Man, which had several camps holding thousands of "enemy aliens"– many of them Jewish refugees. From there, many of the men were deported to Australia or Canada, although they were later allowed to return to the UK and join the war effort.

To serve in the AMPC, Ignatz, who was still stateless and officially considered an alien, had to swear an oath of allegiance to King George VI. This made him one of "the King's Most Loyal

Enemy Aliens", a sardonic title given to Jewish refugees who joined the British Army. Most didn't mind their alien status, viewing it as a temporary inconvenience; they were loyal to the country that had offered them refuge, and at least the word "alien" wasn't prefixed with "Jewish".

Ignatz's enlistment form declared that he was "fit for general service at home and abroad", that he "understood the risks" for both him and his relatives, and that he was willing to be deployed "in any theatre of war".

So, on December 12, 1939, aged 41 and less than 20 years after his discharge from the Polish Army, my grandfather became a private in the British Army with 69 Company AMPC, based at the No. 3 Pioneer Training Centre at Kitchener Camp.

Neither Ignatz nor Frieda would have been happy with the thought of Ignatz once again being a soldier, but there was little choice. As they had always done before, they followed their instincts and made the best decisions in the circumstances.

69 Company was one of 15 alien companies in the AMPC. These companies were the British Army's only unarmed units, as ongoing fears that German-speaking men may be spies or sleeping agents meant they were not to be trusted with guns. This was ironic considering how many of these men had experienced extreme loss, suffering, deprivation, and deportation at the hands of the Germans, something that their fellow armed soldiers hadn't experienced. While the recruits to the Pioneer Corps were regarded as the lowest rung of the army ladder, they had among them highly intellectual and cultured men, who, through no fault of their own, had found themselves in a position they did not ask for. Many of these men later transferred to the Intelligence Corps, as respect for their talents, dedication, and service to the country was recognised, and they played a significant role in the war effort.

The AMPC (which was renamed the Pioneer Corps in November 1940, and then the Royal Pioneer Corps in 1946) was part of the British Expeditionary Force (BEF), which went to France at the beginning of 1940 to complete tasks that were "auxiliary" to the military effort. These included building bridges, roads, and railways, ready for a potential invasion by the British. The Corps' motto, "Labor Omnia Vincit", meaning "Work Conquers All", perfectly expressed its purpose.

All the Jewish refugee recruits were given a number starting with 138 for easier identification; my grandfather's number was 13800351. Marking out the Jewish recruits in this way reflected the inherent suspicion felt towards these men in the army. Even though they were not officially regarded as security threats and had sworn an oath of loyalty to the king, it was still felt necessary to single them out. It is somewhat poignant that the men were given numbers which identified them as Jewish while, albeit under vastly different circumstances, fellow Jews were being identified and tattooed with numbers in Europe's concentration camps. As it turned out, the identifiers for Jewish recruits in the British Army were later altered, so that if the Germans captured the men, they would not immediately be recognised as Jewish and killed.

Ignatz underwent just a few weeks of training then left for France, where he served from January to June 1940. This period is known as the Phoney War because there was barely any fighting.

No stories have been handed down in my family of my grandfather's time in France with the AMPC, nor is there a written memoir. However, one of the best insights into the events of this period is a book published in 1950 by Norman Bentwich: *I Understand the Risks: How those who fled to England from Hitlerite Oppression Fought – Understanding the Risks – Against Nazism.*

According to Norman Bentwich's account, which relied upon first-hand witness statements and 69 Company War Diaries, Ignatz's company was the first alien company to head across the Channel. They left Sandwich in the depths of a cold winter night on January 22, travelled by train and boat via Southampton to Cherbourg, and then proceeded to Rennes, Brittany's capital city. From there, they marched to Verdun Camp – an old French Army barracks – where they stayed until March, undertaking gruelling manual work including the construction of railways.

At the beginning of March, they moved to a camp at Inbonmel, where they were housed in train wagons. Then, they moved on to help construct Oxygen Camp in Rennes. In April 1940, they moved again to help construct Boozeu Camp in Bruz, and by May they were back at Oxygen Camp. Tasks completed during their months in France included camp construction, building railways, and digging trenches for the coming battles.

It was challenging work, and for my grandfather, who was not a young man and not in the best of health, it must have been gruelling. But at least there was no combat, and while their accommodation was largely in Nissen huts, their wider surroundings were pleasant.

By June, however, everything had changed. The Germans had invaded northern France and the Low Countries (Belgium, Luxembourg and the Netherlands) on May 10, circumventing the Maginot Line (a line of concrete fortifications built to deter invasion), and their blitzkrieg saw them sweeping through Luxembourg and France over the next five days. The French government was surprised, and with the French Army capitulating easily, the German Army advanced towards Paris at a terrifying pace. The French prime minister pleaded with the US President Franklin D. Roosevelt to declare war on Germany, but he was not disposed to intervene in a "European war". There are chilling similarities between these American sentiments and those of President Trump today vis-à-vis the war in Ukraine.

King Leopold I of Belgium quickly surrendered on May 28, angering the British and many Belgians, and leaving the BEF critically exposed. An evacuation of British and French troops from Dunkirk was hastily organised. Being Jews, and German Jews at that, the men in the alien companies almost certainly faced death if captured; they were unlikely to be interned as prisoners of war. So, they were moved further west than Dunkirk, towards St. Malo, and were ordered to "hold the line". Their task was to destroy vehicles and ordnance so they would not fall into enemy hands.

Finally, the evacuation order came. Norman Bentwich writes: "Gunfire sounded as they marched to the coast carrying their full kit and any weapons they picked up along the way." Coastal roads were crammed with hundreds of thousands of hopeful evacuees; weary, dirty, disheartened, retreating British forces, and Belgians, Dutch, and other refugees from all over Europe, primarily, but not exclusively, Jews. A babel of languages, such as English, French, Flemish, Dutch, German, and Yiddish, could be heard mingling.

The fleeing throng was subjected to frequent strafing from Luftwaffe dive-bombers, who didn't distinguish between retreating soldiers and refugees seeking safe passage. With each raid, they would dive into ditches on the side of the road for safety.

The locals harried the retreating soldiers for abandoning France to the oncoming Germans. It must have been a terrifying experience for Ignatz and his fellow recruits. They had found refuge from the Nazis in England, and yet here they were, just a hair's breadth away from falling into their hands again.

Ignatz's Company was among those evacuated on June 16 on three unescorted fishing trawlers in Operation Aerial, which came a couple of weeks after the primary evacuation of troops from Dunkirk in Operation Dynamo. They were lucky to make it out alive. Two days previously, members of the Pioneer Corps were among thousands of evacuees killed when Stuka bombers succeeded in sinking the ship they were on, the HMS *Lancastria*, even though the RAF was providing aerial protection. In all, 66,000 men from the BEF were captured, died, or went missing in France.

The drama of their escape contrasted with the warm welcome they received when they disembarked at Weymouth on June 17, 1940, bound for London. However, many men were said to have been angry and frustrated that they were forced to hand over any weapons they had acquired, believing they had done enough to prove their loyalty. A couple of days later, the company was sent to Westward Ho! barracks in Devon, which proved a pleasant place to reassemble and recover, a complete contrast to where they had been just a few days previously.

Despite his best efforts, my grandfather's hopes of reaching the US gradually faded. Shortly after arriving at Kitchener Camp, Ignatz had applied for his visa application file to be transferred from the US Consulate in Vienna to the London office. While serving in France, the Overseas Settlement Office informed him that the US Consulate in London was verifying his initial application in Vienna, and if verified, he would be put on the waiting list in London as of the time of his original registration.

Then, on May 17, Ignatz received some devastating news: the US Consulate in London notified him that his visa application had been withdrawn. The US State Department did not favour Jewish refugee immigration, or immigration generally, and had tightened its visa requirements. They would now only accept affidavits from non-family members if the promise of indefinite, irrevocable support in the form of a trust fund accompanied them.

The consulate advised Ignatz that if he wished to pursue his application, he should "endeavour to obtain assurances of support from some other person in the United States who has a direct interest in your welfare and who is willing and financially able to ensure your support for an indefinite period if necessary".

On May 20, Ignatz wrote to Alex Jablow explaining the new requirements. In his letter, Ignatz stated that he had been informed in a short message from the Red Cross that his mother had died in January, but that he had received no news of his father and sisters since the beginning of the war. In his reply, dated July 12, Alex Jablow said that he was not prepared to enter such an undertaking. He suggested my grandfather contact his cousin Harry Salamon in Philadelphia, but reaching out to Harry proved impossible. He had previously sent a telegram on January 24, 1939, promising an affidavit would be sent the following week, but this had never arrived.

On May 20, 1940, Ignatz wrote to the US Consulate explaining that he had joined the British Armed Forces and asking that his visa application be deferred until after the war. He hoped that he would have solved the affidavit problem by then.

In July, 69 Company was moved to Ilminster in Somerset, where my grandfather continued to correspond with Mr Jablow, while helping to build defences such as laying mine traps, digging trenches, and erecting miles of barbed-wire fencing.

The company continued to work on civil defence throughout the summer, but with the stress of trying to secure safe passage for his family and the heavy manual army work, my grandfather's health was starting to suffer. According to his army service record, he was admitted temporarily to Devon Infirmary, Barnstaple, in July 1940. The details of his condition have not been recorded, but judging by information from his later discharge from the army, it was likely high blood pressure or breathing difficulties.

It was not the first time he had experienced health problems: just after arriving in France in late January, he had injured a rib in an accident and spent a week in a French military hospital.

Despite the challenges, he performed well in the army. He was promoted to lance corporal on March 19, 1940, acting corporal on May 6, 1940, and full corporal on August 6, 1940.

Following the summer of 1940, the military remained the safest place for Ignatz. Civilians and politicians in the UK were increasingly uncomfortable having German-speaking refugees on British soil, and a full-scale effort to intern all potentially dangerous aliens was underway. Winston Churchill, who had replaced Neville Chamberlain as prime minister in May 1940, invoked a redundant law, the Defence of the Realm Act 1914, summing up the sentiment with the phrase: "Collar the lot".

Men in the Pioneer Companies, however, were spared. Frieda wasn't interned either, perhaps exempted as the wife of a serving soldier or maybe because of her domestic service status.

A warmer sentiment was expressed towards the soldiers when Colonel Arthur Evans MP, Commander of the Pioneer Companies in France, praised the alien soldiers of the British Expeditionary Force in a House of Commons debate, saying: "They conducted themselves in a manner worthy of the best traditions of the British Army."

Naturally, more aliens signed up. By September 1940, 69 Company had moved to Ilfracombe, North Devon, where they were joined by the mass of recruits who had been released from the Isle of Man internment camps. They were housed in requisitioned hotels, trained on the local beaches, and undertook manual work to strengthen the area's home defences.

It was tiresome, unrewarding work, but it was about to get tougher. By November, they were in Bexley, South London, clearing up the grim aftermath of German bombing raids during the Blitz. This placed them in greater danger. The following month, members of 69 Company were on a bus that was hit by a German bomb. Five died and 19 were injured.

In the spring of 1941, 69 Company moved north to Doncaster and then to Darlington. But my grandfather's health continued to suffer, and the following year, in March 1942, he was transferred to Kempston Barracks, Bedfordshire, which was being used as a convalescence hospital, with rheumatism and hyperpiesia (high blood pressure).

That February, he was placed on the "Y List" – a list of servicemen who were inactive due to illness, discharge, or death. Medical Board proceedings followed on March 28, 1942, when the Medical Examination Centre, Kempston, permitted him to go to Cardiff, where my grandmother and her three boys now lived, and stay there until April.

Ignatz never returned to the barracks. On April 27, he was discharged on medical grounds. His discharge record states that he was "permanently unfit for any form of military service", having a 30 percent disability due to hyperpiesia. It also says that he was suffering from rheumatism, notes that his military conduct had been good, and he had "carried out his duties as a non-commissioned officer with zeal and efficiency". His discharge papers record that he received a £4 payment in lieu of a suit to start him off in the civilian world.

Home visit, circa 1940. Left to right: Ignatz, Otto, Wally, Sigi, Frieda.

My grandfather spent several years afterwards in a frustrating fight with the Ministry for Pensions for his right to a war pension. His signed enlistment papers stated that he "would not be entitled to a military pension if his health failed or if he sustained an injury, unless the disability was directly attributable to the conditions of military service". He argued that it was.

By 1944, however, the Pioneer Corps Records Office and the Ministry of Pensions had lost all traces of his medical records, so to get a war pension, his claim of being injured in France on active duty would have to be backed up by witnesses.

He gave several names of ex-colleagues who had served with him, and some of those who remained in the army were eventually tracked down. Finding them was no easy task, as many had anglicised their names – something the army had encouraged German Jewish recruits to do to decrease their chances of being executed if captured by the Nazis.

The men who were interviewed either claimed not to remember my grandfather or not to remember the accident, although one man, Saunders (previously Scheib), did recall him having chest pains in France and England in 1940. Ignatz's claim of injury on active duty could not be verified, so his war pension was rejected because his injury was not "directly attributable to his service in the forces or materially aggravated by that service". This was a significant setback for my grandfather, who left the army with almost nothing to build his and his family's future.

Ignatz, Yetti Löwenstein, and the Jablows continued to correspond until 1945. Sadly, only the letters received by Ignatz survive, not the letters he sent; one must read between the lines to imagine what he wrote. A remarkable bond of friendship developed between them, even though Alex Jablow and Ignatz had never met, and Yetti was not even a relative, just an old friend.

In her letters, Yetti recounted her children's stories and various health issues and enquired about my grandparents and the boys. She was desperately worried about the fate of her parents and three brothers, who had remained in Europe and from whom she had not heard. She was keen to receive a photo of the family, and when she did so, she wrote that she thought Sigi and Otto were typical Salamons.

In her final letter, Yetti said she had lost hope of finding anyone alive, although she did hear that her youngest brother was in Russia. She concluded: "We have beaten the scoundrels, unfortunately, too late."

7

Welcome to Wales

Cardiff 1942-1949

My grandmother had left domestic service in 1940 after less than a year, contrary to the terms of her visa. This was possible because the Home Office had lifted the restriction on changing jobs when war broke out. It is unclear why Frieda left; it could be that she was allowed to leave because she had relatives in Cardiff to provide board and lodgings, or perhaps she was no longer required after German-speaking domestic staff became undesirable when war broke out, and still more so after Dunkirk. The most probable explanation is that she lost her job because her place of employment in Kent fell under a "protected area". The Domestic Bureau of the Central Office for Refugees supported 2,650 domestics who could not work, although there is no evidence that Frieda received such maintenance.

For whatever reason, she left and moved with the three boys to Cardiff in May 1940, initially staying with her brother-in-law, Maks, and his wife, Irka, at 174 Column Road – a terraced house close to the areas around Llandaff and Riverside, where there was a growing Jewish population. Maks had moved to Cardiff from Poland with his family in May 1939 after the business he worked for, Aero Zipp Fasteners, relocated from Berlin to the UK in December 1938. With Ignatz in the army, Maks was the only person Frieda knew in the UK, so she inevitably moved to be close to him.

It has always intrigued me how the family kept in touch during this period of so much upheaval and relocation, even across national borders. That they knew where to find each other can only have been through the exchange of letters, yet the postal service wasn't quick or dependable.

Maks and Irka would have been delighted that Frieda and the boys were safe, welcoming them into their home. However, my grandmother didn't know Maks; it's not even clear if they had ever met, so the living arrangements would not have been ideal, and the home wasn't large enough to comfortably accommodate the four new arrivals, with Maks and Irka's children, Roger and Edgar, also living there. And so, by May 23, they had moved to a place close by, at 79 Column Road.

Column Road would become a central theme in Dad's life; not only were his first two Cardiff homes there, but Mum's parents also lived there later. It's probably no coincidence that this is where Dad bought several houses over the years, which he converted into student lets.

*

In April 1942, after three long years apart, the family was reunited in a new world, a new home, if not their first-choice country. A constant reassessment of their options as events unfolded had brought them to Cardiff. They had miraculously survived, but their struggles were far from over.

Frieda had to learn English; she had picked up a little of the language while in domestic service but needed to improve. They had to find schools for the boys and a way to support themselves. Things were particularly challenging with no war pension and my grandfather not in the best of health.

When my grandfather arrived in Cardiff, Maks worked as a development engineer at Aero Zipp and was happy to help his brother secure a job there. Due to the fear of Nazi infiltration, it wasn't easy for German-speaking immigrants to find work in the

UK, so places like Aero Zipp offered a perfect solution for both employer and employee. Uncle Sigi and Dad's cousin Maurice, Ruzia's son, also worked as apprentices at the factory. However, much to his frustration, Maks' son, Edgar, couldn't secure a position there, despite his father's seniority.

Aero Zipp was one of 55 businesses owned by Jewish refugees based in Treforest; they employed 1,800 people between them. The Treforest Trading Estate was set up in 1936 as part of the Special Areas Act 1934, which set out to nurture new businesses in places of high unemployment, specifically Tyneside, Scotland, and South Wales.

With the rise of antisemitism in pre-war Europe, which saw so many Jewish businesses seized, the Act offered a way to escape and start afresh. Residence permits were easy to get, and the rents on business premises were affordable. With British companies not particularly interested in setting up in the Special Areas, there was ample room for new businesses.

Apart from Aero Zipp, other Jewish-owned businesses on the Treforest estate included O.P. Chocolates, founded by Oscar Peschek, an Austrian baker and confectioner; Gnome Photographic, founded by Heinrich Loebstein, a German photographic equipment manufacturer; Pearl Paints, founded by brothers Fritz, Simon, and Willi Stern, German paint manufacturers; and General Paper & Box, opened by Paul Schoenmann, an Austrian businessman from Vienna.

All these diverse businesses had one thing in common: they were started by ambitious Jewish immigrant refugees, eager to progress in their new environment and provide for their families. While there may have been some caution at first among the local communities, they were ultimately happy with the work opportunities offered and soon appreciated the business acumen and ethical values displayed by their foreign bosses.

Aero Zipp Fasteners was set up by Joachim Koppel, a Jewish businessman who had fled Berlin and managed to bring his machinery with him. Initially, the company made zip fasteners, but during the war, it was requisitioned to create aircraft components for the Ministry of Aircraft Production. Because the business was considered beneficial to the war effort in May 1940, the Jewish industrialists behind it, and their employees, were spared from internment. And the company was not only saved from closure but flourished amid a flurry of government orders.

At first, Maks and Ignatz travelled to work by bus, about an hour each way, until Ignatz, always the first to try something new, bought a car.

Maks was a prolific inventor and secured patents for some of his new machinery ideas. The company produced an in-house magazine, *Punch and Die*, that was both informative and fun. It had articles about the employees, and Maks' more off-beat inventions featured prominently in the magazine's pages over the years. These included a device to lift you out of bed and straight into your trousers – a brainwave that pre-dated the almost identical device in the animated Wallace and Gromit movie, *The Wrong Trousers*, by some 40 years. Another clever invention emptied the bath water and flushed the toilet simultaneously. These ideas were just a bit of fun, and it's rather a shame that they were never put into production.

Just as he had in the two armies he had served in, Ignatz worked hard at Aero Zipp, earning the respect of his employer and colleagues. He initially worked as a supervisor in the small works departments, overseeing many female employees. Then, he was promoted to foreman, a role that put him in charge of over 200 employees engaged in various manufacturing operations.

Within a few years, Ignatz and Frieda had saved up enough money to buy a house – an unremarkable, three-storey terraced property at 12 Llanbleddian Gardens, opposite what is today the Sherman Theatre, and where they lived the rest of their lives. The property had a back lane where Ignatz enjoyed tinkering with his car on a Sunday. They took in boarders to make ends meet, with my grandmother assuming the tasks of cooking, cleaning, and washing, while my grandfather worked at Aero Zipp.

At home, Ignatz was strict and could be short-tempered. Dad's cousin, Edgar, spent a lot of time with the family when he was young and recalls: "Ignatz didn't have a lot of patience, and if he didn't have it done properly, he didn't want it done at all."

Perhaps because of how hard they had to work to support the family, my grandparents didn't always have much time for their children, but they did learn English from their boys, who had quickly become fluent at school. My grandfather had, of course, received English lessons at Kitchener Camp, but there was still much to learn.

They were not a religious family; Dad had no recollection of them going to synagogue except on the major Jewish festivals. Perhaps their religion was now too strongly associated with the horrors of the Holocaust. But even before the war, it had been Jozef and Karolina, not Ignatz and Frieda, who had been known for their religious sensibilities. They were, however, deeply proud of their Jewish heritage and passed this on to their children.

My grandfather was more focused on secular, practical activities. He was particularly good with his hands – a trait that he passed onto Dad. He also bought properties to rent out, including 110 Ninian Road, the house my grandmother moved to after my grandfather died. He must have had an astute financial brain, and this was where Dad got it from.

But it was my grandmother who, according to Edgar, was the driving force behind the family. To outsiders, Frieda seemed quiet and meek, but those who knew her well described her as a formidable woman. Her strength and resourcefulness saved her children and enabled her to support the family when poverty and destitution remained a real threat.

*

Since arriving in Austria in the early 1920s, my grandparents had been strangers in a foreign land. The feeling was exacerbated when Ignatz was deprived of his Polish nationality in 1938, making him stateless – a situation that was to last for the next nine years.

Persecuted in their adopted homeland and forced to emigrate, they arrived in the UK penniless, exhausted, and bewildered by the momentous events around them. Officially designated as aliens, they were made to feel unwelcome in the country to which they had fled for refuge. Perhaps what made it even worse was their almost complete lack of English, which made it hard to integrate. And when they could string a few sentences together, their heavy continental accents singled them out as foreigners.

Their roots had been torn up, and the only thing that gave them an identity was their religion and the community of people around them in the same situation.

However, as the years went by, Ignatz and Frieda settled into life in Wales. They assimilated, made friends, and enjoyed spending time with the family. By VE Day's arrival on June 6, 1945, Austria seemed a distant memory. They would have been startled, therefore, by the images of skeletal concentration camp inmates and the horrific stories of atrocities that were gradually emerging from Europe, particularly at the 1947 Nuremberg Trials of surviving high-ranking Nazi officials. It was at these trials that the principle of crimes against humanity was established. Twelve of the defendants, including Hermann Göring, Joachim von Ribbentrop, Arthur Seyss-Inquart and Martin Borman, were sentenced to death, with a further seven, including Rudolf Hess and Albert Speer, sentenced to life imprisonment. Sadly, many other leading Nazis escaped trial, including Adolf Hitler himself, who took his life in his bunker as the war was ending, and Dr Josef Mengele, the Auschwitz "Angel of Death", who fled to South America.

My grandparents' thoughts must have turned to the families and friends they never saw again, those they had they left behind in Europe and who perished at the hands of the Nazis. Ignatz's father and uncle, Jozef and Moses Salamon, killed, starved, or worked to death in the Sosnowiec Ghetto in 1942; his mother, Karolina, and sisters, Manya, Josefina, Anna, and Sabena, perishing in unknown circumstances in their home town of Suchej in 1940 after the Nazis occupied it; his sister-in-law's brother and nephew, Eduard and Ernst Reichenbaum, murdered by the Nazis in Auschwitz and Hamburg in 1940 and 1945 respectively; and his uncle and cousin, Joachim and Jakob Reichenbaum, murdered in Auschwitz in 1942. Likewise, Frieda's parents, Moses and Rosa Stein, killed in the Transnistria Camp in Ukraine between 1942 and 1943.

Those who survived the Holocaust are often described as "the lucky ones". I'm not sure whether Ignatz and Frieda would have considered themselves lucky then. Yes, they were living in Cardiff in safety, having escaped to a country not later invaded and occupied by the Germans, but they had suffered tremendous upheaval and loss. Perhaps they even suffered from survivor's guilt – a shame felt by so many who lived on after their families perished. However, what is almost certain is that they would have suffered the same fate as six million other Jews if they had not shown the tenacity, courage, and strength to follow their instincts and escape.

*

Ignatz and Frieda were not wealthy, but the job at Aero Zipp and Frieda's work supporting the boarders kept the family afloat. Even so, my grandfather had ambitions to run his own business, just as he had in Austria.

While he was still registered as stateless, this was not an option. However, in August 1947, after the requisite five-year wait, my grandparents, Sigi, Otto, and Wally, finally received their naturalisation certificates from the Home Office, granted for "service to the country". He could now set up a business on the same terms as a UK national. It was a seminal moment; they were no longer aliens. They now belonged somewhere.

Home Office No. S.34083.

Certificate No. **BZ** 2915

BRITISH NATIONALITY AND STATUS OF ALIENS ACT, 1914
CERTIFICATE OF NATURALIZATION

Whereas   Ignacy Salamon.

has applied to one of His Majesty's Principal Secretaries of State for a Certificate of Naturalization, alleging with respect to   him self the particulars set out below, and has satisfied him that the conditions laid down in the above-mentioned Act for the grant of a Certificate of Naturalization are fulfilled in   his   case:

And whereas the said   Ignacy Salamon. has also applied for the inclusion in accordance with sub-section (1) of section five of the said Act of the names of   his   children   born before the date of this Certificate and being   minors, and the Secretary of State is satisfied that the names   of   his children   , as hereinafter set out, may properly be included:

Now, therefore, in pursuance of the powers conferred on him by the said Act, the Secretary of State grants to the said

Ignacy Salamon.

this Certificate of Naturalization, and declares that upon taking the Oath of Allegiance within the time and in the manner required by the regulations made in that behalf   he shall, subject to the provisions of the said Act, be entitled to all political and other rights powers and privileges, and be subject to all obligations duties and liabilities, to which a natural-born British subject is entitled or subject, and have to all intents and purposes the status of a natural-born British subject

And the Secretary of State further declares that this Certificate extends to the following minor child   of the said   Ignacy Salamon.
Sigmund - born 25th January, 1929.
Otto - born 28th January, 1931.
Walter - born 30th August, 1936.

In witness whereof I have hereto subscribed my name this 20th   day of

August, 1944

Sgd. A. MAXWELL
Under Secretary of State.

HOME OFFICE,
LONDON.

PARTICULARS RELATING TO APPLICANT.

Full Name	Ignacy SALAMON.
Address	12, Llanbleddian Gardens, Cardiff
Trade or Occupation	Foreman.
Place and date of birth	Sucha, Poland. 19th September, 1898.
Nationality	Polish.
Married, etc.	Married.
Name of wife or husband	Frieda.
Names and nationality of parents	Josef and Karolina Fani SALAMON. (Polish).

(For Oath
see overleaf.)

Certificate of Naturalisation, 1947.

Frieda and Ignatz, circa 1948.

Part Two

The Father

Wally Salamon 1936-2008

8

A New Dawn

Bridge Street Stores 1949-1967

Ignatz had started as a shopkeeper and his happiest times had been running a shop, so it made sense to return to this way of life. The memories of the horrors of war that had brought them to Cardiff were largely unmentioned; the focus was placed firmly on the present and on creating a solid foundation for their children and future grandchildren.

In 1949, he resigned his role at Aero Zipp, leaving with glowing praise. His leaving reference letter read:

> "He always showed himself to possess a high sense of duty and a considerable capacity for bearing heavy responsibility. His work was thorough and painstaking in its attention to details… he was a good disciplinarian and able to control workers in a firm, fair but kindly manner. He is reliable, works with energy, drive, and resourcefulness."

That same year, he took on a property in Bridge Street in Canol Dinas Caerdydd, Cardiff City Centre, put up a sign saying Bridge Street Stores, and stocked it to the rafters with food, getting the shop off the ground with money saved while working at Aero Zipp. It was a small, double-fronted unit, with curved glass windows, laden with goods piled high on either side of the narrow entrance door. Advertising for Echo margarine, Cookeen (a British brand of block vegetable fat, marketed for making pastry), and Capstan and Players – unfiltered cigarettes popular at the time – adorned the shop frontage.

Bridge Street Stores, circa 1949.

Cardiff was granted city status by King Edward VII in 1905. By 1949, it had a population of 243,000, and it became the capital of Wales in 1955. The city centre was tightly packed, bound by the River Taff to the west, Cardiff Castle and the Civic Centre to the north, and two railway stations, Central and Queen Street, to the south and east respectively. Cardiff Docks lay further south.

In the 19th century, the port was one of the largest dock systems in the world, transporting iron and coal around the world. At the turn of the 20th century, coal exports peaked at over thirteen million tonnes. Several docks were constructed to facilitate the rapidly increasing flow of iron and coal: the Bute West Dock was the first dock to be opened by the 2nd Marquis of Bute in 1839, followed by the Bute East Dock in 1855, Roath Basin in 1874, Roath Dock in 1887, and the Queen Alexandra Dock in 1907. At the time, the international price of coal was struck in Cardiff's Coal Exchange building, and it was here that the world's first £1million coal deal was signed.

Iron and coal would be brought down from the South Wales Valleys' coalfields and ironworks, initially on the Glamorgan Canal and later by railroad. The canal, constructed in the late 18th century, ran from Merthyr Tydfil, along the valley of the River Taff, through Cardiff city centre, ending at Cardiff Docks. My father could remember the canal flowing along Mill Lane, running next to Bridge Street, before it was filled in in 1951.

The growth of Cardiff Docks through the 19th century brought many immigrants to the city. Butetown and the surrounding dockland area, later known as Tiger Bay, became a diverse community, with over 350,000 seafarers and dock workers from at least 50 nationalities making Cardiff their home and contributing to the dock's operations and the city's maritime industry.

Some of the largest immigrant communities to live and work in Tiger Bay were the Irish, Somalis, Yemenis, and Greeks. As Tiger Bay became a bustling mix of multi-racial communities, it developed a powerful character and later developed a reputation as a red-light district and for gambling dens. It is said that during the early part of the 20th century, such was the rate of immigration growth that South Wales absorbed immigrants at a faster rate than anywhere in the world, except the US.

Between 1881 and 1914, over 120,000 Jews fleeing antisemitic pogroms in Central and Eastern Europe also emigrated to Britain. Around 4,700 are estimated to have arrived in South Wales, almost half of whom settled in Cardiff, with Jewish communities growing throughout the region, especially in Merthyr Tydfil, Swansea, and Newport. These Jewish immigrants were not generally employed in the traditional industries of South Wales, such as coal mining and iron working, but were merchants and pedlars seeking business in working-class areas. Lionel Bernstein, a customer who grew up in Merthyr after his grandparents emigrated there at the turn of the century, remembers the small but vibrant Jewish community, where many Jews were shopkeepers. He recalls: "When we walked along the high street to synagogue on the High Holy Days, shop after shop would have signs saying, 'closed due to holidays'; that's just how it was."

Before and after the Second World War, Cardiff experienced a further wave of immigration. During the 1930s and early 1940s, around 80,000 Jewish refugees from Nazi-occupied Europe flocked to the UK seeking safety, and many settled in South Wales, particularly Cardiff, where, as we've seen, government-backed schemes enabled industrialists to open factories in Treforest. Their numbers were swelled by thousands of evacuees from other parts of Britain, many of whom remained or returned after the war, and later by former German prisoners-of-war who had been interned near Bridgend and who, on their release, either stayed or returned to Wales. In the 1950s, refugees from Soviet-occupied Eastern Europe arrived, escaping the clutches of communism. Many of them were Jewish, and the Jewish population in Cardiff grew rapidly from just a few families in the mid-19th century to a peak of around 5,500 in the 1960s, with three synagogues, kosher shops, and several Jewish youth and cultural groups.

Large numbers of economic migrants from Italy and Spain also arrived in the area in the inter-war period, and again after the Second World War, seeking employment after economic depression at home curtailed any opportunities. Large communities were established, particularly in the South Wales valleys, where many cafés, fish and chip shops, and ice-cream parlours were opened. A customer recently told me that many Italian cafés opened to keep the men out of the pubs! A few of these businesses still exist and thrive today in the hands of the next generations, such as Sidoli's, the famous Italian ice cream manufacturers founded in Ebbw Vale in 1922.

These immigrants had one thing in common: they fled their homelands and settled in a foreign country. They lived and socialised together, sharing common languages and cultures, and longed for things that reminded them of home. Food was central to these memories.

One of our current customers, Marta Phillips, aged 93, and her sister Frieda, aged over 100, were Czech refugees who came to Cardiff in 1938. Marta recalls: "I remember the barrels of gherkins and the 'stinky *käse*' (smelly cheese), which my sister insisted had to be stored outside." These loose gherkins, which had to be fished out with a net, were coincidentally known as Wallies. The name emerged in the late 19th century, when Eastern Europeans arrived in London and enjoyed pickled cucumbers served with olives. Olives were known as a "wally" in Cockney rhyming slang, and the word stuck.

The whole area around Bridge Street was a cluster of Jewish-owned businesses. As well as Bridge Street Stores, there was Krotosky's, the Kosher butchers; Rapport's, a clock and watchmaking business; Rivlin's, a garment importer and distributor; Glicker's toy wholesalers; Jacob's antique market; and Gaba's, a goods wholesaler. By the 1950s, more than 20 businesses were owned and run by Jewish immigrants around Bridge Street.

I am not aware whether these Jewish businesses, or the wider Cardiff Jewish community in general, suffered from any significant antisemitism during these years. There had been antisemitic riots in Tredegar in 1911, but these feelings had long abated. Rather than being attacked, immigrants were celebrated for the employment they provided and admired for their entrepreneurial spirit. There was also still quite a degree of sympathy for the plight of these refugees as news of the horrors of the war emerged.

Bridge Street was a central location in Cardiff, with easy access to the docks and the train and bus stations nearby. However, by the

1950s many premises in the area were run down, the street having originally been established in 1839 as a route from the city to the gaol. Because of this, properties were cheaper to find there than elsewhere in the city centre, making it a natural place for immigrant Jews to set up their businesses. Redevelopment of the city centre has meant nearly all these businesses have been demolished or are no longer in Jewish hands. However, a couple still exist today, in the shape of Rapport's and Jacob's Antique Market, as well as Wally's Delicatessen. Today, the Jewish History Association of South Wales runs a historic trail of Jewish businesses and other Jewish landmarks in the city.

Seven ornate Victorian and Edwardian arcades could be found in the city centre. These arcades gave shoppers a unique experience, showcasing an eclectic mix of owner-managed businesses. They are still integral to the city's retail landscape, and Cardiff has recently embraced the marketing brand, "City of Arcades".

Initially just a grocery store, the shop struggled in the post-war austerity years, which saw widespread rationing and price controls. Then Ignatz had an idea that would save the business and enable it to thrive in the following years.

He began stocking the shelves with continental products. He knew these foods were now in greater demand in Cardiff following the influx of immigrants from Europe, escaping persecution, deprivation, and shattered economies after the war. He had the goods shipped by road and rail from speciality food importers in London, although I'm not quite sure how he knew where to source these hard-to-find products. I suspect he may have had some help from some of his more business-savvy customers.

Throughout the 1950s and 1960s, the shelves brimmed with jars of loose spices and specially imported goods, from Krakus sauerkraut and pickles to exotic jams and sauces. I vividly remember jars of Krakus pickles piled high in pyramid formation, and Krakus jams, which were known for being fruity and not too sweet, displayed in wire baskets in the window. Krakus products are still sold in the shop today; it is a brand that has spanned the decades and connects today's shop to that of my grandfather.

The chilled counter was replete with continental cheeses, hams and sausages, and the floors were stocked high with barrels of gherkins, pickled fish, and other delicacies you couldn't find elsewhere. Salamis hanging from the ceiling gave the shop an authentic European feel, and Ignatz never returned to his grocery days.

The variety and uniqueness of the product range is encapsulated by Irving Lewis, now aged 95. Perhaps the shop's oldest living customer, having been visiting since the 1950s, he says: "I bought cashew nuts, coffee beans, white crab meat, and tins of crayfish, which I used as 'currency' while in the army and for a decent cup of coffee in the NAAFI.[3]"

The changes brought in by Ignatz changed the shop's appeal, and as word spread among the city's European communities, customers flocked to the store from near and far. The shop began to thrive, despite not being in the most salubrious location. It sat in a run-down part of the city, a short distance from Queen Street, the main shopping street, comprising a collection of ramshackle Victorian buildings spread across a maze of small streets. The shop was next to The Greyhound, an infamous pub known for rowdiness and brawls that tumbled onto the street. The shop's outside toilet sat against The Greyhound's backyard; drunken voices spilled over the wall along with the occasional flung boot or old shoe.

There were dramas at the front of the shop, too – drunken fights that on more than one occasion resulted in a broken window, leaving shattered glass all over the produce, which then had to be discarded. Money was also lost to thieves. The back office was next to the pub, making it easy for people to climb over and break in.

In addition, the area had problems with pests, so Ignatz brought in a cat to patrol the property. He was driven to succeed in the business, no matter what, and he did all he could to give himself the best chances. After all they had been through, his goal was to

---

[3] The Navy, Army, and Air Force Institute, which provided food for the UK armed forces

create a business that would provide his family stability far into the future.

It is fair to say that the shop was unique in Cardiff, and possibly in the whole of the UK, with its range of imported continental products, most of which hadn't been seen in the country before. Ruth Morris, the daughter of Joachim Koppel, who had established the Aero Zipp factory where Ignatz had worked before setting up the shop, remembers her parents referring to the shop as a "trinket box" and that they loved everything about it.

Ignatz now spoke fluent English, albeit with a strong accent, and had adopted the Anglicised name of Ivor to assimilate better. However, he chose not to amend his surname as some other immigrant Jews had done. Perhaps this was a step too far, having already lost so much; it was the last connection he had with his parents. However, English was not the dominant language in the shop. It was full of Germans, Czechs, Poles, and other Eastern Europeans, all delighted to find the much-loved foods they had been unable to buy elsewhere in Cardiff, such as herrings, pickled cucumbers, carp, rye breads, cheeses, and a seemingly endless variety of cured meats and sausages. It had a delicatessen's hallmarks before the UK was even familiar with the concept.

Bridge Street became a place not only to shop, but also to socialise, reminisce, and catch up on the latest gossip. Many of the shop's customers had been accomplished industrialists before coming to the UK, either as wartime refugees or escaping Eastern European hostility after the war. Like my grandfather, they had drawn on their earlier experience to build successful businesses in the UK, and some had become very wealthy. While the imports at Bridge Street Stores often didn't come cheap, this wasn't a problem for these customers, and some would place regular orders for home delivery.

These cultured people craved a taste of the foods they grew up with now they lived in a strange land with vastly different culinary traditions. Bridge Street Stores gave them a feeling of familiarity and nostalgia and became a haven.

Perhaps because of that (but also because this is how people tended to shop in those days), most customers were regulars and would only buy what they needed for the next few days before returning to the shop to buy more supplies.

These customers prized personal, attentive service, so they loved the warm welcome and honourable, old-school shopkeeping delivered by my grandparents. The aim wasn't to serve someone quickly and then pass on to the next person, but to take time to talk and connect. One current customer, Kath Smith, who visited the shop with her father, told me how he and my grandfather would chat across the counter, putting the world to rights, while he was serving other customers simultaneously. Another customer, Michael Racz, who came to the shop with his Hungarian father every Saturday, recalls: "We went in for *wiejska* for our Hungarian goulash but would usually be tempted into buying something extra."

Another lifelong customer, Mr Engl, started going to Bridge Street Stores at seven. His father, a factory owner from Budapest, arrived every Friday to shop and socialise. Mr Engl recalls being frightened by my grandfather's gold-capped teeth, and how the chilled goods were displayed on a marble slab instead of a refrigerator. He also remembers the countless barrels piled high with loose products such as herrings and cucumbers. Mr Engl's mother would make breakfast rolls with liver sausage bought from the shop, something he says he has had for breakfast every day since.

Mr Engl also recalls Ignatz's distinctive gravelly voice – likely due to years spent chain-smoking. Later, Dad became a heavy smoker too, undoubtedly influenced by his father's habit.

At work and socially, Ignatz was sometimes quite gruff. "He was very outspoken and didn't suffer fools gladly," Dad's cousin Edgar recalls. "If I were standing in the shop with my hands in my pockets, he would say, 'Get your hands out of your pockets!' He was quite a strict disciplinarian. I think that stemmed from his army days: he was a leader."

My grandmother worked alongside her husband but was quieter than he was. She was very much the image of an obedient wife supporting her husband, and most people who remember the store recall Ignatz rather than Frieda. However, her importance to the business cannot be underestimated.

Ignatz and Frieda in Bridge Street Stores, circa 1960.

Despite scaring the young Mr Engl, my grandfather is widely remembered as a kind man who was in his element serving customers. He would happily give customers' children tasters of food and often offer customers little gifts, especially at Christmas.

These are all skills that passed on to my father, Wally, who joined his parents in the business at the age of 14 in 1950, after working there on weekends and school holidays from an early age. Dad had been given a good schooling at Cathays National School and later at Clark's College on Newport Road. Like other children of German and Austrian immigrants, he likely suffered from some xenophobic antisemitism at school, with his foreign accent making him stand out as different. His education might have widened his prospects, but he was always expected to enter the family business like his elder brother Otto. I never knew whether my father was agreeable to this or resented it, but it became his life, and he got on with it. Outside work, Dad enjoyed going to the Jewish Youth Club, Habonim, where he particularly enjoyed the camping trips and camaraderie, and playing table tennis for Cardiff Maccabi.

When Dad donned his Bridge Street Stores overalls, my uncles Otto and Sigi were doing their National Service. Before that, Otto had worked in the store, while Sigi had trained as a tool and die maker at Aero Zipp, a job he loved. Sigi's desire to pursue this work, rather than go into the family business, caused much tension between him and his father.

And there was more: Sigi also nurtured a desire to go to Israel. His National Service, during which he was frequently on the end of antisemitic jibes by his fellow recruits, strengthened these Zionist urges, and in 1951, shortly after completing his National Service, he boarded a ship to Israel, where he felt he belonged. He had never truly felt settled in the UK, and after so much upheaval, he longed for somewhere he could call home. Unlike his parents and brothers, he couldn't find this in Cardiff, where my grandparents had built a strong family life, which included regular visits from Maks, Irka, and their sons Roger and Edgar. "Fritzi was lovely," Edgar fondly recalled. "She was the driving force behind Ignatz. She was my favourite auntie. It was just her general manner – always hospitable. Whenever there was a birthday, we gathered in each other's houses with presents."

In the early days, the families used to play cards together, but soon my grandfather, who was always the trailblazer and the first to adopt new inventions, bought a television. Naturally, everyone else followed. "When the television was on, you couldn't say a word, you just had to sit there and listen to it," Edgar recollects. "It was one of those 10-inch black and white sets stuck in the corner with two channels, but he would just sit there and enjoy it. He loved his detective programmes."

Edgar also remembers how Ignatz enjoyed watching the horse racing on television. This hobby seems somewhat at odds with my image of my grandfather, but I'm pleased he found ways to relax outside of work (I don't know whether he indulged in the occasional flutter).

I am glad to have had the opportunity to learn something about my grandparents' character from Edgar. It's not something my father ever talked to me about, and of course, by the time I wanted to know more, the opportunity was no longer there. I wonder why Dad didn't speak much about his parents. Was it because my sisters and I didn't ask much about them, and he thought we weren't interested? Or did it reflect something of his upbringing, of his relationship with his parents? I have never had the impression that they were particularly close or that home was a warm and loving environment, but as they had both died by the time Dad was 31, maybe it was all just a long time ago.

Edgar's mother would occasionally take him to the Bridge Street shop, which she described as an "Aladdin's cave", where he was particularly struck by the huge barrel from which pickled cucumbers would be fished out with a pair of tongs and placed into jars brought into the shop by customers (a sustainable custom before the term was even thought of). However, his mother wasn't a regular customer, considering such specialised food too expensive compared to the prices in regular supermarkets.

On February 17, 1955, aged 18, my father's fledgling business career was interrupted, like his father's before him, when he was conscripted into the army to do his National Service. The National Services Act 1947 mandated that all non-disabled men between the ages of 18 and 30 were to be called up for two years of service. He joined the 29th Field Ambulance Company of the Royal Army Medical Corps, attached to the 12th Infantry Brigade. His army number was 23116459. He enlisted and did his initial training at Crookham in Hampshire. On May 10, 1955, he was posted to Clive Barracks, Hildesheim, in the Harz Mountains in Germany. Edgar remembered him coming home on leave and sitting in the kitchen painting his sergeant's stripes on his uniform white.

Wally in the Royal Army Medical Corps, 1955.

Dad did well in the army (just like his father) and was promoted to lance corporal on November 9, 1955, corporal on January 7, 1956, and sergeant on August 11, 1956. Edgar was immensely proud of his older cousin: "It was incredibly good to rise to sergeant in two years. He was a good leader. That's how he got on so well later, because he was a real businessman."

Wally was discharged on March 10, 1957, and his discharge record read:

"This man has attained the rank of sergeant, which clearly shows his intelligence, initiative, and all-round usefulness. He is honest and thoroughly reliable."

Wally was then enlisted into the Army Emergency Reserve for three-and-a-half years and reverted to the rank of acting corporal. His attachment was to the 158th Welsh Field Ambulance (Territorial Army) based at Westgrove Drill Hall, Cardiff, although he was never called upon to attend. He was finally discharged from his engagement on August 16, 1960, and from all Army Reserve Liability on February 28, 1964.

He always said that his army days were his "university years" and that he never saw any active casualties, only played war games. He made many good friends amongst his fellow recruits, and his photo album from those years, annotated with nicknames and funny quips, is one of my most treasured possessions today.

Overall, life for the Salamon family was good. My grandparents had successfully built not only a shop, but also a community. Compared with their lives in Austria, where they had probably been the only Jews in the village, they were now embraced by the Jewish community in Cardiff, or at least sections of it. Because the shop sold *treif* (foods that are not kosher according to Jewish dietary laws), the Orthodox Jewish community largely shunned it.

In fact, the established, assimilated Jewish community in Cardiff did not generally look fondly at the newly-arrived immigrants from Europe. Not only was their lack of religious observance frowned upon, but their very arrival caused fear that a rise in antisemitism would follow, which might affect their positions, as they had heard what had happened on the Continent.

A considerable proportion of the shop's customers were immigrant Jews, but for them, Jewishness was more about their cultural identity than a commitment to rigid religious observances. They ate non-kosher foods and didn't strictly observe Jewish laws. This chimed with my grandfather's sensibilities, and with their encouragement, he left the Orthodox community at Cathedral Road Synagogue, where Sigi, Otto and Wally had celebrated their bar mitzvahs, and joined the newly established Reform Jewish community, Cardiff New Synagogue (now Cardiff Reform

Synagogue), which took over a former Methodist chapel in Moira Terrace, Adamsdown.

This synagogue was founded in 1948 by two prominent Cardiff businessmen – Max Corne, a cinema owner, and Myer Cohen, a solicitor. At least one-third of its congregants were refugees from Continental Europe, many of whom had lost close family in the Holocaust. In 1953, a memorial tablet was erected in the synagogue in memory of relatives and families who had perished during the war. The plaque reads:

"This tablet is erected in memory of the relatives of members of this synagogue who perished by Nazi oppression and whose graves are unknown. May their dear souls rest in peace."

These immigrants became known collectively as "the Continentals" – a term used derogatively by the established Jewish community in Cardiff to highlight their differentness. No doubt they were shocked and upset by this attitude; it would not have been what they expected from fellow Jews, especially after all they had been through.

By 1949, the young congregation had appointed a full-time minister, Rabbi Dr Louis Gerhard Graf, who was from Berlin. He followed the more modern approach to Judaism emerging from Germany in the 19th century, which aimed to reconcile Jewish tradition with the changing world and evolving Western thought, and which emphasised the developmental nature of Judaism.

One aspect that was particularly challenging for these immigrants was the question of Jewish status, especially when they wanted to marry. The Orthodox synagogue in Cardiff demanded that they see their parents' *ketubahs* (Jewish marriage contracts) to prove their Jewish lineage. For most, this was simply impossible; they either no longer existed or were impossible to get. The Reform synagogue took a different approach. They recognised a Jew as a Jew, regarding the person, not the piece of paper, as paramount.

Among the Reform community were many Holocaust survivors. I grew up around people who arrived in this country on the Kindertransport, others who had spent time in concentration camps (and had the tattoos on their arms to show for it) or worked as slave labourers. One woman, Mrs Bergman, a Czech Holocaust survivor, spoke of when she was working as a slave labourer in a German armaments factory in Dresden. She and her fellow prisoners heard Allied bombers overhead and wished they would drop their bombs on their factory. Mrs Bergman's story was harrowing. She was pregnant when sent to Mauthausen concentration camp in 1945, not long before the American liberation of the camp. Although she was malnourished, she managed to keep her pregnancy a secret. She would have been sent straight to the gas chambers had they not been blown up by the Germans the day before her arrival, to cover up their atrocities. As the Americans advanced, the German guards loaded the inmates into cattle wagons to move them to another camp, but with the Allied soldiers so close, they ended up simply abandoning them there, locking them into the wagons with no food or water. Mrs Bergman gave birth to a daughter on the cattle wagon on May 2, 1945, three days before the camp was liberated. Her daughter, Eva Clarke, has been a lifelong Holocaust educator. Sadly, Mrs Bergman's story was just one of many distressing stories among the early members of the synagogue.

My family remain members of this synagogue today; it's where my three children and I had our bar and bat mitzvahs, and I have served as treasurer for most of the past 26 years.

*

Dad's marriage followed his return from National Service in 1957. He was 22 when he first started dating my mother, Laraine Bassett, following a bit of careful choreography by my grandmother, Beatrice (Beattie).

Mum's family were based in Bridgend, where they had moved from London when my grandfather, Ernest (Ernie), took a job with a furniture manufacturer. My grandmother's family were from Minsk, in modern-day Belarus, and had come to the UK at the end of the 19th century to escape the wave of pogroms sweeping Russia then. They settled in London's East End, eking out a living while housed in cramped tenement flats. Mum recalls hearing tales of her grandmother having to share a cooker with the woman living in the room next door, who, like her, had four children to feed.

Like many immigrants who had endured such hardship, my grandmother (we called her *Booba*, the Yiddish word for grandmother, also spelt *Bubbe*) was eager to ensure her daughter had a better start in life. As far as she was concerned, this meant making a good match with an eligible young Jewish man.

With that in mind, she started taking her daughter to a Jewish club for teenagers in Cardiff, where the mothers enjoyed tea while the teenagers socialised and danced. Mum learned to jive there and had a couple of dates, but nothing came of them, and she sensed that her mother was getting worried.

Then, one day, *Booba* announced that she was going shopping at the Bridge Street shop and that Mum must go with her. Outside the shop, she instructed her to go and talk to Dad. As Mum recalls:

"She said to me, 'Right. Now, I want you to go in and have a nice chat with him. If you do as I ask, then we will go to C&A and buy you a new dress.' And that was a big thing, as I didn't often have new dresses; I had hand-me-downs from my mum and shared clothes with my sister. Things were tough in those days.

"I was really geared up, so I went in there and stood in front of the counter and said to Wally, confidently: 'Are you going to the Silver Ticket ball?' This was a big Jewish ball in May.

"'No, I'd really like to go, but I've got nobody to go with,' he replied.

"Was he primed as well as me? I could see his mother standing there with a big grin from ear to ear. I said, 'Oh, that's funny. Me too. I've got nobody to go with.'

"'Shall we go together?' he shyly suggested.

"'What a good idea,' I said."

And so they went to the ball, Mum got the new dress from C&A, and six weeks later they were engaged. Dad's parents put on a lovely engagement party at Bindles dancehall in Penarth, and one year later, on July 21, 1959, the young couple married at Cardiff New Synagogue, aged 18 and 22 respectively. I don't know for sure, but I would not be surprised if the wedding date was arranged to minimise disruption in the shop.

Wally and Laraine's engagement party, July 10, 1958, with a happy Frieda in the background.

Unfortunately, Ernie had recently lost his job, so Dad's family stepped in at the last minute to help their *machatonim* (the parents of your child's spouse) arrange the wedding. This was a massive financial stretch for them, as they were not well off themselves, and Mum was forever grateful for their generosity.

My parents, maternal and paternal grandparents, and other family members look so happy in a photograph of the bridal party on the synagogue's steps. The bride, still so young, glowed in her beautiful white wedding gown, with a flowery headdress and petite bouquet. The groom looked resplendent in a top hat, dinner jacket, and bow tie, sporting a floral horseshoe on his lapel for good luck.

Wally and Laraine on their wedding day, July 21, 1959.

One of the wedding guests was Maureen Goldstein, a cousin of Mum's on their mother's side (their grandmothers were sisters). Maureen and Otto hit it off at the wedding, and not long after, they were engaged to be married.

Looking back at her whirlwind romance with Dad, Mum is stunned at how quickly her life transformed: "I was just over 18 years old when we married," she says. "It all happened very quickly. It just took over. And that's how my life began. We had a lovely marriage and three wonderful children. It was a good life. But it's just strange how it all unfolds."

From the time they started dating, Mum began visiting the shop to see Dad, and she also started chatting with the customers. She described the scene:

"There was a chair, I think for elderly ladies to sit on, right next to the refrigerated counter where all the meats and cheeses were on display. I didn't know what to do with myself when I went there in working hours, so I would just sit there most of the time. I remember feeling so awkward and uncomfortable, but I got to know all the old customers like that, because they were all a bit taken with me. I was very young, just 17."

From the outset, the prospect of joining the Salamon family business hovered over Mum, but she had other ideas. She had worked in retail as a Saturday girl since the age of 15, mostly selling ladies' underwear and hosiery in a drapery shop, and already knew this was not the job for her. She recalls:

"I decided I was going to be a secretary, so that's what I did. I went to Port Talbot to train at the Steel Company of Wales, as it was called in those days. It was a very prosperous business; it had a little college of its own, and you could go there from school. It was one of the first training colleges. My mum had found out about it, she was good at stuff like that, and she arranged for me to go there for six months of training, learning shorthand, typing, filing, and things like that. After six months, you got a job in the steelworks."

She had only worked there for about a year when she married my father. Dad wanted her to work in the shop, but much to her relief, she fell pregnant quickly, and motherhood beckoned.

Dad's parents were, of course, delighted. They had no girls, and Mum remembers them saying she was a "pretty little thing" who was very much in love with their son. The two of them would sit together holding hands in the dining room at the family home in Llanbleddian Gardens, and Mum recalls my grandparents exclaiming how lucky they were to have her in their lives. "They were lovely to me, and they were very, very good to my parents. They were very sweet, charming people who had a sort of lost look about them somehow – not surprisingly, with what they had been through. They came here with nothing, but they had somehow, despite everything, made themselves a life in Cardiff."

Before their marriage, Mum lived with her parents in Bridgend, and Dad lived with his parents in Llanbleddian Gardens. Dad's parents lent them some money to put down as a deposit on their first home, in Kyle Avenue, Rhiwbina, where they moved when they married. By 1965, when they moved to Llyswen Road, Cyncoed, they had two children: my sister Belinda, born in 1961; and me, born in 1963. My younger sister, Rochelle, followed in 1967. This is where they raised their family and spent many wonderfully happy years.

Despite the family's success in creating a new life in Wales, the spectre of the war and the Holocaust sometimes reared its head. The trial of Adolf Eichmann in 1961 would have been a particularly poignant moment for Ignatz and Frieda, who no doubt watched the television broadcast of the trial with interest. Eichmann had handled the Nazi's forced emigration policy in Vienna, which saw my grandparents evicted from their home, and from where they escaped with their lives. Eichmann tightly controlled the IKG in Vienna and was personally involved in many of the emigration decisions. I do not know if either of my grandparents ever came face-to-face with Eichmann during their emigration process, but his menacing presence would never have been far away as their nightmare in Austria unfolded.

Eichmann had been kidnapped in Argentina in 1960 by Israeli Mossad agents and taken to Israel to stand trial. He was charged with 15 counts: four for crimes against the Jewish people; three for crimes against humanity against Jews; one for war crimes; four for crimes against humanity against non-Jews; and three for membership of enemy organisations. He was convicted on all 15 counts, sentenced to death, and hanged on June 1, 1962.

Meanwhile, business was booming amid a Yiddish, Czech, German, and Polish hubbub at Bridge Street Stores. Despite financial losses caused by uninvited visits from The Greyhound's more troublesome customers, everything on the surface was going swimmingly.

However, the burden of running the business was falling heavily on the shoulders of my grandparents, with Otto and then Dad away for extended periods on National Service. The almost inevitable outcome of this was that my grandfather's health (we children call him Papa), which had been in decline since his army days, worsened dramatically. Edgar recalls him having a series of operations in his last few years, and that he never took time to recover from these before returning to work. He was deeply suspicious of doctors and was inclined to soldier on as much as possible.

Edgar remembers being admitted to hospital in his youth with suspected appendicitis and finding himself on the same ward as Ignatz, recalling: "He came over, asked how I was, and said, 'When the doctor comes to see you, tell him you feel fine, and don't let them put a knife into you.' I did exactly that and was discharged. That showed his fear of hospitals and operations."

For all his determination, his health continued to fail, and he finally died on October 24, 1963, in Llandough Hospital, Cardiff. Many years later, at my father's 70th birthday celebrations, Dad and Sigi disagreed over their recollections of how their father died and for how long he had been able to continue working in the business. Their memories, faded by the passage of time, were quite different. What is known for sure is that the cause of death recorded on Ignatz's death certificate was inflammation of the abdomen, a blood clot in the abdomen, and narrowing of the arteries. This should have acted as an early warning sign for Dad, who would later in life suffer from major heart issues and cancer of the stomach.

Frieda and Ignatz, circa 1955.

I wonder if Papa ever felt truly at home in Wales. Indeed, he built a good life, with a business, family, and friends around him. But was he settled? Had he reconciled with all the upheaval and loss in his early life? I will never know for sure, as things like this were seemingly never discussed in the family. However, the memoirs of other immigrants who arrived in similar circumstances are revealing.

Many Continental Jews who arrived in Wales after fleeing Nazism never felt truly Welsh or British, despite living most of their lives in Wales and being naturalised as British citizens. Perhaps this was because they couldn't shake off the early trauma of being seen as outsiders upon arrival. Many claimed that their continental accents were the main issue, marking them as foreigners and hindering their employment prospects. Strangely, they didn't feel Austrian, German, Czech, or Polish (or from whichever country they emigrated) either. In many instances, they had not lived there for long and, for understandable reasons, felt let down by these nations. Many never returned, including my grandparents.

The only identity they retained was being Jewish. This wasn't a question of religious observance but an ethnicity – an identity based on family, tradition, and heritage. Some said they felt a duty to keep their Judaism alive in memory of the six million who had perished.

They maintained this identity by joining synagogues, observing Jewish festivals and traditions, educating their children in the Jewish faith, and naming them after deceased family members. I can see these behaviour patterns in Ignatz's life. However, I know he never lost his connection to Poland altogether, probably nourished by his work and social life rather than by an allegiance to his country of birth. Although his identity was complex, and how he felt about it was unknown, from what I now know, I would say my grandfather identified as a Polish Jew.

After Papa's death, my grandmother (we call her Mama) moved out of 12 Llanbleddian Gardens into the property they had bought many years earlier at 110 Ninian Road, closer to where their sons lived. Belinda and I only have vague memories of Mama, but we share one recollection of her handing Parma Violet sweets to us when we visited her at home.

After Ignatz's death, and free of the responsibilities of looking after the shop and her husband, Mama went to Israel for a long-awaited reunion with her beloved brother Yaakov and his wife Zila. They walked in the Tel Aviv parks and talked about their experiences since they had last been together.

Frieda died a few years later, in October 1967, from heart failure. Undoubtedly, the strain of losing her husband and the difficult challenges she had faced in her life contributed to her poor health. Both losses were deeply mourned by the family, who had relied on Papa's strength and leadership and on Mama's similar qualities, which were softened with warmth and kindness.

Reunion in Tel Aviv, circa 1965. Left to right: Frieda, Zila, Yaakov.

Frieda Salamon, 1902-1967.

They are buried together in the Reform Jewish cemetery in Ely, Cardiff. Using the anglicised version of his name, Papa's headstone reads: "In Loving Memory of Ivor Salamon."

It is a Jewish custom to name a child after a deceased relative, but this does not necessarily mean giving them the same name. Some people choose a name that begins with the same letter; others use the deceased relative's name as the child's middle name; some use the Hebrew name of the deceased person; and some people anglicise it. So, for example, if the relative's name was Yitzhak, the child might be named Isaac, or even Ian, as is the case with Otto's son Michael.

I was born just before Papa died, so by Jewish custom I couldn't be named after him. My middle name is Joseph in English or Jozef in Hebrew, in memory of my great-grandfather. Therefore, my full Hebrew name is Jozef ben Zvi, meaning Joseph, son of Zvi, which is Dad's Hebrew name.

Daniel, my youngest child, is named after Papa. Ivor is his middle name, Yitzhak is his Hebrew name, or Yitzhak ben Jozef in full. Rochelle is named after Mama (her middle name is Frieda), and Belinda is named after Mama's mother, Rosa.

It is also a Jewish tradition to recite *kaddish* (a memorial prayer) in memory of deceased parents. Dad would quietly recite this prayer to himself every Friday evening at the family *Shabbat* (Sabbath, the Jewish day of rest) table, after the blessings had been completed for wine (*kiddush*) and bread (*hamotzi*). As a young boy, I didn't know what he was doing or saying, but I knew that you didn't interrupt or disturb him for the minute or so it took Dad to get through the prayer. As a teenager, I wanted to socialise with friends on a Friday night, but I knew I had to be at home for the *Shabbat* dinner and hear Dad recite *kaddish* before I could go out. Today, I remember Dad by reciting *kaddish* for him on the anniversary of his passing and at certain times in religious services throughout the year.

9

Business Evolution

Continental Delicatessen 1967-1981

By the time of Ignatz's death, Otto and Wally were already well equipped to take the helm at Bridge Street Stores, thanks to their father's mentorship and having worked there since the age of 14. Dad, who was short and sturdily built, took after his mother. Otto, who was taller and slimmer, looked more like his dad.

In the years immediately after their father's death, the brothers changed little about the shop, continuing to provide the same personal service and broadly the same goods. But in the early 1970s, spurred on by Britain's entry into the Common Market and emerging food trends, they gave the business a name incorporating a newly fashionable word: Delicatessen. A sign spelling out the new name, Continental Delicatessen, was erected in large blue capital lettering above the entrance.

As the Continental Delicatessen, they started selling more Western European foods and foods from further afield, such as spices, nuts, and dried fruits, which had become easier to source due to Britain's enhanced links with Europe and the rest of the world. The shop benefited massively from the expansion of international travel from the 1970s onwards. People were experiencing international foods on a much broader scale and wanted to buy them when they returned home. Then and now, the shop has always stocked the actual brands sold overseas, so customers know they are buying authentic products.

Continental Delicatessen, Bridge Street, circa 1974.

Looking for new trends to follow, they started stocking health foods and wholefoods, and Dad, together with their supplier Nature's Table, invented several new muesli recipes: Super Hi-Fibre, Deluxe, Fruit, Tropical, and Fruit & Nut, each with a prescribed quantity of cereals, dried fruits, and nuts. Fuelled by the popularity of the F-Plan diet, these were a huge hit and remain popular with customers today, some of whom, such as Richard Owen, have eaten the shop's muesli for breakfast since the 1970s.

Entering the booming wholefood market was a wise move: many of the shop's original customers were no longer alive, and their offspring had adopted more typically British foods and healthier eating habits. Besides the mueslis, Dad created a new snack called Crunchy Mix, later renamed Trail Mix, and when a new spicy Indian snack made its way onto UK shelves for the first time, he christened it Chana Chow. It is now widely known as Bombay Mix, but Wally's older customers still refer to it as Chana Chow.

Dad also created two new curry spice blends: a hot Spiced Madras Curry Powder, and a medium-strength Asian Special Curry Powder, the latter with whole cinnamon sticks, bay leaves, and cardamon pods. These blends continue to be mixed, packed, and sold in the store today, where they are still reliably popular with customers.

These spices, grains, and nuts were all sold loose from open sacks, tins, or other containers, and scooped out into brown paper bags for weighing on the old-fashioned scales. The scales had a dial from which the cost of the goods had to be manually calculated, requiring some rapid calculations while weighing goods. Selling loose products this way may seem old-fashioned from today's perspective, but they were working sustainably then, even though they didn't know it. The business was sustainable before it was fashionable to be so.

Current-day customers Gavin and Gail Kinsella remember visiting the shop in the 1970s. They were vegetarians – a relatively new food trend at the time – and they recall: "It was the only place you could get TVP (Textured Vegetable Protein, a meat substitute) and Indian spices."

Another modern-day customer, Louise Meaden, remembers her mother taking a continental cookery course in the 1970s, saying: "Bridge Street was the only place you could get all the ingredients."

As its customer base and range of stock continued to grow, the brothers seized the opportunity to expand into the unit next door when it became available – not for customer-facing space, but as a warehouse where, as a teenager, I remember lifting and stacking sacks of nuts and rice.

My sisters and I used to love going into the back room to pet the little ginger cat that Otto kept there to patrol for pests, and who sometimes, to our delight, had kittens, which were often given away to staff. A favourite activity of mine was diving into the mountain of discarded cardboard packaging that used to accumulate in the passageway. The shop also had an upper floor, which in the distant past had been residential, but was now a place of mystery, darkness, and danger for us children. You had to tread very carefully and stand on the joists, because there were no floorboards; I remember Dad once put his foot through the ceiling. We used to venture up there but were nervous of ghosts and rats, and falling through the ceiling.

Another source of fear was the courtyard's outdoor toilet, which backed onto The Greyhound pub. By the time we children were visiting the shop, Dad had erected barbed wire to stop people coming over the wall, but the stench and noise of the pub still travelled, mingling with the smell of hops from the nearby Brains Brewery. You could hear the pub-goers fighting and swearing, and at kicking-out time, you would see all the drunks come onto the green opposite the shop. They would lie there to sleep off their drunkenness in the afternoon then go back in at opening time. Sometimes I would see them urinating and fighting. It was a very rundown area.

As Dad was so tied up with the shop, my sisters and I frequently visited him at work, especially on Saturday mornings after the children's service at the synagogue, or after school visits to the Guildford Crescent swimming baths. On our way to the shop, we would get a bag of chips from the fish and chip shop next door, which we would eat in the back room of the shop with salami or garlic sausage, which Dad sliced for us and wrapped in paper.

My cousins Karen and Michael, Otto's children, were regular visitors too, especially on a Saturday when our mums would help in the shop. Michael has fond memories of those days, recalling:

> "If we couldn't go to one of the houses, we'd go to the shop and play shop. In the back room there was a table, and a sort of kitchen. We used to take things off the shelves into the back room, where we would build a little shop for ourselves and just stay out of the way. For lunch, we were allowed to go to the fish and chip shop on our own, where we bought the chips for pennies."

Karen remembers they were encouraged to behave well, with the promise of fudge sweets or chocolate-covered plums – popular Polish sweets still sold in the shop today.

The shop itself was a symphony of exotic smells: salami, cheese, herbs and spices, dried fruits, and fascinating physical sensations, too. Rochelle loved to plunge her hand into the rice sacks on the floor, feeling the tickle of dozens of grains on her skin.

Wally and Otto in Continental Delicatessen, circa 1976.

Otto and Wally were raised to work hard and always prioritise the business. When Mum and Dad were courting, he once told her in a letter that he couldn't meet up with her that weekend as he was needed in the shop. "Business before pleasure," he wrote.

Dad rarely, if ever, went on holiday with his parents when he was growing up. Perhaps this is why he later struggled to take time out to go away with Mum and us children. We only had occasional holidays, about once every four years, to places like the Costa del Sol and Malta.

Because Dad was always working, Mum had to shoulder most of the responsibilities for my sisters and me. In his absence, she took us on trips to the seaside, to activities such as piano lessons, judo, horse riding and ballet, and played sports with us. I remember being taken along to her regular rehearsals with the local amateur dramatic group, Orbit, which gave me a lifelong love of musical theatre.

As time moved on, we children grew up largely oblivious to the horrors our grandparents had escaped. Dad seemingly knew little of his parents' story, as they had been reluctant to talk about their wartime experiences, nor had they talked much about their lives before the war. This was common among refugee survivors of the Holocaust, who often didn't talk about their past, or at least not until many years later. There are various theories as to why this is the case: the need to protect their offspring from the horrific realities of what their parents had experienced; shame at the debasement they had suffered; the need to escape the pain of reliving the memories; or perhaps a desire to leave the past behind, assimilate in their new countries, and focus on building new lives.

In a memoir written by Debbie, Sigi's oldest child, she writes of Sigi talking about his father:

> "There were few occasions when he wanted to go into it. He said it was so long ago, he'd wrinkle up his face. Clearly his early memories, the ones that stood out in his mind, were not pleasant, and he preferred not to think about them."

But there were traces of the family history everywhere. Sigi, Otto, and Wally all spoke English with a slight German accent. This was more pronounced in Sigi and Otto, who were older than Wally when they arrived in the UK. They could also speak German to greater or lesser degrees, although by the time I joined the business, Dad's German was mainly limited to food vocabulary. He always said he could understand German being spoken better than he could speak it.

The Eastern European products, the continental customers, and the Eastern European workers in the shop all painted a picture of a prior life in Europe. Several of the shop's Eastern European customers – tough, strong men from Lithuania, Poland, and Latvia –

were employed by Dad to work on the student houses he had purchased, or in our home. I remember him rewarding them with smoked sausage or salami. They were ex-merchant seamen or ex-miners, often with large tattoos on their arms, missing or gold teeth, with heavily accented, gravelly voices and lined, worn faces. I was so scared, I could barely look at them.

The spectre of the Holocaust arose from time to time. Belinda recalls how Dad came home one day bearing a gift from a customer in the shop:

> "It was a gold necklace – a Star of David. I was already obviously quite aware of Jewish history and the Holocaust, and Dad said that the customer had seen me as a little girl in the shop, and he had no-one else to give it to, and he wanted to give it to a little Jewish girl. I remember being very touched, and that was all part of the resonance, this connection between Europe and the shop and being Jewish. Here was somebody else who had escaped the Nazi regime and who had no family, and gave it to me because I was the only little girl he knew. It was very touching."

The foods enjoyed at home were another sign of the family's European heritage. Mama had taken my mother under her wing and taught her the traditional Eastern European recipes she cooked at home. One of Dad's favourites was a classic but simple Polish dish of sour milk served with boiled baby potatoes, known as *siadle mleko* – "a dish for kings". I can still vividly remember Mum placing a bottle of milk on the windowsill in the sun until it soured and a layer of cream formed at the top, then scraping it off and spooning it onto the potatoes.

My father ate everything with *chrayne* – a grated horseradish relish mixed with beetroot. This was a typical Polish condiment, which Dad would eat with meat or fish. It was so strong it would make your eyes water, but I got a taste for it and still have it today with the occasional meal.

Dad would only eat rye bread made with caraway seeds. This is a staple in Polish households. In the early days, this would be sourced from London or Scotland (we knew it as London or Scotch bread) and delivered by train to Cardiff Central station, where it was collected. This bread was great when fresh, but due to its high rye content, it had a long shelf life and was particularly tasty toasted when a few days old. I also like this bread, although I have struggled to find a consistent supplier for it. It is something I enjoy on my visits to London.

Other Jewish foods I remember from childhood include *latkes* (small fritters), usually made with potatoes, but made by my mother with fried *matzo* meal (a ground form of the unleavened bread *matzo*) left over after frying fish and eaten dipped in sugar. Looking back, this was very unhealthy but so very tasty. We also ate *gefilte fish* (stuffed fish) from time to time – a dish made from a mixture of ground white fish, which my mother served with a slice of carrot on top.

I also remember having *tzimmes*, a type of Jewish stew made from carrots and flavoured with honey or sugar, and *kugel*, a baked casserole made from potato or noodles, which my mother mixed with carrots. On reflection, carrots seemed quite a staple in our household.

My favourite desserts were my mother's apple strudel and cheesecake. Apple strudel is a traditional Viennese pastry that originated in the Austro-Hungarian Empire. Traditionally made with hand-stretched dough, my mother used the more convenient filo pastry as a shortcut. It was filled with stewed apples and raisins and served warm with cream or ice cream.

My mother's cheesecake was to die for; a traditional Polish-style baked cheesecake (*sernik*) made from curd cheese and flavoured with vanilla, atop a base of crushed biscuits. Baked cheesecake differs from classic cheesecakes, which use cream cheese or ricotta and are not baked in the oven but left to rest. We still sell an authentic Polish cheesecake in the shop, which we have sourced for many years from a Polish bakery in London.

*

The seven weeks leading up to Christmas were always an intense time for the family. Dad woke at five every morning to leave for work and returned home late. Mum was regularly roped in to help in the shop, and my parents would be visibly exhausted. Belinda recalls:

"It was an ordeal because it was just non-stop. Christmas week was especially exhausting, and Mum still had to make Christmas day lovely for us, even though she was dog tired. And Dad's exhaustion was off the scale. He was working eighteen-hour days, on his feet nonstop, and carrying heavy, heavy stuff. You just never knew how he did it. He was so stoic and so strong. But he got a buzz out of it as well, because that was the time of year when there were loads of customers."

It was a similar story for Otto's family: he was out before the children got up, and home after they went to bed. Sometimes the children would be grouped together to make childcare easier. Karen recalls: "If our mum or Laraine were working, the five of us would be shoved together somewhere so that they could work. During December, we didn't see Dad – if we wanted to see him, Mum took us into the shop to see him."

Even though there was no Sunday trading in those days, it was still a seven-day week, because Otto and Wally would spend Sundays restocking the shop for the week ahead, making trips to the Cash 'n' Carry, or doing bookwork.

Following family tradition, it was inevitable that all the Salamon children would be called on to work in the shop as we hit our teens. Karen recalls how her father came home one day and declared: "We need some Saturday staff." She started work the next day.

"I was probably 14 when I started working there on a Saturday and school holidays," she says. "It was hard work, very hard work. I was serving, but I didn't serve the meat and cheeses on the counter because we weren't allowed to use the cutter. I'll never forget the shelf of different pastas. Pasta was just coming into fashion, and every Saturday at some point, Wally would get me to sort out the pastas. They were on a long shelf, and I had to tidy them all up for him. Other times, I would have to take down telephone orders for Dad and Wally to deliver."

Karen got to know plenty of regular customers, who usually visited at the same time every week, including George, who would spend time chatting and shopping, while his wife and daughter browsed at Bird's the Jeweller next door, and the customer who pulled up outside each week in a three-wheeled disability car. The staff had to go out, take her order, and bring the goods to her.

The shop had just one till, and on the counter where we children usually worked was a cash drawer, which was periodically emptied into the till. After the drawer was taken away to be emptied, there would often be a sudden rush of customers, and Karen remembers having to put money into her pockets to be counted later.

Wally usually took charge of the back-office tasks, while Otto stayed out front serving customers, and the children did whatever was asked of us. "Sweep the floor, serve a customer, fill a shelf, you just did it," Michael recalls. "We didn't know any different. That was how we were brought up, so we weren't missing being at home watching television. It got you out of the house. That was just our life."

Belinda worked in the shop from the age of 13 to 18. She remembers the long days but notes: "Dad worked longer." She particularly recalls selling loose spices such as turmeric and cumin, measuring them out on an old-fashioned set of scales, a task that turned her hands yellow and made them smell of curry.

Meanwhile, Otto and Wally oversaw everything with the help of David Pike – a young man who joined the business in 1971 – just as everyone, staff and customers alike, was having to get used to decimalisation, the new monetary system replacing pounds, shillings, and pence.

David, who was to become a core staff member in the business for decades, still clearly remembers his first meeting with Wally. He arrived at the Continental Delicatessen feeling nervous. His neighbour, Clive, who worked at the nearby Dewhurst Butchers, had told him there was a job at the shop, but David knew nothing of the food they sold. He felt daunted meeting Wally, because he was originally from Austria and David had never met a foreigner.

Nevertheless, the meeting went well and he got the job. "I was quite a shy boy; I was only 14 coming up to 15, but Wally was always very kind, very approachable, and very lovely. He became like a father to me," he says.

David had a passion for fishing, and soon after joining the business, Dad arranged for David to take me, aged 10, on a fishing trip. He even bought me a fishing rod. David took me to Roath Park Lake, where we tried our luck but caught nothing except the proverbial old boot. David would continue fishing for recreation and competitively for the whole of his life, but this was a one-off for me. The fishing bug didn't take hold of me, and my fishing rod never saw the water again.

At the time of David's arrival, the store was a unique business. Cardiff had a Greek and Polish shop, but no other Eastern European shops. As David recalls:

"It was unbelievably busy, especially on a Saturday, when you would have people almost two, three deep at the counter for cooked meats. We would have deliveries once a week from London on the back of a lorry: fresh produce just in butter boxes. You would have maybe 20 boxes, say with thirty pounds of meat in each one. The salamis and sausages used to come covered in fat, and I used to wash them in a sink before hanging them up. Once they dried, they would go into our cold room, where there were sausages hanging everywhere."

There was nowhere else for Italian and Spanish customers to get a taste of their home country. One current day customer, Jose Ramon Suarez, often went to the store after working his shift at Asteys café around the corner, to get chorizo, mortadella, and Manchego. He recalls: "It was the only place to get food from home." Mr Suarez still regularly visits the shop today and buys Spanish *turron* (nougat), which is hard to find elsewhere in Cardiff. Mr and Mrs Spinetti remember talking to Wally about their hometown of Parma in Italy, saying: "The shop was not central; you had to make your way there, but it was worth it."

Certain foodstuffs made an impression on David: the yard-long Polish sausages, from which sections were cut for customers; the barrels full of loose gherkins and sauerkraut; and the dreaded big wooden barrel of pickled herrings. David remembers these well:

"If somebody said, 'Could I have two schmaltz herrings?' that was the job that nobody wanted. They came from Norway, and they used to be put into this barrel: a layer of fish, a layer of salt, a layer of fish, a layer of salt. You would have a big battle and had to go right down to the bottom of the barrel and get them out. The male fish had a sort of white milk in it, and the female fish had eggs, and sometimes a customer would say, 'Can you get me two with roe?' and you'd think, 'Oh my god' and you'd have to go in this barrel, sort all these herrings out, and try and find the right ones, which we then wrapped up in newspaper. And as you can imagine, having been put down six months before in the salt, and cured, they had a strong smell."

As a young man, he dreaded The Greyhound, whose customers – Scrumpy-loving Irish boys who worked on the roads – frightened him to death with their brawls on the grass at the front of the shop. He used to share a taxi home with Clive, who, much to 15-year-old David's dread, would often propose a pint in The Greyhound while they waited for the cab. "It was unbelievably rough, you can't imagine," says David. "I used to sit on the stool in the bar with him and have a shandy while he was having a pint. I would be looking around, and all these really rough people – it was frightening."

The shop's other immediate neighbour was the Asian Spice Box, which sold loose spices and was far less threatening.

David quickly fell in love with life in the shop, its multinational customers, and its fascinating range of stock with strange names and flavours. There was no modern till, and he had to learn how to add up quickly: each customer's receipt, with the calculations, would be written on the back of a paper bag. To make this easier, prices would be displayed in easy-to-add-up values ending with 25p, 50p, or 75p. We still price goods like this in the shop today, even though our electronic tills can add up and work out the change. David developed excellent mental arithmetic skills; I was always amazed at how he could calculate the price of a single product from the case price quicker than I could do it on a calculator.

David was tasked with delivering the shop's takings to the bank daily – a walk that took him past Lipton's, the local supermarket, where a young woman called Tricia worked. She used to catch his eye as he went by. Then she and her friends stood outside the shop where David was serving, pretending they were going to the fish and chip shop. In response, David got into the habit of waving at her as he passed Lipton's, and the rest, as Tricia puts it, is history. In due course, they would marry, and Tricia (known by everyone as Tric) would come to work in Wally's with David.

David did well in school, and at the age of 16 he was offered several apprenticeships, but he decided his heart was in retail and chose to stay on at the delicatessen. When he passed his driving test at the age of 17, Dad bought a little blue Bedford van for him to run around Cardiff in, delivering orders to customers. He recalls:

"On Friday mornings, we used to do about 30 or 40 orders. All the Jewish and Continental families would ring up, we would write the orders down, and then we would make up the orders and I would deliver them to all the posh families up in Cyncoed and Lisvane. They would pay me, and I'd bring the money back."

He was stunned by the grandeur of the houses: one family, who owned a chocolate factory, had a large house on Llandennis Avenue in Cyncoed, with stables at the rear. He describes his trips there:

"I can remember driving this little cronky old blue van up the drive. I would take the order in and stand in the hallway. It was a massive house; they had a big sweeping staircase. I used to give the order to one of the maids, and she would go and get the money. They had these little dogs – I think they were Chihuahuas or Pekingese – which would come snapping at my feet. I remember flicking them away. That family had a big chalet in Switzerland, too, in the Alps. These were all people who had come over as displaced people and set up businesses. A lot of the clientele had factories. We used to see these people on a regular basis, just so they could get their food from home."

I was 14 when I started working in the shop during school holidays, though not on Saturdays as a rule, because that was when I played rugby. I was given the standard crisp white overalls to wear, and like my sisters and cousins, I was kept clear of the cheese and delicatessen counters due to the danger of cut fingers. I served the customers with nuts, herbs, and spices, and put out products.

I had grown up surrounded by the delights and occasional frights of the shop: smells ranging from glorious to heavy and pungent; the secret rooms and corners where kittens played and we children became imaginary shopkeepers; and the ghostly attic and threatening outside toilet, which you had to be brave to visit. Until now, however, I hadn't known the customers or the finer details of how the business was run.

As I continued working in the shop, I understood more about the business side of things, as opposed to it just being a place where my father worked. I remember I would be in the back room, and he would come in with the cash to count the money. I remember him standing up to count the money – it was all cash in those days, not cards. He would clear his desk and count it out in piles of hundreds. I still count the money like this today, although there's less cash now.

I was enormously proud of the shop, even from a young age. The shop was well known amongst my friends, and I used to brag that it earned more per square foot than Marks & Spencer. While this was not true, it reflected my pride in the business. The shop was just part of the family and formed the basis for most conversations in the house, especially around Christmas.

In the shop, we children saw a quite different side of our father, who was quiet and reserved at home. Belinda says:

"The shop was his kingdom. That was where his personality came out, chatting and guiding people, telling people what to do, and everything else. He would be there with the customers, chatting away and busy, busy, busy. It was where he was the most confident and the most outgoing. That's where you saw a dad that you never saw at any other time. Although it was exhausting, he did love it. It was his life."

Dad left his outgoing persona in the shop – he once told me that if he didn't feel exhausted at the end of the day, he didn't feel like he had done enough work. It was a show; it was what he needed to do for the business. This was his theatre; he was the director and leading man, his staff the fellow actors, and the customers the audience.

Karen agrees, noting that while her parents were quite sociable outside of work, this was the last thing Wally wanted after a day in the shop, preferring to enjoy some peace and quiet.

However, he never rested when he wasn't working in the shop. He didn't need downtime or relaxation. Working in the shop or on his projects was his form of relaxation. He did a lot of renovations himself, both in the shop and at home, notably building the wooden furniture in our bedrooms. He built the kitchen too and did most of the carpentry on the student houses he bought and converted into bedsits. Beyond the carpentry, he relied on his trusty Eastern European labourers and a few locals with whom he developed strong relationships. I remember there was a man for everything: Peter the electrician, Brian the plumber, Fred the painter, George the builder, and Luka the labourer. They loved him: he treated them well, and they would always work hard for him.

Gardening was also a passion, and in the little time he had available, Dad enjoyed landscaping the garden at home. He was always fond of a pond, and I remember him building one in our back garden, complete with rockery and waterfalls.

I was occasionally roped into helping with one of his projects – stripping walls, removing rubbish from sites, and the odd bit of painting. But Dad wasn't good at delegating, preferring to do everything himself whenever possible. It frustrates me that he never taught me building skills, although I understand his reasons. He would always say: "Hold the ladder", "Pass the hammer", "Pass the screwdriver", not "You go up the ladder". He didn't want me to make mistakes and was protecting me, but he was also a perfectionist and felt he could do it better.

One reason behind Dad's deep drive to succeed may have been the glimpses he got of his customers' affluent lives. He saw grace, elegance, and what money could buy, which spurred him on.

Mum remembers how, when she and Dad were still courting, she admired the elegant European customers she met while sitting in the shop – how they dressed, held themselves, spoke and behaved, which usually included a gentle kiss on the hand for her. She is convinced that Dad learned much of his charm in the shop from these customers.

A typical example was Mr Zinger, who used to enter the shop with a confident swagger, his coat flung loosely over his shoulders. Mum recounts:

"He was a handsome man, and wearing the coat over the shoulders was a very continental thing to do, especially if you were rich. Running the shop taught Wally very good English; these people were terribly well-spoken and very polite, with all this shaking of hands and 'How are you, madam?' Wally learned about how people behave, how they comport themselves, how they spoke to each other.

"Some of the conversations would have pricked up his ears, I'm sure. His customers gave him ideas about things we might never have considered. He picked up things about holidays which he'd never heard of. He heard people say, 'I think we might go on a cruise,' or 'We might go on a holiday.' He just picked up little nuggets of information, as you do. As a young person, you pick up all sorts of stuff. You don't realise it's soaking into you, and then it trickles out in later years."

Dad's fortunes improved, but he was never showy with it. The one notable luxury he permitted himself was a nice car. Over the years, he owned three Jaguars. His first two were old-style Daimler Jaguars with the classic Jaguar hood ornament, then he treated himself to a low-slung S-Type. I remember how Dad used to park it on Tyndall Street, on the other side of the railway tracks in what was then a red-light area. On one occasion, Dad and I arrived there after a day's work to find a prostitute lounging on the bonnet of the car.

"Fancy a bit of fun, love?" she said.
"Oh, I'm too tired, darling," Dad replied.
"Don't worry. I'll do all the work," she rallied.

Significantly, he vowed never to own a German car. He hated German things because of his background, which was ironic considering that he sold so many German products. But when you put that to him, he would shrug his shoulders and say: "You know, you've got to make a living."

However, the incessant workload, the stress of running the business, and no doubt his heavy smoking, all contributed to Dad developing heart problems. Like his father, Dad was a lifetime smoker. In photos from his army days, he can be seen holding a cigarette in every picture. One of my earliest memories is of Dad collecting Green Shield Stamp coupons from his cigarette packets. He had shoe boxes full of them, which he would exchange for goods from a catalogue.

When he first developed heart problems, Dad gave up smoking for about five years. Then he started smoking Hamlet cigars, but he inhaled the smoke into his lungs, as you would with a cigarette, which was worse because there was no filter. Eventually, he went back to smoking cigarettes.

For years, he had complained of angina but, with his usual stoicism, had shrugged it off. These angina pains were later classified as heart attacks by doctors. Then came a crisis he could not ignore. On September 2, 1979, he was returning with Mum from a beautiful walking holiday in Austria. At Munich airport, waiting to board their flight, he suffered a major heart attack. We were all devastated, and I remember the anxiety of not being able to visit him. He spent three months recovering in a hospital in Munich, where the care was first-class, but the experience ravaged Dad. He went out as a bull of a man, quite chunky, with thick fingers and massive forearms, but came back a shadow of himself; he had lost a lot of weight, which he never regained.

Rochelle was about to start high school then, and I remember helping her with her tie for her first day. Meanwhile, Mum flew back and forth from September to November until Dad was fit enough to come home.

Within days of his return, he was back at work. Nothing could keep him away from his beloved shop… like his father before him.

10

A Fresh Start

Wally's Delicatessen 1981-1993

Continental Delicatessen could have rolled on indefinitely, but on June 19, 1981, Otto and Wally received a devastating letter. Bridge Street had always been situated in a less-than-salubrious area, and now a plan was in place to remodel and gentrify it for modern shoppers. Immediate plans included an ice-rink, a large department store (Toys "R" Us), and a multi-storey car park above some small shop units. Forty-three years after the Nazis confiscated the family business in Austria, a compulsory purchase order informed the brothers that their business would also have to close. Notwithstanding the different circumstances and gravitas of the situation, this was nonetheless a momentous blow – one which, for me, and surely for Wally and Otto also, represented a painful reminder of past experiences.

This was a fatal setback for the many Jewish-owned businesses clustered together in the Bridge Street area. Some were forced to close altogether, while others relocated to other parts of the city, including Krotosky's the butchers, who moved to City Road. One or two remained, notably Rapport's, which still trades out of the same premises on the slight stretch of Bridge Street left intact following the redevelopment. This ended a period when Jewish businesses dominated this part of central Cardiff, and today just a handful of Jewish businesses are operating in the city centre.

Finding themselves at a crossroads and facing an uncertain future, the pair bravely decided to go their separate ways. They had worked together in the family business for over 30 years, and while our families spent some time together outside work (religious festivals mainly), and we children got on well, Dad and his brother had some disagreements about the way the business should go forward, which meant changes had been minimal.

Each brother now had a chance to do things his own way. Otto and Wally had quite different personalities and strengths and decided to see where these would take them.

After initially toying with the idea of opening a restaurant, something he and Mum had long hankered for, Dad took the safer option and settled on a shop unit in Royal Arcade. In contrast, Otto opened a small delicatessen around the corner on Caroline Street.

It was a bold but carefully considered move. Cardiff had grown to a population of 285,000, swelled over the previous three decades by immigration from Europe, Asia, and Africa. The city was fast becoming a major retail destination in the UK, with increasing numbers of visitors from west and mid-Wales, the south-west of England, and locals attracted by shopping trips to the newly built St. David's Centre. With this wider catchment area and shifting population demographic, the brothers reckoned on a prosperous future.

They negotiated long and hard over the compensation for the Bridge Street shop. They were happy to go their separate ways, although they argued that they both opened shops because they thought the Royal Arcade shop would not be able to support two families with its high overheads.

After much back-and-forth, during which the brothers pressed on with getting their new businesses up and running, on August 23, 1983, the valuation officer eventually agreed to split £18,500 between them. Even though they weren't entirely happy with the amount, they needed to end the protracted negotiations.

Dad negotiated with the landlord of the Cardiff Arcade Company – owners of the David Morgan department store, which dominated The Hayes – for a 15-year lease on 42 Royal Arcade and a separate lease on 44-46 Royal Arcade, where he purchased an existing business (a Greek deli) from Mrs Lambros. This was an astute move as, despite the additional premises being small, it provided the new business with an instant flow of new customers.

With its gracious glass-vaulted ceilings and flagstone floors, Royal Arcade – Cardiff's oldest arcade, built in 1858 – vastly differed from Bridge Street, despite being just a few minutes' walk away. Today, it retains many hidden corners that are not accessible to the public, including upstairs rooms that the Cardiff School of Art once used, and a hidden street behind the shop fronts running to St. Mary Street, known as Kingston Court, comprising 13 little houses built in the 1850s to house migrant dock workers. The Morgan family incorporated Kingston Court into their retail store when it expanded in the early 1900s. While it is out of sight to the public today, visitors can still see blocked-up doorways and windows at street level, and empty rooms at first-floor level behind the shops.

Royal Arcade backed onto the Tabernacle Chapel, a Welsh-language Baptist chapel, built in 1821 and developed further in 1840. In 1849, a few years before Royal Arcade was developed, a cholera epidemic spread through Cardiff's slum housing areas, including The Hayes. The Chapel's small graveyard would likely not have been big enough to accommodate the mass burials required, so a pit was probably dug beside the cemetery to accommodate the bodies, as happened in other well-documented areas.

Interestingly, the shop units next to the graveyard have no basements, and 42 Royal Arcade is one such unit. It has only a low void below the floorboards, filled with compacted soil and rubble. Units 44-46, on the other hand, have a deep basement that was originally part of the David Morgan department store.

*

Dad threw himself into designing the new shop with his typical enthusiasm, pride, and eye for saving money. He had always had a flair for design, and now he seized the opportunity to shape a shop to his vision. Mum and Dad had spent months in the run-up to the opening, sketching out the layout and design for the shop. As Mum recalls:

> "We'd sit there in the evenings, night after night until midnight, sketching and drawing layouts, where we would put the stalls, the aisles, the gondolas, and so on, and trying to make the most of the space we had. We drove each other mad but were on the same page."

Dad started by building all the shelves himself. The compensation for the closure of Bridge Street was still unpaid, so this was a way to save vital funds and create a unique design that can still be seen in the shop today. It includes a mix of low, high, and round shelving that enabled him to cram as much stock as possible into the available space, which was extremely limited at the time.

His idea was that things had to scan with the eyes. He would look at something and say: "It doesn't scan right." He didn't like straight lines and wanted everything to be higgledy-piggledy. If you had a row of signs, one would be short, one would be tall; on the floor, one basket would be round, one would be oval, and so on. Nothing was uniform.

Despite the ingenious shelving, fitting all the stock in was challenging, and then the space got smaller. Soon after the initial agreement was drawn up, David Morgan issued notice of their intention to redevelop 44-46 Royal Arcade for a fire escape and end the lease. All that would be left of that unit was a long, narrow windowed area at the front, which they assumed Wally would be unable to do anything with. However, Dad was anxious that he would not have enough space for his new venture, so he decided to keep it.

The resulting unit, which was separate from the main store and had its own entrance, was initially used for storage. However, during the hectic Christmas period, to ease the pressure on the shop, it was turned into an overflow shop selling nuts and dried fruits, piled high in wicker baskets. Mum would help to staff this overflow shop, often with Tric's help.

From the outset, Dad wanted to give the shop his name, Wally's, reflecting the old-fashioned personal service that had always been his hallmark. I wasn't happy with the choice of name as it was the cause of much teasing from my friends, due to the word's insulting connotations.

Mum cleverly used her calligraphy skills, creating the handwritten font that still adorns the windows today. Inside the shop, a collage of the Wally's logo she created from dried pulses still hangs from the ceiling in its exact same location since the opening day. The logo included the main product categories sold then: "Health foods, Wholefoods, Herbs and Spices", written around the inner rim of an oval border, with the shop's name, Wally's Delicatessen, at the centre.

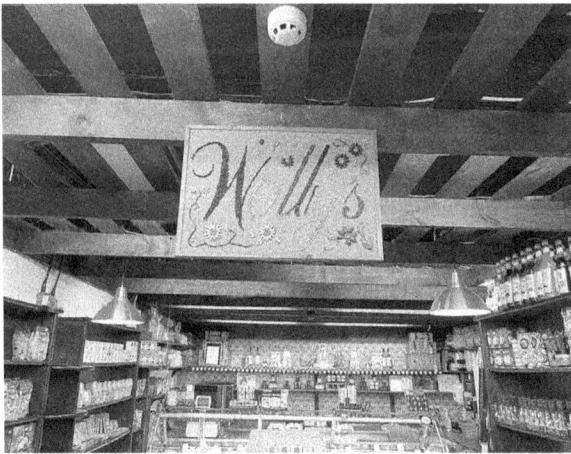

Wally's sign, made from dried pulses, hanging in the shop in 2025.

Although Dad modernised elements of the shop, notably by investing in electronic scales and tills, he also wanted to keep the old-fashioned look and feel that had always been its hallmark. To achieve this, he happily indulged in his love of antiques, buying vintage pots, pans, scales, and even a beautiful old brass cash register to decorate the shop (you can still see the cash register and scales in the kaffeehaus today).

An old butter churn – one of Dad's favourite purchases – was used to display pasta near the entrance to the shop. He saw it as a statement piece, but as with many other things, this didn't last because it was not practical, taking up too much space and not displaying enough product. The butter churn ended up being a plant holder in his garden.

The whole family mucked in to help get the shop ready to open, and so did David, who had recently returned to the business. A few years previously, after David had completed four years at Continental Delicatessen, he and Tric, now married, had bought a business in the Rhondda Valley – a mini market in Ystrad Rhondda that they ran together for four years.

They had kept in contact with Dad and bought stock for their store from him, particularly pasta. But then a supermarket opened in Talbot Green, and buses began taking customers to the supermarket free of charge. It was the death knell for their business, so when Dad approached David and asked if he would become his manager in the new shop, David happily agreed.

David Pike behind the deli counter, circa 1981.

David recalls an intense month leading up to the opening, which was spent staining the shelves a vintage deep brown and then filling the whole shop with stock:

> "It was very hard work and very stressful, because Wally put everything on the line for that shop. When he and Otto inherited the business, it was already up and running because it was their father's business. But this was Wally's own project, so it was all his own financing, and he was taking on a 15-year lease with David Morgan, so there was a huge financial commitment as well. But we felt confident it was going to work, because Wally was a very good businessman: he knew how to buy and sell things. He also had an excellent rapport with customers. I don't think there was much doubt it was going to work."

Tric came in to help too, initially as a temporary arrangement before finding herself a job. The night before the shop opened, they were all still there late in the evening. One of the final jobs was to fill the narrow shelves behind the cheese counter with a big display of honey. "As I put the last jar of honey on top of the display, the whole lot collapsed, and there was honey everywhere, all down my leg, in my shoes," Tric recalls. "I could have cried. We were all scrubbing the floor and cleaning up until 11 at night."

When the shop opened the next day, everything was in order, everyone was smiling, and the familiar faces started to come through the doors, as did many new ones. Dad took centre stage, now dressed in his suit, which he decided to wear to stand out as the owner, while the rest of the staff wore the traditional white overalls. There was a sense of excitement and anticipation. Looking back, Mum says there was an inevitability about it all. "After the compulsory purchase, we had to go somewhere: Wally knew nothing else, and he loved it," she recalls. "It was not a trial for him to go to work and come home in the dark, because he loved what he did."

Wally outside the shop in Royal Arcade, 1981.

By December 1981, Dad was engrossed in the intense run-up to his first Christmas in the new shop. I was home for the holidays and, as usual, was helping. This routine continued unhindered by the parties my old school friends and I enjoyed whenever we were home. On one occasion, at about three in the morning, with the party still ongoing, I had to drag myself home because I knew I had to be in the shop early the next day. It was ingrained in me, as it was with my father; it was always business before pleasure.

However, one early morning, I was woken before my alarm by Mum entering my room. She told me that Dad had been taken to the hospital at night by ambulance. I hadn't heard any of it. At five in the morning, I had to pick up David from Fairwater, where he was living, to take him into the shop. It was an incredible worry, but we knew Dad would want the "show to go on".

Dad had suffered another heart attack and, following his major heart attack in Munich two years before, this was the second clear sign of the toll the shop was taking on his health. It hit Rochelle, who was still living at home, particularly hard. "This is a big part of my memories. I found it a traumatic time," she says. "I grew up with a sense of fear about losing Dad from the age of 11, when he had his heart attack in Munich."

Dad made a speedy recovery and was back in the shop before Christmas, but it was clear that his health was deteriorating.

*

The following year, the dynamic in the shop changed when Otto's business closed, and Dad invited Otto and Michael to come and work with him. Dad wanted to help his brother and nephew but also needed experienced staff, as the new business was taking off and his health was causing him issues.

This arrangement suited both brothers for a time, but before long, Otto, his wife, Maureen, and Michael opened Swallows Café at the St. Mary Street end of Royal Arcade. Maureen had always been a great home cook and caterer for communal events, and they wanted a business that suited their skills and that Michael could run after their retirement. Together they ran a successful business, with Maureen's cooking driving a vegetarian menu built around salads, lasagnes, macaroni cheese, jacket potatoes, and toasted sandwiches. Everything was home-made on the premises. After a while, however, Michael left the business and moved to London to be with his fiancée, Deanne, which prompted Otto and Maureen to sell up and retire.

Otto in the shop, circa 1982.

Dad suffered yet another heart attack in the autumn of 1982. The stress of the long-running dispute for compensation at the same time as setting up and then running the new shop, and dealing with the landlords on the leases, had affected his health more than he realised or admitted.

This time, his doctors recommended that heart surgery was necessary if he were to prolong his life. It was an extremely anxious time, but there was little choice. He underwent triple bypass heart surgery at the University Hospital Wales, followed by stern advice from the doctor to change his lifestyle or risk death. It was clear to everyone that things would have to change.

Unlike his long recuperation in a Munich hospital following his heart attack a few years earlier, the medical opinion this time was to get him up and about as soon as possible, so Dad was back at work in three weeks. However, he did take the advice on board enough to start taking more frequent holidays.

On one such holiday in 1986, spent in the Costa del Sol, he and Mum were meandering through a mountain village when they spotted a small development of new townhouses being built overlooking the coast. Their interest was piqued enough to take a closer look, and the developer, who happened to be on site, got talking to them. He took them to a bar in the village overlooking the development and, over a few glasses of wine in the Spanish sun, sold them a dream. On the spot, they decided to buy, and so began a love affair with the Spanish village of Benalmadena Pueblo.

The house sat in a row of six others, with a shared pool, and they named it *Casa Ensuena* (House of Dreams). They loved their time there and enjoyed socialising, visiting flea markets, taking afternoon siestas, and doing up the house.

The trips to Spain became frequent, three or four times a year, for four to six weeks. Mum and Dad were talented artists and spent time there sketching and painting. The lifestyle change was exactly what Dad needed to relax and recuperate.

Belinda, who by now was 24 and living in London, recalls the relief she felt at seeing Dad slow down, saying: "We knew he needed it for his health, because this man just did not stop working. When he wasn't working in the shop, he was working to build Mum a kitchen, or a study, or cupboards in my brother's and sister's rooms – he was always busy, busy, busy."

When Dad was away, David ran the shop. "David was his sidekick," says Mum. "He was very capable, which meant Wally could get away for extended periods. I think Spain prolonged his life by ten years at least. He loved it so much. He was so happy and relaxed there — it was just his heaven, and it made an enormous difference in our lives. He came back refreshed, ready to go again. Those were extremely good years for us."

*

After Tric helped to set up the shop, Wally invited her to stay on, overcoming his initial cautiousness about employing husbands and wives. Luckily, everything was to prove so harmonious that she would still be there four decades later. She particularly loved the community that built up around the shop, recalling:

> "The regulars would come in every Friday around nine in the morning. You'd think, 'It's ten to nine, we'd better start getting ready now,' and you knew exactly what they were going to buy. There was Mr Engl, Mr Zinger, Lilo, Mrs Kavana, Margaret, Leda — they all used to come in at the same time. It seemed like their Friday club. There would be five of us serving them behind the counter, and they'd all be there chatting until after ten. It was lovely because you knew them, and it was like a family. It was a lovely place to work."

David and Tric remember how the shop quickly became filled with the same hubbub of European languages, particularly German and Polish, that had been a hallmark of the Bridge Street shop. They were a mixed cast of characters, all originally from overseas. However, the one difference by now was that the shop no longer had so many Jewish customers. The Jewish community in Cardiff had dwindled in size by the 1980s, due to intermarriage and relocation, mainly to London. The remaining community was well assimilated and generally affluent, so they tended to shop more in London and eat out more. After the move to Royal Arcade, the wider community no longer associated the shop with being a Jewish shop.

Mr Zinger spoke German and owned a factory. He was very thin, upright, smart, and well-groomed. Tric remembers him driving a fancy car, maybe a Bentley, and always buying liver sausage, Hungarian and German salami, and Black Forest ham.

Mr Engl also owned a factory and was always immaculately groomed, with his pristine shirt, tie, and overcoat. After Mr Engl died, his son continued visiting the shop with his wife, granddaughter, and great-grandchildren. Tric and the staff loved the whole family.

Lilo was an eccentric lady of German heritage who lived alone in the valleys. Tall and thin, with mousy, curly hair, she made a special trip down to Cardiff on the bus every Friday morning and always wanted to be served first because she had to get her bus back, which prompted protests from the other customers. She would always order liver sausage, *fleischwurst* (meat sausage), and *bierwurst* (beer sausage, so-called not because it contained beer but complemented it), but just five slices of each. And it would be a challenge to cut all the slices in time for her to rush for her bus. If Tric accidentally cut too much, Lilo would admonish her, but always in a friendly way. Her son, Roy, and his daughter still visit the shop today and feel a close affinity for it.

Leda was a petite, cheery old Greek lady from Ely, with dark hair, a big smile, and a penchant for pasta and feta cheese. Tric always found herself laughing with her when she called in. She always demanded a kiss on the cheek from Wally. Leda was one of the shop's longest-standing customers. Her daughter, Veronica, told me: "I remember your grandfather taking my father into the back room of the shop for scarce Polish products which he gave to him to take on humanitarian lorry runs to communist Poland." They would frequent the Polish House (*Dom Polski*) in Newport Road together. Veronica says: "My parents regarded your grandfather and his family as the extended family they never had."

Another Friday regular was Joe. He was of Caribbean origin, lived in Taff's Well, and was a massive fan of the Kolos bread – a rye bread from a Ukrainian bakery in Bradford, made with a 50-year-old sourdough starter. It was incredibly popular with customers and many still ask for it today, some six years after the family that made it retired.

And there were others, too: Mrs Egan, a smart, blonde, bespectacled German lady who used to come in with her daughter; and Mr Stein, a small and charming man who, like most of the regulars, favoured soft meats – a staple for a traditional German afternoon tea. He would buy German and Hungarian salamis, frankfurters, and kabanos (dry, smoked sausage with caraway) – usually about a quarter pound each of ten different meats, enough to see him through until his next visit a week later.

They all used to visit like clockwork every Friday, and the staff delighted in their loyalty. When not on the counter, Tric recalls she would often be busy weighing out food from the sacks that filled the shop floor, putting the measured quantities into paper bags, and then taking them to the till to take the money, as in the early days there weren't enough staff to split the tasks.

I helped in the shop when I could, as did Mum. Meanwhile, David and Dad worked six days a week in a routine that would continue for the first two years of the shop's life. David, now very experienced after his years in retail, took on the managerial role easily, freeing Dad to do what he enjoyed best: spending time with the customers.

By now, two Davids were working in the shop. 16-year-old David Richards joined not long after the shop opened, on the Youth Training Scheme (YTS), a government-backed scheme designed to help young people into work. As he puts it, he was "One of Maggie's Boys". He had grown up in the Riverside area of

Cardiff and had never even considered a retail job until the Jobcentre sent him there. He remembers his first days fondly:

"Wally was a lovely man – I got along with him immediately. All the staff were nice and friendly. I had no issues with anybody. We all got on. The foods were alien to me, though; as a Welsh boy growing up in Riverside, I didn't know much about sauerkraut and gherkins. It was a multicultural shop, both in its food and its workforce. When I first started, I was a warehouseman working with George Slegelis, a Latvian. He took me under his wing and showed me the ropes – we got on great, and he was a very hard worker."

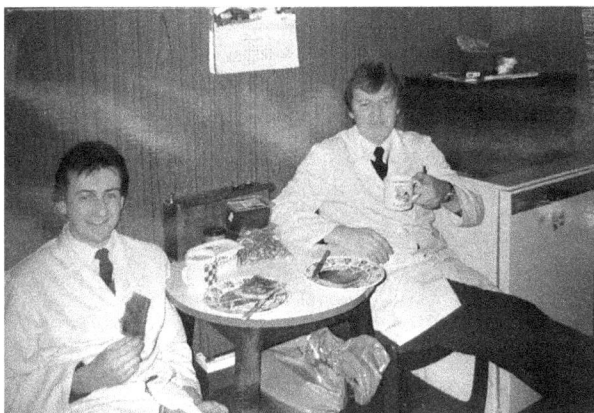

David Richards (Dai) and David Pike, taking a break, circa 1981.

The newest David became known as Dai to avoid confusion, although many customers often called him "Young David". That was in 1981, and Dai is still with the shop today. Some customers still call him "Young David", even though he has just turned 60!

Dad was, by now, a very experienced retailer and businessman. He understood the importance of the customer experience long before this became a buzzword in business schools. Establishing a customer rapport was fundamental to his approach, and he imbued this in all his staff. They would chat with customers, get to know them by name, learn about their families, and remember what they liked to order each week. Over the years, this ensured customers stayed loyal to the shop, and this loyalty was passed down to the next generations, many of whom continue to frequent the shop today. Some customers even became friends with staff members and met outside the workplace.

The shop's staff in the 1980s included three notable Eastern Europeans who worked as warehousemen: one from Latvia, called George Slegelis, who was short, with a heavily lined face, and had previously worked in Bridge Street; one from Poland, called Leo Etmanski, who was tall and lean; and finally George Reminnij, a large bear-like man, who claimed to be from Russia. The two Georges and Leo had been my grandparents' lodgers. After arriving illegally in the UK after the Second World War, they had worked manual jobs in flour mills and factories, where they developed immense strength. Now in their 60s, they were happy to help at Wally's, where the work was hard but not backbreaking.

They had exciting and interesting stories about their exploits when they were young. George Slegelis once told me how he arrived in this country, still a teenager, by jumping from a ship where he had been working as a merchant seaman. Leo told matter-of-factly how, as a young man, he was in a concentration camp during the war. He recalled how, when people escaped, the Nazis would line them all up and shoot every other man as they tried to find out how the people had escaped. The man right beside him was shot. George Reminnij told of how he lost a finger during an Allied bombing raid while working as a slave labourer on the railway lines in Germany, and how, while in the Russian Army, he would urinate on his wounds to disinfect them.

George, however, had a darker past that only became known after his death. He had concocted a cover story that he told everyone, including my grandparents, that he was from Russia and had come to the UK after fleeing the Nazis. But after he died, a different story emerged. George was Ukrainian and had fought in the German Army during the war, likely one of the many Ukrainians who collaborated with the Nazis to fight the occupying Russians. A photo found in his house after he died shows him as a young man posing in his German uniform. This was the first anyone in the family knew about it.

It seems incredible, knowing what we now know, that George would first live as a tenant of, and then work for, a Jewish family after serving in the German Army during the war. Was this his way of making up for his past actions? Somehow, I doubt it; without the necessary papers, his options would have been limited, and when he found himself in a position to live and work somewhere comfortable, he would have grabbed the opportunity. I want to think that George wasn't antisemitic. Although he was a German soldier, his reasons for signing up were to fight the Russians, not to support Nazi persecution of Jews.

George's story was covered on the TV show, Heir Hunters, after it was revealed that the seemingly penniless George, who had died intestate, had left an estate, including the house that he owned in Cardiff. I am relieved that Dad died without ever knowing his family had employed someone who had fought for the Germans, as this would have made him very upset. (Heir Hunters did eventually find a distant niece in Eastern Europe).

The warehousemen's job was to bring the goods into the shop for storage, and then, as needed, onto the shop floor. They were known as "bluecoats" on account of the colour of their overalls. Then, as today, everything had to come into the shop via the arcade, as the shop has no back door. In the 1980s, there was no external warehouse to store the goods, so everything had to come into the shop and go upstairs for storage.

The shop would receive deliveries on Sundays at Christmas, as it was closed in those days. Sacks of nuts would be placed in the arcade to be counted and checked. Such was the number of sacks that the shortest delivery route would be taken. However, this was abruptly stopped when Dad received a letter from Richard Morgan telling him that the delivery driver couldn't drive his vehicle down the arcade!

The warehousemen made an impression on us children, and Rochelle was especially fond of Leo. She recalls:

"Unlike the other two warehousemen, who were oxen, powerful men, Leo was much slenderer. He looked like he would have been the most handsome man when he was younger. He still had a full head of hair and a sort of Errol Flynn 1940s moustache. He was shy and unassuming; he only spoke if spoken to. But he was such a sweet man."

Rochelle also remembers having a lot of fun with the staff:

"It was always nice to see Dai, David, and Trish. I wasn't a diligent pupil, so missing study time was not my prime concern, but I missed out on socialising. The shop was hard work – you were on your feet all day, especially in the later months of the year when it started to become 12-hour days, so I was too exhausted to go out in the evenings. But then there was a big social element at the shop, because the Saturday girls were great fun and were older than me. I learned a lot from them, and then in the later years, I brought in my friends to be the Saturday girls. It was very sociable and interesting, because you were exposed to people you wouldn't have been exposed to just by going to school every day."

Rochelle and the other Saturday girls usually worked on the nut counter, where shelves of wooden boxes and jars stored all the goods: dates, apricots, herbs, and the item she dreaded – pungent dried egg powder, a popular rationed ingredient from the Second World War that people were still using widely in the 1980s. "We used to fight not to have to serve somebody dried egg powder," she says. "It had the most horrific smell, and you had to scoop it out. We had sweetie jars full of that sort of thing, or herbs and spices, and you had to weigh everything out." Another foul-smelling product from those days was Bombay Duck, which, despite its name, was dried fish. It was eventually banned in the UK in the 1990s for food hygiene reasons, and has made abortive comebacks now and again, but it is now gone forever.

Around this time, Dad also took on, as Saturday staff, Sian, my mother's niece, and later Grant, her nephew. Dad always preferred to employ people he knew, be they his family or employees' family, and I have continued this practice.

Another key staff member was Maritza Norman (now Sloman), a Greek woman who had joined the team six weeks after Wally's opened. She had seen the job advertised in the South Wales Echo and decided to apply. Like Dai, she had no prior experience with the type of goods Wally's stocked. "I walked in, and I thought, *Oh gosh, I don't know. There's an awful lot of stuff in here*," she recalls. Mum interviewed her, she got the job, and was duly thrown in the deep end. As she remembers those first few days:

> "The first day I started, Wally took me down to the counter and said, 'There's all the stuff, there's a price list on the wall.' It was a big price list, but he didn't have a single item labelled, and he walked out and left me as they were having a big delivery. Somebody came up to me and asked me for something, and I didn't know what it was. I thought, *Oh no, I can't cope with this*. But that was Wally – 'Here's the price list, get on with it.' By the time we got to the other side of Christmas, I will admit he had put markers on everything, so I knew what everything was. After that, I just absolutely loved the job."

One day, after she had worked there for a couple of years, Wally called Maritza to the office. "I thought, *Oh my god, what am I doing wrong?* I was always doing something wrong. But he offered me a full-time job. I could have snatched his arm off," she recalls.

She loved working for Dad, and she loved the rest of her colleagues, too. There was occasional larking about: she recalls grabbing Dai's legs with the help of Linda (Tric's cousin, who worked part-time) when he reached into the counter to wash it at the end of the day. "He'd be shouting, 'What are you doing? What are you doing to me?' We said, 'We're making a wish.' If Wally saw any of that, we'd be in the doghouse. There were many things like that, but we also worked very hard."

She recalls how, on Saturdays, she would look up from her work to see customers queuing up to the shop door. "We were a very, very busy shop. You had to have the stamina to keep up with it."

Christmas time was hectic and stressful. Tric and Maritza recall how Dad reduced them to tears during one stressful run-up to Christmas. They were tasked with fulfilling specific orders, and on one occasion they brought down the wrong products. Dad, clearly feeling the festive stress, shouted at them. Tric cracked, saying: "Right, that's it. I'm going," and Maritza added, "If she's going, I'm going. We're not being spoken to like that."

The women went upstairs, hastily followed by Wally, who begged them to return. Maritza replied: "We will stay but leave us alone. Go down the other end of the shop with the nuts."

That afternoon, Dad disappeared, and when he returned, he had a pot plant and a little box of chocolates from Thornton's for each of them. He asked for their forgiveness, which was granted on the condition that he leave them alone in the future. Suitably cowed, Dad obeyed.

This incident aside, Maritza and Tric agreed he was an excellent employer. "He was very good to us – like a father figure, very gentle," says Tric. "But when it was busy, he'd be saying, 'Don't do this, don't do that.'" Maritza adds: "He was such a nice man to work for – very caring and generous towards his staff. I loved my job. Our regular customers used to come in and joke with us, and we were like a family."

Maritza and Tric knew this personal touch was essential to the job, but it could create tension at Christmas. "Wally would get very uptight at Christmas and when things were very busy," Maritza recalls. "It was just his makeup: when things were steady, he was fine, quite laid back about things. But when the shop got busy, he wanted you just to serve, serve, serve, which was fine, but he couldn't quite grasp that people wanted to talk to you."

However, Maritza recalls that Christmas at Wally's was also magical. It would begin a few weeks in advance, when the Christmas goods came in: huge salamis, *stollen* (German Christmas cake, with or without marzipan, covered in icing sugar), German gingerbread, chocolate cakes, *pfeffernüsse* (small round spiced cookies covered in a white icing glaze), Maritza's favourite, *kourabiedes* (Greek shortbread biscuits), and *panettones* (Italian Christmas cakes with candied peel and raisins), which were hung by strings from the ceiling along with the salamis. "It was so lovely," says Maritza. "If you've seen programmes on television about the continental shops in Italy and Spain, that is how it looked. There was just so much of each country's specialities for Christmas, because people wanted that, and they'd order it a few months before."

Wally in the shop, circa 1981.

Rochelle remembers it as an Aladdin's Cave, beautiful and brimming with Parma hams, gingerbread hearts, and a cornucopia of other continental foods. Mum, who helped in the shop at Christmas for many years, recalls:

"It was a wonderland, decorated not with balloons but with cake. We never used decorations because the food was the decoration. It was very colourful – bright reds and yellows on the wrapping – and everything stood out. And, of course, it was the smell as well. People always came in and said: 'I've been dying for this smell. I couldn't wait to get back here and have another smell.'"

Dai's Christmases were all about the chaos of the meat counter, where he and about six other staff members would clamour to serve the endless queues. He remembers:

"It's a wonder we managed to get the tills to balance, but we managed to get through it. We had stock everywhere: stock hanging from the ceiling, we sat on stock, we had stock underneath cupboards. We worked long hours over Christmas, horrendously long hours. My longest day started at 6.30 in the morning and finished at 10 at night. I used to work every day in December. We all did: me, David, and Wally. We were allowed one day off the first week in December, and then we put our foot down. Yet in some ways, January was worse. Sometimes, even now, I wonder which is the hardest month, December or January, because in December, even though you're so busy, there's so much to do and so much going on. The days and weeks fly. January is so quiet; you're looking for things to do, and the days are so long, and at the end of it, you think, *Thank God January is over*."

During the 1980s and early 1990s, trade continued under David's stewardship, with Wally enjoying his time away. These were particularly good times for the business, and at the heart of it was the much-loved and trusted original crew – David and Tric, Dai and Maritza.

Part Three

The Son

Steven Salamon 1963

11

A Change in Career

Wally's Delicatessen 1993-2000

I had a happy childhood growing up in Cardiff. I attended Rhydypenau Primary School and then Cardiff High School, where I enjoyed playing football and later rugby. I achieved some academic success, driven to study hard by an obsessive fear of failure. Outside of school, I played squash – a sport I continued to enjoy into my 50s – took piano lessons, and went to the Jewish youth club, the Jewish Lads' and Girls' Brigade (JLGB), where I would later become a leader upon returning to Cardiff.

The Jewish Lads' Brigade was founded in 1895 by Colonel Goldsmith, the highest-ranking Jewish officer of the 19th century, to support Jewish immigrants by providing an interest for the children of the many impoverished immigrant families arriving in England at that time. The aim was to offer young Jewish immigrant boys the opportunity to learn skills that could assist them in securing employment, and to transform them into exemplary Englishmen. Girls were granted membership in 1963.

JLGB was a uniformed organisation based on army principles of rank, discipline, and training. The Cardiff Company was established in 1977, and my mother, who was running a local Girl Guides group, was one of the first officers. At JLGB, I learned army drill and would proudly demonstrate my steps and manoeuvres to my father. An annual summer camp was held at Deal in Kent – near the site of the Kitchener Camp – where the young boys and girls slept in canvas tents, and where I would wear my father's army shirt, adorned with his sergeant's stripes.

Since my grandfather spoke little of his early life and my father knew nothing about Kitchener Camp, I had no idea then that JLGB played such an important part in my grandfather's escape story.

My parents instilled in me moral values, a strong work ethic, and respect for money. As a teenager, I would rise early before school to deliver newspapers, and naturally I assisted in the shop on some Saturdays and during school holidays. Through this early foundation, I developed positive character traits that have served me well.

My parents were not particularly religious. Like many descendants of immigrant Jews, the spiritual aspect of their Judaism had been diluted, possibly in response to the terrors and atrocities perpetrated against their families during the war; many wondered if there could be a God. Instead, for them, being Jewish was about heritage, cultural identity, and a sense of how to live and behave in society.

They were keen, however, to instil in their children a certain level of Jewish practice, customs, and traditions. My sisters and I attended *cheder* (religion school) on Sunday mornings at the synagogue, where I celebrated my bar mitzvah in 1976, at the age of 13. My teacher was Julius Weil, a Kindertransport refugee from Cologne, Germany, who was the last boy to celebrate his bar mitzvah in his home synagogue before it was burned down during Kristallnacht. He taught me to read Hebrew from the Torah, and I vividly remember the tears rolling down my father's cheeks as I recited my *parshah* (weekly Torah portion) on the big day.

As a family, we attended synagogue on religious festivals such as *Pesach* (Passover), *Chanukah* (Festival of Lights), *Rosh Hashanah* (New Year), and *Yom Kippur* (the Day of Atonement). While the services could be dull for children at times, there were also enjoyable moments, such as dressing up and playing party games. We often gathered with Otto's family for *Seder* (traditional ritual meal during Passover), where we would read the *Haggadah*, the story of the exodus of the Jewish people from enslavement in Egypt. We would also come together in each other's houses to 'break the fast' after a day of not eating or drinking on *Yom Kippur*. The sighs as the first mouthfuls of food were consumed after the fast ended – usually a piece of *challah* (ceremonial Jewish bread made with egg, usually braided, and often sprinkled with sesame or poppy seeds) – were, and still are, amusing.

I enjoyed a happy childhood, and I'm pleased to say that growing up, I encountered little antisemitism. I attribute this to how assimilated we were both as a family and a Jewish community in Cardiff generally. Most Jewish children in Cardiff didn't stand out from the crowd regarding how we dressed, spoke, or behaved. We kept our Jewish identity behind closed doors and within our synagogues. Although we lived in what we considered a 'Jewish area', close to the Orthodox synagogue in Cyncoed, where Jews began to move in greater numbers from the 1950s onwards, for non-Jewish kids my age, that was simply where we lived, near the school.

There were occasional racial slurs, but I didn't feel overly insulted or intimidated by them. I thought they were simply part of the cultural language used in the 1970s, when racial sensitivities were not as heightened as they are today. The only times I felt singled out for being Jewish were when I voluntarily excluded myself from school assemblies, entering at the end of the religious assembly with the few other Jewish children to hear the notices. I could not look up as I filed into the hall, but I could feel all the eyes burning into my soul. There were only a few moments in my life when I wished I were not Jewish, but that was one of them.

I left for Sheffield University the same year Wally's opened, to study for a BA in Economics, Accountancy, and Financial Management.

Despite my Jewish upbringing, I had never visited Israel, and the long summer holidays gave me the perfect opportunity to explore my Jewish heritage. I wanted to understand the essence of the Jewish story; after the Passover meal each year, we recite a prayer: "Next year in Jerusalem." For me, the time had come. It was a rite of passage, a bridge between my childhood Jewish life and my journey into the adult Jewish world. This was more about the religious and ethnic aspects of my identity than my lineage, which would come later.

I spent two summer holidays in Israel, six weeks at a kibbutz (a collective settlement where residents share resources, property, and decision-making processes), and two weeks exploring the country.

These trips were transformative experiences for me. On the kibbutz, I worked in the fields picking pears and in the kitchens. I met many Holocaust survivors who had settled in Israel after the war to rebuild their lives. I heard stories of people's horrific wartime experiences, including one gentleman who had been in the Warsaw Ghetto as a child and had acted as a runner, scurrying through the sewers to fetch and carry stolen food and messages to those on the outside. Forever psychologically affected by his experiences, this man now showered several times a day to rid himself of the terrible smell from which he couldn't escape.

As I travelled throughout Israel for the first time, I felt connected to what it meant to be a Jew. Living in the diaspora – a population scattered throughout the world that is separate from its geographic place of origin – and in a small community, one can lose sight of the broader picture and story of the Jewish people over the centuries. At various locations across the country, I experienced almost out-of-body spiritual sensations that I had never felt before or since. At the *Kinneret* (the Sea of Galilee), where Jesus is said to have performed miracles and walked on water; at Masada, an ancient fortification built by King Herod atop a mountain in southern Israel, where the last Jews held out against a Roman siege for months before taking their own lives rather than falling into the hands of the Romans; at the Dead Sea, the lowest place on earth, where Jewish manuscripts were discovered in caves dating from the 3rd century BCE (Jews refer to the period before Christ as the Before the Common Era); and in Jerusalem, the holiest of cities and the centre of the three major Abrahamic religions – Judaism,

Christianity, and Islam – where the Western (or Wailing) Wall, the most sacred site in the Jewish faith, stands as a reminder of the last Temple.

After these visits, I realised that my Judaism would remain a part of me forever. I wanted to raise a Jewish family to carry on the thousands of years' legacy of the Jewish people and, more importantly, that of my grandfather and father.

During one of these trips, I visited the Tel Aviv home of Dad's cousin, Yitzhak Stein – the son of Frieda's brother Yaakov and his wife Zila. Yaakov and Zila had lived in a neighbouring village in Austria to Ignatz and Frieda and had similarly lost their home and livelihood after the German annexation of Austria. Yitzhak fled to Palestine on an illegal ship with his parents in 1940, during the British Mandate. His wife, Dalia, who is the daughter of Warsaw Ghetto survivors, still lives in the same apartment in Tel Aviv today. Meeting Yitzhak and his family strengthened my understanding of my family history and the history of the Jewish people; one marked by persecution and displacement throughout the world. Here was another piece of my family's fractured wartime story and yet another example of survival against all odds. My sisters and I are still in contact with their sons, Amir and Yuval, today.

*

Following my degree, I completed my accountancy training at Peat Marwick Mitchell (now KPMG) in London. Significantly, there was never any suggestion that I should follow Dad into the family business; it was not even discussed. When I decided to study accountancy, Dad was delighted. He always said accountancy was an excellent qualification, and "accountants are never out of work".

I enjoyed the work, but a new idea formed after a few years. I might like to go into retail. I didn't know whether it would be in my father's shop, but having been brought up with a retail background, I wanted to learn more about it. So, I joined a department at KPMG which specialised in retail clients. I felt that if I could learn something about how retail businesses worked, it might be beneficial to me in the future.

As my career progressed, so did my love life. In January 1988, I began dating Corrine Ser. Corrine lived near Richmond in Surrey, worked for the tax office, and was Jewish. We shared a lot of common ground regarding family history and pride in our Jewish roots.

After a whirlwind romance, we got engaged in July 1988. A particularly poignant engagement gift was given to us by Mrs Schuerman – a lifelong friend of my family from Vienna, who had also escaped to Cardiff and whose memories of Kristallnacht are recounted earlier: a silver teapot which was saved from being looted by the Nazis, which remains one of my most-treasured possessions.

On September 3, 1989, Corrine and I were married at the Northwest Surrey Synagogue. The Master of Ceremonies (MC) at our wedding, Harry Polloway, had also served as MC at my parents' wedding 30 years earlier. Harry, the son of immigrant refugees, was a stalwart of the Newport Jewish community and later became the MC for the Royal Family. After our wedding, Corrine moved into my flat, but we soon began considering a life outside London, as we hoped to start a family, and Cardiff seemed the natural choice.

Through a recruitment firm, I secured a position as a management accountant with Chemical Bank, a US investment bank, working in its back office in Cardiff. Initially, we stayed in my old family home, but we had our own house before long. Our first child, Benjamin, was born on April 19, 1991.

By 1993, everything was starting to point towards me joining Wally's. Chemical Bank had announced a merger, and the newly-merged bank would be based in Bournemouth. I was offered a promotion if I relocated, but I did not want to uproot my family, so I opted for voluntary redundancy. I was aware that Dad's health hadn't been good, and I thought that if I went into the business, I could work with him for a while and then he could retire.

It was unusual for young Jewish adults who had grown up in Cardiff but moved away for university and work to return home, and even less so to take over their father's business. However, I had ambitious plans and envisioned a chain of delicatessens by the time I reached 40. I hadn't discussed this with Dad, nor was there any substantial conversation about how my joining the business would work. In hindsight, I decided largely on my own, believing I was doing the right thing for Dad and me. I wanted him to take more time away from the business and enjoy his retirement.

What I had not appreciated at the time, because I had been living away for most of the last 10 years, was that Dad's health had improved sufficiently that he did not need, or particularly want, to retire. His extended breaks in Spain, with David managing the business in his absence, had considerably lightened his workload and stress levels.

However, with the decision made, I joined the business in September 1993. The first thing I took on was the bookkeeping; it was the natural choice. Dad was initially happy for me to be in the office, as it gave him freedom to be on the shop floor. Then I gradually started getting involved in the buying decisions, which Dad and David had done together for years.

Shortly after I started, I learnt a painful lesson about the dangers of the meat slicer. I was slicing a salami when, suddenly, I had sliced off the tip of my thumb. David calmly picked it up off the floor with greaseproof paper, placed it in my suit pocket, and went to the next-door neighbour who had a van and asked him to take me to the Royal Infirmary. It was early in the morning, and I felt a bit faint on the way to the hospital. I had lost a lot of blood, which was soaking through a tea towel wrapped around my thumb. The nurse stitched it back on there and then. To this day, I have no feeling in the tip of my thumb. However, I quickly learnt how to use a meat slicer safely.

A few customers came early in the morning while we set up the counters. These people had time to chat and were happy to do so while David and I served them and continued our work. Just like Wally before, work could stop for no man.

One customer, Mr Kolb, a gentle man, had been a regular at the shop since he first visited the Bridge Street store with his German immigrant father in the 1950s. A jeweller and engraver by trade, with a shop in Grangetown, Mr Kolb always ordered the same: liver sausage, smoked ham, and rye bread. We would chat about many things, including the economy and politics.

I also remember Mr and Mrs Valek. Mr Valek was a Czech man who had lost his entire family in the Holocaust. Small and wrinkly, he had a quiet demeanour and always seemed to be one step behind his wife, who was taller, thinner, and appeared the more dominant of the pair. His wife would order Hungarian salami and liver sausage, just enough for the week, and they would return the following week like clockwork. However, Mr Valek was a war hero. You would never have guessed it by the way he carried himself, but during the Second World War, he was a decorated officer in the Czech air force, known for his fearsome reputation for downing enemy aircraft. Such was his contribution to the war effort that in 1991, he was invited back to Czechoslovakia by President Havel to be officially recognised for his war service.

Doris Moritz was a formidable German woman with a stern manner and forthright views, who came to the UK on the Kindertransport in 1939. She would order rye bread and liver sausage, which she always claimed was a taste of home. Her husband, Alfred – a distinguished man who became a Professor of Classics at Cardiff University – spoke clearly and precisely, though with a marked German accent, having arrived in the UK from Germany in 1937 after being sent there alone by his parents. Their son, Michael, moved to the US in the 1970s and founded Sequoia Capital, the venture capital firm that famously invested in Google, PayPal, and YouTube as startup companies. Michael is now a billionaire and the richest Welshman in the world.

Lillian Bogod visited the shop to order matjes herrings (young herrings preserved in salt and oil) for making chopped herring – a traditional Jewish dish – for her Friday night dinners. Her husband, Michael, now aged 96, is one of the oldest living members of Cardiff Reform Synagogue.

Following the morning setup, my day would involve placing orders, restocking the shelves, assisting with deliveries, and serving customers. It was fascinating to observe Dad interacting with the older customers, those who remembered him as a young man and knew his parents. He would chat with them while I got what they wanted from the counter. I'm sure the discussion veered into how I was faring in the business, but the hushed words meant I could never quite catch what was being said. Over time, I began to build relationships with these and other customers, becoming part of the dialogue.

The one thing I was determined to do was prove myself in what Dad valued most: hard work. I had never forgotten Dad commenting: "If I'm not exhausted at the end of the day, I do not feel I have worked hard enough." So, I worked extremely hard, constantly racing up and down the stairs to fill gaps on the shelves. I was shattered at the end of the day, but I knew Dad valued hard work more than anything else.

Even after I slipped a disc, I ruled no task out. I would clamber about in the basement void or above the roof slats, even if I were wearing my suit; there was nothing I would not do. It was how I felt Dad would look upon me the best, not in the office doing the book work, but doing the physical stuff like that.

Working every Saturday meant I wasn't around as much as I would have liked for family outings, taking the children to activities, or watching them play sports. Like Dad before me, I missed much of their growing up. However, I was determined to be a more hands-on dad than my father and to be present for my children as much as possible. While this didn't occur to the extent I would have liked, I still played a significant role in their childhoods.

Meanwhile, Dad found it hard to let go; he felt that everything he did was one less task I would have to manage, and he wanted to lighten my workload. That's how he explained it, but I don't believe that was the only reason. I think he was concerned that the transition might adversely affect the business. He often recounted tales of how the sons of people he knew had ruined their fathers' businesses, and I realise this was a significant worry for him. He aimed to protect the legacy he had inherited from his father.

It was true that, excepting my stints in the shop as a Saturday boy, this was a new world for me and I had much to learn. Retailing was in Dad's blood, literally. As a young boy, he had joined his father in the business and didn't know anything else. On the other hand, I didn't know much about it, so I had to learn everything from scratch, from buying to profit margins, merchandising to window displays and sign writing.

Each sign was handwritten with a marker on a small board and inserted into the end of a sawed-down broom handle, into which Dad had cut a slit. I wasn't good at writing these signs; I could never get them to scan nicely. In the end, I decided to create the signs on a computer instead, but in old shop photographs, you can see that all the signs in the shop were handwritten.

Dad surprised me two years after I joined him by deciding to legally transfer the business to me. I don't know whether he was considering retiring now that I had learned the ropes, but if he was, it never materialised. I hadn't pressured him into it, but it caused a dilemma, because I was now the owner, yet he remained the boss. He had recruited and trained all the staff we had at that time. In their eyes, I was the new boy and didn't know the business that well. It was confusing for them and challenging for me. It would confuse customers, too, and I was frustrated when customers approached me and asked: "Where's the boss?"

Wally and Steven in the shop, circa 1994.

As I learned the business, there were some areas where Dad and I disagreed, including the use of loss leaders to attract customers into the shop, and the number of product facias. What we did agree on was the importance of customer sampling. Dad firmly believed in offering samples to customers – a practice that continues in the shop today. He instinctively felt that if a customer tried something, they would be more likely to purchase it, and he was right. However, Dad would sometimes become annoyed if customers returned for too many samples. One woman came back three or four times, and I remember he tapped her lightly on the wrist, saying: "It's not lunch."

As time went on, I got to know Dad better than I had while growing up, when we had not spent much time together. David and he had a stronger father-son relationship than I did, which was perhaps understandable as David had been working for him since he was 14. David had known Dad for over 20 years when I joined the business, so they were quite close. However, by being in the shop, Dad and I developed a better relationship, even if it was mainly centred around the business, and I value that.

It was not only Dad who had to adjust to my presence in the business; it was also a significant change for the long-term staff. I realised how challenging it must have been for David to have me join. Despite this, he warmly welcomed me into the business and helped me learn the ropes as best he could.

Dai, who was just a year younger than me, found that we had plenty in common, but he was also aware of the differing approaches Dad and I took as we tried to steer the shop forward. "Being roughly the same age gave us the same outlook on life. You were ambitious with the business when you came in, wanting to expand it, but I think you were keener than your dad," he told me.

Dai's observations were correct. Dad couldn't conceive a way of running the shop without always being there. He was risk-averse, and the one shop provided all the work and stress he could cope with. He was also wary of people's honesty and often told me tales of friends of his being ripped off by their managers when they weren't there.

Nevertheless, I persuaded Dad to look at premises in Swansea. We found an excellent unit in a suitable location, and I wanted to go ahead. But on the drive home, Dad dashed my aspirations by saying: "It's too much of a gamble and would put my pension at risk." After that bombshell, I couldn't possibly proceed.

While I had expected Dad to retire, his health continued to improve, perhaps due to the additional support I provided. So he remained at the helm. In hindsight, I don't believe my joining the business was beneficial for him, as it was somewhat imposed on him; he didn't want to relinquish his baby and wasn't ready to retire. However, at 60, he was compelled to take a backseat, which he found difficult. Consequently, there was some friction between the two of us.

I want to believe I made the right decision going into the business, but there were times during those first 15 years when I questioned it. However, I was a very respectful son and didn't want any disputes or arguments about work that might affect our family life, so I bit my tongue.

I spent those years watching, listening, and learning from my father, just as I'm sure he had done with his own father. One valuable lesson I learned was the importance of timekeeping. Dad lived by the clock during the day. Breaks and tasks had to be on time, and everything had to run like clockwork. Otherwise, the day would slip away from you. Dad often said running the shop was like "holding a tiger by the tail".

Gradually, I gained more confidence as I transitioned from an accountant to a retailer. While I was initially a bit apprehensive about moving from my previous profession into retail, I was now proud to be at the forefront of the family business and excited to drive it forward.

By then, my parents had upgraded their Spanish home to a villa just outside the village, which Mum named *Valterrena*. With its stunning grounds and swimming pool, this became Mum and Dad's favourite place. They began to spend more extended periods in Spain, a month to six weeks at a time, which benefitted Dad's health and provided us with a break from one another. I would take charge for four to six weeks and could relax. However, I worked very hard to ensure the shop looked good when he returned.

When he wasn't in Spain, he often came into the shop after we had opened. He might reorganise a window display without discussing it with me, or ask a staff member to do something contrary to what I might have asked; they were being dragged from pillar to post. It was frustrating. I wonder whether he felt the same frustrations with his father when he joined the business. I imagine my grandfather and father were quite similar in that respect.

Nevertheless, the shop remained busy, especially at Christmas, when Corrine and I would work exceptionally long hours. Our children spent the week leading up to Christmas at Mum's house, and there was always great anticipation about reuniting with them after the shop closed on Christmas Eve. By the end of the 1990s, Corrine and I had two more children: Natalie (born July 30, 1994), and Daniel (born June 2, 1999).

Space in the shop was so limited that at Christmas, salamis would be hung on hooks from the roof slats in the unit next door, which was no longer being used as an overflow nut shop by then. *Bacalao* (dried salted cod) would also be hung from the slats, and I still remember its awful smell. The shop ceiling would be overloaded with hanging *panettone*, and I even had to take some boxes home to store in our front room and garage, as storage space was so limited.

The shop remained a magnet for Polish customers, just as it always had been. I recall how they would purchase vast quantities of *kielbasa* (the generic term for Polish smoked meats), pickles, cakes, bread, and spirits. They would arrive at the counter and buy whole rings or sticks, sometimes three, four, or even five at a time. They were buying for large family gatherings and catering for the entire festive period.

The only brand of Polish meats available back then was Pek, a name that became synonymous with quality. Although it has since vanished from the UK market, customers still request it, often refusing to buy any other brand. Popular Pek products included *wiejska* (a smoked pork boiling ring), *krakowska* (a smoked sausage made from lean pork seasoned with spices), and *kabanos* (a long, thin, dry sausage made from pork and seasoned with caraway). These products can still be found in the shop today. Very often, descendants of Polish immigrants – second, third, or even fourth generation – stop by to buy these products and regale me with stories of how they remember enjoying them with their families when they were young.

Other Polish meats that were stocked since the earliest days of the shop in Bridge Street have long since disappeared, including: *oganowa* (a smoked shoulder ham, tied with a sting), *tuchowska* (a garlic boiling ring), *kilimetrova* (a long, coarse boiling sausage, folded at intervals), mysliwska (a dry smoked sausage, also known as Hunter's Sausage), and *kashanka* (a blood sausage). Their very names conjure evocative memories of tastes and smells and family members who shopped for these foods and enjoyed them together.

The staff and I became accustomed to taking orders from these Poles and then prompting them with a suggestion of something they might have forgotten. It was amusing. We might say: "How about some poppyseed cake, you've forgotten that?", hoping they might buy an extra item. And they would respond: "Oh, yes, I did, give me four."

We also tried to greet the customers in the little Polish we knew. We could say "hello" or "good day" (*dzień dobry*), "goodbye" (*do widzenia*), "thank you" (*dziekuję*), and a few Polish names of products we sold (and still do today), such as *krufki* (fudge sweets), *sliwka* (plums in chocolate), *makowiec* (poppyseed cake), and *wiśniówka* (cherry brandy).

The customers appreciated our efforts to use their language. When speaking to customers today, I still try to incorporate the odd word or two from their language that I pick up, whether it be Italian, Spanish, German, or Greek.

Another language often heard in the shop, particularly in the early days, was Yiddish. This is the thousand-year-old language of Ashkenazi Jews, originating from Central and Eastern Europe. During wartime in Europe, Yiddish became the common language of the concentration camps and ghettos.

Dad used several Yiddish expressions in the shop over the years, which became so commonplace that they rubbed off on the staff and became part of the shop's language. Examples included: "Pass the *shmatta*", meaning pass the cleaning cloth; "*Schlep* this downstairs", meaning carry this heavy load downstairs; and "Don't be a *schmendrick*", meaning do not do or say something stupid. He also liked to start the end-of-day close-down routine by saying: "Let's make *Yomtov*", a reference to getting everything clean and tidy for the Jewish holiday.

Dad had several other favourite expressions that he used regularly, such as: "Where do you think you are, your father's yacht?", which was said when someone got too big for their boots; "This is for thinking, this is for dancing," pointing first to his head and then his feet, said when someone wasn't using their brain to think about something; and "No *yentzing* tonight," adapted by Dad from the Yiddish word *yentzen* (to copulate), meaning no sex tonight, said when there was a big day the next day and an early start.

Another favourite expression Dad used was: "*Meine tante hatte auch ein*" (my aunt also has a), said as a sardonic put down if someone was boastful about having or doing something. This was typical of Dad. He wasn't easily impressed by material possessions, preferring to build his family and his business and, quite literally, build.

When I was young, Dad used to call me a "*lobbus*", a Yiddish term for a good-for-nothing, but used affectionately. I believe Dad's use of Yiddish and the occasional bit of German connected his past with his present. It likely reminded him of his parents and the language spoken at home when he was young; it was a piece of them that he could carry with him and pass on. These words and expressions transcended time and place, creating a legacy of a bygone and never-to-be-returned-to world. Today, I cling to and use as much Yiddish as I can, although I worry about how much will be passed down to my children and grandchildren.

12

Gradual Changes

Wally's Delicatessen 2000-2006

By the time I had worked with Dad for a couple of years, I had grown accustomed to certain facts. One was that while I did all the bookwork and a lot of the buying, and could run the shop smoothly, Dad would never find it easy to take a back seat. He liked to be hands-on, directing staff, changing displays, and being present in the shop. We shared a small office, and Dad was often in there when I needed to be, making me uncomfortably aware that I should get back onto the shop floor if I wanted to please him. Another indisputable fact was that the business would not expand to further sites while Dad was involved. As in many aspects of running the business, my father still held the reins.

Nevertheless, I always felt the need to prove my worth, and despite Dad's reluctance to open in new locations, I found other ways to grow the business. My first significant development was setting up a website and selling online. This was in 2000, during the early years of the internet, when Wally's online presence was strong, often ranking at the top of internet search results for "speciality foods".

This had the unintended result of making us appear like a larger business than we were. For a couple of years, we supplied Fortnum & Mason in London with German frankfurters, shipping them by post. Fortnum's discovered us through an online search for suppliers of speciality meats, and I believe they were unaware that we were merely a small independent shop in Cardiff.

Initially, Dad, David, and I packed the orders on the shop floor after closing. After a short while, Corrine, who had been working part-time, took on the responsibility of packing the orders. We were so busy with internet orders; we have never done as much of our turnover online as we did in those first few years. As the popularity of online retailing soared over the next two decades, it became increasingly difficult for a small business like ours to find its place online and make its presence felt. Our online business has since declined, bucking the trend, but that has made us even more determined to ensure that our bricks-and-mortar business, the shop, is as good as it can be, offering customers an in-person experience that cannot be found online.

I successfully introduced further changes. In 2000, we expanded into the unit next door, which was being used for storage. The space was costly due to its long window run, which is the most expensive floor area for rent and rates. I wanted to expand the shop to sell a broader range of products. We weren't using that space as an overspill shop at Christmas, as my father had done in years gone by. By combining the two units into one, I finally allayed my father's fear, expressed 20 years earlier when he surprised Richard Morgan by accepting this reduced-sized unit, that he would not have enough retail space.

Naturally, Dad took it upon himself to fit out the unit for retail purposes. He reused much of the original shelving, installed a new slatted ceiling and wooden floor, and created new window display cases.

However, the change caused a problem, as the shop lost vital storage space which was already in short supply. We spoke with Richard Morgan, our landlord, who was a proper old-school gentleman, and he provided us with some unused space at the far end of the arcade, above the shops and spanning the arcade. This storage space was more than adequate for our needs, but the issue was that it was up two flights of stairs. With the help of a local

Wally, with drill in hand, fitting out extension, and Steven, 2000.

engineering firm, Dad ingeniously planned and built a hoist to enable us to lift the goods up and down in a cage. This was typical of Dad; he was always capable of finding ways to solve a problem and wasn't fazed by it. As I have already made clear, I regret not inheriting his practical skills.

The first product range we introduced in this new sales area was South African foods. During the 1990s, there was a significant influx of South Africans from an Afrikaner background into the UK, following the rise to power of the African National Congress. Around the same time, the NHS recruited nurses and other staff from Southern Africa to bolster their staffing levels. Like other immigrant groups, both these communities sought a taste of home. We had been selling beef biltong (air-dried beef; the name comes from the Afrikaner language, meaning bull's tongue, due to the way it looks when hung up) for some time, but we now began stocking a wider range of goods, including *mielie meal* (a coarse flour made from maize), a South African staple. We offered such an extensive range of products that customers thought we were a South African shop. However, demand began to dwindle after immigrant South Africans started opening shops around the country, and these goods became increasingly available online.

My next step was to purchase a wholesale business from one of the shop's Greek suppliers. This gave us access to a small wholesale delivery round and, more importantly, introduced us to new suppliers in London. The acquisition added new tasks, such as securing orders and taking a van to London to collect customer goods. The monthly van trip enabled us to call on other suppliers and buy items directly. Once back in Cardiff, customer orders were loaded into my car for delivery around the local area, reaching as far as Barry – a task carried out by me or David.

We brought so many goods back to Cardiff that the van occasionally became overloaded. On one occasion, David and Dad were stopped by the Highways Police on the way back and taken to a goods weighing station. All the goods had to be unloaded onto the tarmac there and then. At about four in the afternoon, I received a call from David while I was in the shop: "Help. We're in trouble," he said. I urgently had to hire a transit van and drive to meet them to collect the excess stock from the roadside.

On another occasion, David and Tric were stopped. They had to unload the excess stock into a garage repair workshop owned by strangers in Watford and return the next day to collect it. The police charged David, and Dad wrote a letter to get the charge dropped.

Another market we were able to significantly develop for a time was the shop's Polish trade. We had been selling Polish products since the original shop opened on Bridge Street. But, after Poland joined the European Union in 2005, there was a massive influx of young Poles into the country, and a few large cash-and-carry wholesalers selling Polish goods opened in London. Seeing the range of products available was mind-blowing, and I realised that the new customers would be buying them for everyday use, not just for a reminder of home.

These Polish immigrants were economic migrants, in contrast to the Polish refugees of the 1930s, such as my grandfather. They were often young families seeking better job opportunities and living conditions. Most were employed in manual labour and received low wages, which meant they had to look for cheaper foods rather than higher-quality options.

We stocked a wide range of products, from drinks to confectionery, fruit juices to crisps, and preserves to pickles. This was a tremendous new market for us for several years, until a wave of *Polski sklep* (Polish shops) opened (at least four in Cardiff), which undercut our prices. The shops weren't located in the city centre, as we were, facing high rents and rates, but in suburban areas with lower overheads. The Polish community frequented these shops to such an extent that our Polish trade fell below its previous levels.

This was disheartening yet unavoidable. Even some of our older Polish customers would purchase from these shops, only visiting Wally's for specific products where the quality offered elsewhere was considerably inferior. By this point, we realised we could not rely on our Polish trade and had to seek new markets elsewhere.

One market we developed was for US confectionery. Demand for these products soared during the 2000s, as product placement on television soaps and comedies brought them to the attention of the UK public. We stocked various American foods, including cereals, drinks, and jellies (jams). However, like the Polish and South African trades, demand for these products declined after dedicated US shops opened nationwide.

These experiences highlight the ongoing shift in population demographics and demand that the shop faces. The composition of immigrant communities in Cardiff has evolved over the years, and we have responded accordingly. My grandfather introduced European delicatessen products to his grocery store in the 1950s. My father introduced health and whole foods in the 1970s and 1980s and expanded into western European foods, particularly Italian and Spanish. I have introduced new product ranges from countries like America, Southeast Asia, Africa, and the Far East, to meet the shifting demand.

A significant change in 2000 was the mandatory introduction of metric weights and measures for products sold loose by weight. Imperial units (pounds and ounces) had been the standard measurement system in the UK since 1824 and were ingrained in the British shopper's mindset. The transition to grams and kilograms caused considerable confusion for customers and employees, and it took some time before it became second nature. Some older customers have never transitioned and still order in what they call "old money" today.

A significant disruption to the smooth operation of the shop occurred around this time, when David announced he was leaving to run a fishing tackle business with a friend. David had long desired to be his own boss, and this, combined with his passion for fishing, seemed the perfect move. Tric, meanwhile, continued to work at Wally's. I was extremely worried about how we would manage, as David had been so central to the business, but I hoped we would get through it with effective recruitment.

Then, six months later, I received a request to complete a reference for David for a position at Marks & Spencer. I rang him immediately and asked what had happened. David explained that the new venture had not worked out, so he was on the job hunt. I invited him to return to Wally's, as this was what he knew best, and David agreed to come back, not even missing a single Christmas.

*

My three children became regular visitors to the shop. For Natalie, the smell of the shop on me and her Papa (Wally) is one of her earliest memories. From the shop itself, she vividly recalls the old-fashioned tills and the gingerbread Santa biscuits that arrived every December.

For Benjamin, Christmas also loomed large. He recalls:

"My earliest distinct memories of Wally's are entirely tied up with Christmas. For most of the year, the shop was where

Dad went during the day. He left before we went to school, and I remember so clearly that six in the evening was the exciting time when we could expect Dad to walk back through that front door. I can't recall when the shop wasn't a part of our lives in this way.

"But Christmas was different. Throughout December, we saw less and less of Dad – he gradually left earlier and came home later. Mum worked part-time in the shop, too, at this point, and the week before Christmas was so intense, with long hours for both, that the three of us children would go to stay with our Booba (Grandma).

"The build-up to Christmas Eve is exciting for any child, but for us, it was even more intense because Christmas Eve meant we could run and hug our exhausted parents when they came to pick us up and take us home. I can remember those hugs, and now, looking back, I can only imagine how lovely it must have been for Mum and Dad to see us, too.

"Christmas is special for most families, but for the three of us, it was extra special because it meant we could finally have uninterrupted time with our dad again, despite him contentedly dozing off on the sofa as we excitedly played with our new toys.

"And, of course, Christmas wasn't Christmas without some classic Wally's treats – especially the gingerbread iced hearts and Santa Clauses. That's the taste of Christmas for me."

Daniel remembers visiting the shop when he was five or six years old, when he would run to the meat counter to snack on meats and cheeses.

"My diet as a child was delicatessen. Besides running in to see this unbelievable mass of fresh cheeses and meats, I used to go to the warehouse and hide in the boxes where they packed all the goods for delivery. When I was growing up, it wasn't just a shop – it was where I'd go to have fun.''

These memories closely resemble those of my sisters and me when we were the same age. The baton had truly been passed, and history was beginning to repeat itself.

My parents' home served as a second home for the children while they were growing up. Ben cherishes fond memories of his childhood spent with his grandparents:

"Thanks to Dad spending so much time in the shop, I enjoyed a beautiful, close relationship with my grandparents. I also had the added benefit of being their first grandchild (although there were nine more to come after me). They were both extremely loving and very warm, and their home was a very comforting space for me, with only happy memories.

"As I grew older and began learning German at school, I have fond memories of sharing what I had learned with Papa. He had spoken German at home as a child but was out of practice. I loved seeing the light in his eyes as he enjoyed slipping back into his German, with all the songs and sayings that would pour back into his memory. 'Messer, gabel, schere, licht. Dürfen kleine kinder nicht,' he would sing to me (this must have been a song from his childhood – it translates to knife, fork, scissors, fire. Little children are not allowed).

"I loved Papa dearly, and you could feel that everyone in the family looked up to him. He was the centre of our family. As a young child, Booba says I used to climb into bed with them and happily play with the Star of David necklace around Papa's neck – an heirloom that Booba passed down to me after Papa's passing. It's my honour to wear that same Star of David today."

When Natalie saw him, Wally was always in one of two places: either in the shop or at home. "He was incredibly hard-working and always so smart in his suit," she says. "In his downtime, he would enjoy spending time with his grandkids or pottering in the shed or garden."

I am, she adds, just like my father – incredibly hard-working and with my heart always in the business. This quality rubbed off on the children. As she describes:

> "He had a routine like clockwork; home by six-thirty every evening and every Tuesday off. Dad would have my brothers and me spend time stocking shelves in the shop, providing us with experience and skills we could use going forward. We were always taught to be hard-working, determined, and striving towards a goal, something Dad has always done even to this day."

Ben agrees, stating that his Papa and I are among the hardest-working people he has ever known. "I have heard the stories about Papa and his talents – building, often literally, every element of the shop and his family homes. He seemed to know how to do everything regarding construction and DIY, seemingly never stopping.

> "Dad inherited that trait 100 percent. Dad's skills lie less in the DIY department – but the man is no less hard-working. Indeed, he finds it difficult to switch off (ask any of his staff)."

My children didn't know their great-grandfather, Ignatz, and neither did I. However, the understanding I have gained of him through my research for this book makes me realise that the traits my children describe in me come not only from my father but also from my grandfather. The three generations of men who have run the family store over many decades have essentially shared the same outlook: determination, hard work, and a desire to instil this in their children.

13

The End of an Era

Wally's Delicatessen 2006-2008

By 2006, the shop had reached its 25th anniversary in the Royal Arcade, and I organised a party to celebrate the occasion. Amid the speeches, I said this about Dad:

"None of us would be here today if it were not for you, especially me, for obvious reasons. You started this business, having previously achieved the twenty-five-year milestone with the old shop. You designed it, fitted it out, staffed it, and stocked it; nurtured it during the early years; worked it to the bone, and loved every minute. Your stamp is all over the shop, and whatever fine reputation we have got is just recognition for your talents.

"Your energy is remarkable for a man of any age, let alone a man approaching seventy. I am sure I will never come across another person who can work with the consistent dedication and enthusiasm you have always shown and continue to show. I know from personal experience the cost to you in terms of your time with your family and your health, but I also know that you would not have had it any other way. You have had a mission in life, and you have achieved it.

"Dad, you are a much-loved man – by your wife, family, staff, and customers."

I felt that reaching this milestone was an achievement to be celebrated, both for the family and for the long-term employees. Dad, however, was more relaxed, almost indifferent to the whole idea. "Do it if you must," he said. I'm not quite sure why he had that attitude; I know he was proud of Wally's and its longevity, but perhaps, for him, the story didn't begin in 1981 with Wally's, but rather in 1949 with his father's shop, Bridge Street Stores. Whereas Wally's Delicatessen felt like the starting point for me, I think for Dad, it was merely the continuation of the family business his father started.

Wally and David, on the 25th anniversary of Wally's in Royal Arcade, 2006.

Meanwhile, the shop continued to evolve. In 2005, after 125 years of trading, the David Morgan store was sold to a property investment company, Helical plc, which planned to convert it into smaller retail units, with apartments above. Simultaneously, a significant redevelopment of The Hayes (the commercial area in which the Royal Arcade is situated) began. A new shopping centre, St. David's Dewi Sant, was to be constructed to extend the existing St. David's Centre. This latest development would be built over the site of my grandfather's original shop in Bridge Street. The entrance to the John Lewis department store now stands roughly on the spot of the old shop. The owners named the two malls that cross the centre Grand Arcade and Bridge Street Arcade, recognising the area's history.

Helical had different ideas about utilising the space that Wally's had been given for storage, so they proposed an alternative site that had become available. Situated in the former Works Department, it comprised a large ground floor room, first floor rooms, and a basement, still occupied by the massive machinery used by David Morgan decades previously to fabricate shop fittings for the store which proved too large and heavy to be moved (and can still be found there today).

True to form, Dad worked around it, fitting extensive wooden racking in both the ground floor and the basement, and re-engineering the hoist from the old storage area to work for loading and unloading goods to the basement. This was no small task, and Dad was almost 70, but he found a sense of purpose in tackling this now that he was relied upon less on the shop floor. As we constantly carried heavy goods downstairs, Dad devised the idea of sliding the goods down the stairs on a long scaffolding plank.

Eventually, the insurers deemed that area unsafe, necessitating it to be mothballed. We were then offered storage space in the basement beneath the arcade, comprising a few small rooms which had previously been behind-the-scenes storage for the David Morgan store. The brick-built arched supports for the arcade floor and the low ceilings create a Victorian feel to this cramped space. We are still using this storage space today, and we still use the plank mechanism for sliding goods downstairs.

As the redevelopment of The Hayes progressed, it became evident that Cardiff's retail heart would shift from Queen Street to The Hayes, transforming it from a tertiary to a primary shopping location. However, many businesses suffered in the meantime. The combination of the upheaval on The Hayes and that caused by the redevelopment of the David Morgan store created an extremely challenging period for traders in the arcade.

I was eager to find ways to grow the business in ways that would win Dad's approval, so I began exploring franchising. I devoted considerable time, money, and effort to researching this, as I felt that if I couldn't physically expand, perhaps this would be a way to realise my ambition.

However, during this unsettling period, Dad received devastating news that would forever shape the shop's future. Despite being a lifelong smoker, Dad had never developed lung cancer, but by early August 2007, he had been diagnosed with incurable stage four stomach cancer. He received the news with typical Salamon stoicism, refusing to tell me about it until after Natalie's bat mitzvah at the end of August, so as not to spoil the celebratory mood.

When Dad told me, I couldn't grasp its seriousness. I assumed he would receive treatment, pull through as always, and be back in the shop in no time.

Initially, Dad continued to visit the shop, but once his chemotherapy treatment began, his visits grew less frequent. When he did come in, he would use his mobility scooter and remain seated behind the front counter, taking everything in and chatting with the staff and customers. Even at his most unwell, this was the place he wanted to be.

The staff and I did our utmost to maintain business as usual, but as the seriousness of Dad's ill health became increasingly apparent, everyone – both staff and customers – was distraught.

However, I knew that the one thing Dad would want above all else was for the shop to continue operating as usual.

Amid the upheaval, the double unit next to Wally's, 38-40 Royal Arcade, became available, and I recognised an opportunity. For many years, this unit had been home to the Treasure Galleon, a gift shop, and, more recently, a children's furniture and clothing store.

I thought we should secure a lease on the building and open it up to create one large shop. I realised we needed to become a bigger store to capitalise on the forthcoming new trading environment. I felt we would struggle to survive if we stayed as we were. I had long since given up on my early enthusiasm for expanding to other locations, but this was an opportunity to grow and keep everything close by.

Another advantage of the unit was its equally spacious first floor, which I knew we could utilise. Various ideas were suggested for the combined space, including expanding the delicatessen upstairs or opening a café downstairs. However, I wanted the ground floor to be exclusively a delicatessen, as I had yearned for a larger retail space for many years.

I had been visiting trade shows since joining the business, and one stall that had always caught my eye was the German Food & Drink Federation's stall, with its glossy leaflets showcasing various ideas for using German charcuterie and cheeses in sandwiches and culinary dishes. They looked fantastic, and we were already selling all the products suggested as fillings. I recognised an opportunity to bring my café idea to life.

David and I discussed several options, including opening a bagel bar or a salt beef bar, but I preferred the idea of a café selling continental open sandwiches. I also wanted to reflect the shop's heritage, as my grandparents came to the UK from Austria. While there were already plenty of Italian sandwich shops and cafés, I believed a Viennese-style kaffeehaus would be unique, while paying homage to Dad's background.

The Viennese coffee house tradition began after the Austrians defeated the Turks in 1683, leaving behind sacks of coffee beans – a previously unknown delicacy. Kaffeehäuser became venues for people to meet, read newspapers, discuss current affairs, and engage in intellectual and cultural pursuits.

Dad was becoming frailer as David and I began planning the kaffeehaus. When former warehouseman Leo passed away, it heightened Dad's sense that his era was coming to an end. "Dad had heard that Leo died, and he wanted to go to his funeral, so I went with him," Rochelle recalls. "He cried, because this was a reminder of the old days; it was the passing of everything, and he really respected the people who worked for him and their hard work ethic."

With his work ethic as strong as ever, Dad helped me with the plans for the expansion and the opening of the kaffeehaus. I shared my idea with him, as I sought his blessing, but not only that, his guidance, expertise, and ideas. Thankfully, he supported me, saying: "If you think it's the right thing to do, go for it." This was the encouragement I longed for but was not used to; without it, I'm not sure I could have followed through with it, even after his death.

I believe that Dad had finally accepted that I could, and needed to, grow the business on my own terms. This boosted my confidence and energised me for the challenge ahead. Dad's ill-health was a factor in his thinking, but I would like to think that, after a 15-year apprenticeship, I had finally won his respect, and that he believed I would successfully carry his legacy forward.

He sketched out a few ideas for how the enlarged shop could be designed and even found units in Ikea that could be transformed into shop display units with care. We purchased one, and he set me to work sanding it down in his garage, varnishing it, and adding pelmets and lighting. Throughout, he supervised from his mobility scooter, undoubtedly frustrated that he couldn't engage in the work.

Mum also recalls how Dad's commitment to the business endured until the very end. "The man's determination was remarkable," she says. "I think somebody like that could have done or been anything in his life – a good sportsman, a good musician –

because he had the determination that anybody needs to get anywhere. But he had nowhere to put it except into the business."

Dad also organised every detail of his affairs and established financial plans for Mum. This included advising Mum to sell the villa in Spain, where many happy family memories had been created.

Some of Natalie's final memories of her Papa are from the family holiday at the Spanish villa for his 70th birthday. "This was the last time everyone, including Papa's oldest brother Sigi and our cousins from America, were all together as a family," she recalls.

My most vivid memory from that holiday is Dad singing songs from his army days. He adored the camaraderie and tunes from the army. If he were a bit tipsy, he would often break into an army song about marching across the Rhine or something similar, which were usually rather rude. On the way back from the party, he sang song after song. I had never seen him unwind like that; Spain was the only place he truly relaxed. The pressure of running the business at home never allowed him to do so.

*

Christmas 2007 was an emotional time. By then, we all knew it was likely, barring an unexpected recovery, to be Dad's last Christmas in the shop. I recall the emotions as David, Tric, Dad, and I locked up the shop on Christmas Eve and walked to our cars. No words were spoken, and we all tried hard not to let our feelings show, but the tears in David's eyes conveyed everything that needed to be said.

I was in the same situation as Dad and his brother had been in the early 1960s when their father became too ill to work. By then, they had years of experience working alongside their father, and the baton passed seamlessly. I hoped that the same would hold true for me.

When Dad finally became too ill to visit the shop, I often went to see him at home. We chatted about the shop and what had occurred during the day, shared stories, and discussed business.

He would not necessarily ask about the takings or want to hear the finer details of the day-to-day running of the shop. He wanted to know which customers had been coming in and how they were. He would ask: "It's Friday. Did Mrs Egan come in this morning?" or "How's Mr Engl doing? Is he still getting his liver sausage?" He would enquire about David, Tric, and Dai, eager to hear if they were alright. These questions made me properly appreciate, perhaps for the first time, that the shop was not merely about business for Dad, but it was his life. The customers and staff were as much family to him as Mum, my sisters, and me, and he loved them all.

Dad inherited this trait from his father, and now I truly understood that, to continue their legacy, I needed to take this on board.

The love and affection he felt for his customers and staff were reciprocated and extended to several suppliers with whom he had dealt since the Bridge Street days. One such supplier was Mr Sandhu, an Indian immigrant who had established a highly successful Cash 'n' Carry in Bristol. Dad had been buying from him since the early 1970s, and I recall seeing Dad jump up onto the back of his lorry parked outside the shop to choose what to buy. When Mr Sandhu learned that Dad was dying, he requested to visit him at home with his wife, and they spent a lovely afternoon reminiscing about the old days. Their relationship was unusual; it had transcended a business relationship to become one based on mutual admiration and respect for what these two immigrants had achieved through their sheer hard work and perseverance.

Other shopkeepers in the Royal Arcade also admired Wally. He received a lovely card signed by more than 20 of them, several of whom had traded alongside Wally's for many years. Among the good wishes was this message:

"This card is from all your friends in the Royal Arcade, whose thoughts are with you. People always refer to this arcade as the one Wally's is in when asking directions to find us all."

Dad wasn't nostalgic and rarely got sentimental, but I wish he had been. I regret not asking him more about his background, family life, and childhood. But he never looked back. That was something he inherited from his parents.

He only told me to look after Mum after he had gone. I remember him saying: "Don't underestimate her, she's a formidable woman." That statement stayed with me, but that was about as sentimental as he got. Other than that, it was all very practical stuff.

On another occasion, when he was near death, he remarked that if I propped him up against the shop door after he had passed, he could serve as security, saying: "The customers would not know any different."

There was a certain truth to this. Dad had been a permanent figure in the lives of his customers and staff, who repaid his care and kindness with unwavering loyalty. The family feel of the business had come to extend, quite literally, to the staff: not only were David and Tric a married couple, but Dai met his wife Tammi when she came to work at Wally's.

Dad recognised that his unwavering work ethic had been both a blessing and a curse. During one of my visits, I spoke to him about this and asked whether he had any regrets. His answer was illuminating and somewhat sad. He told me that he could see there was a different way of living, one that involved spending more time with children and family, enjoying hobbies, and relaxing more. He admitted that he didn't know if the way he had lived his life was the right or best way. But he said that, if he had his time again, he would not do it differently, as he didn't know any other way. This shows his selflessness, but my sisters' and my regrets regarding the lack of quality time with him demonstrate that the right balance was not always achieved.

Dad was quite young when he arrived in the UK, and I'm not sure he ever viewed himself as anything other than British, despite being born in Austria to a Polish father and a Romanian mother. His parents had both passed away by the time he turned 31, and he spent most of his life without them, causing their continental influence on him to diminish over time. Had it not been for the shop, I believe Dad would not have maintained much of a connection with his European heritage. He allowed his German to deteriorate, and he didn't delve deeply into his family history until late in his life, when he visited his birthplace in Austria and later secured an Austrian pension, although he never travelled to Poland.

His nationality was complex, and his lineage perhaps too confusing. However, even though he lived almost his entire life in Wales, I don't think Dad ever viewed himself specifically as Welsh. He enjoyed living in Cardiff and was proud of his contribution to its commercial life, yet he never embraced a Welsh identity, whether in language or culture.

Like his father, he was connected to his Judaism, though he wasn't religious. Had he had more time, I think he might have enjoyed going to synagogue and playing a greater role in the Jewish community in Cardiff, as he enjoyed this growing up. I would say Dad identified as a British Jew.

In the final stages of his life, Dad had to be moved into a care home for palliative care. I remember visiting him one evening after work. After knocking gently on the door and receiving no response, I let myself in. I noticed Dad was asleep and crept in as quietly as I could. Suddenly, he awoke and immediately checked his watch. I wondered why he needed to know the time, but of course, this habit stemmed from a lifetime of running the business like clockwork. I take pride in wearing his watch today.

When Dad finally passed away on July 13, 2008, the loss felt by customers and staff was immense. "It was like losing one of our family," says Tric. "He knew all our family – my sisters and brother – and had seen everybody growing up. It was a sad time."

"It was a massive blow," agrees David. "It was like the ending of the old guard. Wally set the standard, and we took it all on board."

Dad was, as David says, an old-fashioned retailer. He expected the staff to say "good morning" or "good afternoon" and "thank you" to every customer, and he always thanked his staff at the end of the day. "A huge part of the business was the meeting and greeting," says David. "Towards the end of my time there, it was the only difference between coming to our business and going elsewhere. You could get what we sold in many other places, but the difference was the rapport with the customers and the relationship with them, which was an important part of my job and everyone else's job."

Wally's many loyal customers mourned him as well. One, Peter Muller, the son of a Kindertransport refugee, sent the following message to Mum after Dad died:

"I was so saddened to hear of Wally's passing and realise what a great loss this will be for you all. My memories and association with Wally span more than 50 years from those bygone days in Bridge Street, which as a family we visited on a weekly basis. It was a far cry from the successful business that he built up to what it is today. Nevertheless, Bridge Street was a focal point for the European community in Cardiff and has left a lasting impression on me from my infant days to the present day.

"As fellow traders in the city centre our paths crossed regularly, and we would chat, joke and consult each other (about whether business was good or bad). In Spain he was a different person, on the few occasions we met out there, he was so relaxed and seemed to enjoy life to the full. Wally was acknowledged as an expert in his field, but more importantly, he played his part in keeping the community together by providing the special food that was the tradition and cultural lifeblood of so many refugees from Europe. This important part of my family's history will live on in the many fond memories I have of these times. I know Wally was also a committed family man and will be sadly missed.

"Our thoughts are with you all at this sad time. I wish you all a long life."

Peter's words eloquently encapsulate everything about Dad and the business that he, his brother Otto, and their father established. In just a few words, several key messages emerge: the longevity of the shop and its role as a focal point in the weekly lives of its immigrant customers, providing them with a sense of community and a connection to home; the notion that food was central to uniting this community, enabling exiles to experience a taste of home and fostering a sense of belonging, which served as a reminder of their heritage and cultural traditions. And, of course, Wally stands out as a devoted family man who, while happy discussing business, was only truly relaxed and at ease in his home in Spain.

It is traditional in Jewish homes to sit *shiva* (mourning period) for seven days after a person has died. However, when Dad was dying, he told the family that he only wanted us to have two days of *shiva* – probably because he was concerned about the impact on the shop. The *shiva* period is intended to comfort the mourners, allow friends and family to pay their respects, and wish them "a long life" (a greeting derived from a concern that a mourner might not see the point of living after their loss).

Dad had never been particularly religious, but I fondly remember how he enjoyed sitting in synagogue all day on *Yom Kippur*, the Day of Atonement. As the years passed and the congregation aged, he would lean over to me and whisper who this or that person was, or comment on those who had passed away. When I go to synagogue now, that is what I remember: him sitting beside me.

I closed the shop as a mark of respect on the day of his funeral (held the day after he died, following Jewish tradition); it was the first time the shop had ever been closed on a trading day. The funeral was attended by hundreds of mourners, from family to friends, as well as current and former staff and customers. Even the local newspaper, the *South Wales Echo*, sent a reporter. Quoting from my eulogy, their headline read:

"A giant of a man in all but stature."

When it became clear that Dad didn't have much longer, I began to think about my eulogy. I wanted to ensure that nothing was overlooked and didn't want to be caught out by a lack of time. This was a moment to tell everyone what a great man, father, and husband he was.

I had coped with Dad's death well up to that point, but when I stood to deliver the eulogy, my voice cracked. Somehow, I managed to carry on:

"Dad was unique: intelligent, creative, skilful, artistic, caring, passionate, gentle, firm, honest, trusting, trustworthy – a true patriarch to the Salamon family.

"Dad did everything for his family. He wanted nothing but to see his family taken care of. To this end, he sacrificed himself."

Whenever I attended funerals without Dad, he would always ask me whether there had been a good turnout, as this was how he gauged a person's standing in the community. So, I told him in my eulogy: "There was a good turnout, Dad."

Dad is buried in the Reform Jewish cemetery in Ely, Cardiff, near the graves of his mother and father, Ignatz and Frieda, his brother and sister-in-law, Otto and Maureen, and his parents-in-law, Ernie and Beattie. The inscription on his headstone reads:

"A rare and remarkable man who inspired us and won the respect and affection of all who knew him."

Like our fathers did before us, Otto's son Michael and I uphold a Jewish tradition of tending to the family graves each year during the High Holy Days, between the festivals of *Rosh Hashanah* and *Yom Kippur*. We are joined by our children whenever they are available, which assures us that this tradition will endure when we are no longer here.

My favourite photograph of Dad hangs proudly in the shop. Not a day goes by without a customer commenting on the photo, remarking what a lovely man he was. I usually agree and then add comically: "He is still keeping an eye on me."

And so, the story's second chapter, which began with the opening of Bridge Street Stores, ended.

Wally Salamon, 1936–2008.

14

Expanding Horizons

Wally's Delicatessen 2008-2013

Following Dad's passing, it fell to me to guide Wally's into the future, and I felt the pressure from the very beginning, particularly as it hadn't been my life plan to follow Dad into the family business. I had worked there for 15 years by that point and wanted to demonstrate to the world that I could run the shop as effectively as Dad had, now that he was gone. I wanted to uphold his legacy, for the family, the staff, and the community of customers who had always been connected to their homelands through the shop.

When Dad died, a few older customers stopped visiting the shop. This was sad, as they had frequented it regularly for many years and had not even been served by Dad in the last few years. I suppose they had been coming out of loyalty or for nostalgic reasons, and that all ended for them when Dad died.

I made a concerted effort to ensure that nothing changed in terms of style, atmosphere, or approach. Dad's ways were deeply ingrained, which made it easy.

I hadn't yet secured Helical's agreement to expand the shop, but plans were still well advanced and continued to progress. I engaged planning consultants, as the Royal Arcade is a listed building, and there were strict restrictions on what was and wasn't allowed.

The building works commenced in April 2009, and the walls between the two buildings were finally knocked through on Easter Sunday. The shopfitter arranged for the supply of high-quality shop fittings from Italy, which were far superior (and more expensive) than the Ikea units Dad advocated.

The grand opening was scheduled for July, but with only a few days remaining, the shelving had not yet arrived. A moment of panic ensued before I decided to purchase temporary metal racking to fill the shop and make it look presentable for the opening.

Wally's Delicatessen, circa 2015.

Mum delivered the opening speech at a launch event in the shop for friends, family, and customers. Champagne flowed, and canapés were enjoyed by all. I gave a speech of thanks to everyone who had helped Wally's reach this stage. It was an emotional day for me, as I was both excited about realising my dream yet incredibly nervous about how it would go and whether I could pull it off.

Following the completion of The Hayes redevelopment, the shop was now in a prime retail location, opposite a new, glossy shopping centre, designer stores, high-quality restaurants, and a new Central Library. The area's transformation was completed through a pedestrianisation scheme, which saw The Hayes and St. Mary Street, at the other end of the arcade, closed to traffic. I was initially opposed to this scheme, but aside from logistical difficulties with deliveries, it has benefited the business overall.

The city's population had grown to 345,000, and, bolstered by visitors, as many as two million people would visit the city centre annually.

The new shop allowed us to expand our product range. We had separate meat and cheese counters, and an olive bar. However, we also began selling loose Belgian chocolates, Italian gelato, hampers and gift sets, teas and coffees, and a much broader range of confectionery. Crucially, we also started to sell a significantly larger selection of wines, beers, and artisan spirits.

David had the bright idea of placing the olive bar front and centre in the shop, and it became an immediate hit with customers. At 12 feet long, it created a tremendous visual impact, featuring an array of Greek, Spanish, Italian, and Moroccan olives, with vibrant colours and enticing aromas being amongst the first things to greet customers as they entered.

Equally eye-catching was the chocolate cabinet, filled with rows of high-quality Belgian chocolates. The gelato freezer has also proven to be a popular addition, allowing customers to choose from any of the nine delightful flavours.

At this time, two crucial new team additions were Mark Pask and Stuart Meyer, whom I had known for years as they had worked for one of our suppliers. Stuart was a bull of a man, as strong as an ox, having always worked outdoors and in manual jobs. He had an incredible work ethic, which I knew had always impressed my father. Mark was slighter, yet no less hardworking. I also took on a colleague of theirs, Nicola. Fast forward to today: Stuart is the shop manager, with Mark his assistant, and Nicola and Stuart are married, continuing the trend started by my father of having married couples as key staff. I even employ three of their children as weekend and holiday staff. The business truly remains a family business in the broadest sense.

The enlarged shop was an immediate success. Existing customers appreciated the new range of products and the fact that I remained faithful to the style of the former shop. I installed a suspended ceiling for hanging products in the traditional Wally's style, laid a wooden floor, and tiled behind the new counter area. The shop now attracted a new clientele, as I had predicted when planning the expansion.

The customer demographic, however, had changed. The expanded range of products attracted many more locals to the store – by which I mean not just indigenous Welsh people, but also third- and fourth-generation descendants of immigrants. By this point, it was becoming hard to distinguish the differences, as they had largely assimilated. That's not to say we didn't still cater to the needs of their grandparents and parents. The shop had become less of a magnet for Eastern European immigrants, such as Poles, Czechs, and Germans. However, it still drew Western Europeans, particularly Italian and Spanish customers who had resided in Wales for a few decades yet maintained their cultural identity. Customers like Mrs Pinotti, a petite Italian woman burdened with shopping bags, often complaining about the buses, the crowds, or her bad back. Nevertheless, she continued to visit the shop weekly for mortadella, provolone cheese, and Italian pastries.

We were now stocking more traditional British products such as hampers, teas, coffee, and chutneys. We also expanded our range of Welsh products, as Cardiff was increasingly becoming a destination on the tourist trail, both from within the UK and abroad. This marked the beginning of an emerging food tourism trend, from which Wally's has benefited substantially, making us a regular destination for food tours in Cardiff.

Our local clientele was becoming an integral part of the customer base. Well-travelled individuals sought foods they had experienced abroad, and knew they could find quality, authentic products at Wally's. "Foodies" desired a range of products that are hard to source elsewhere, all within a welcoming atmosphere. Individuals such as Tony, a Cardiffian through and through, visit every week for continental meats and bread, and to chat with the staff. And Hugh and Ruth Jones, a young couple from west Wales now living in Cardiff, who collect ingredients for home and treats for their children.

*

Meanwhile, I began planning the layout of the kaffeehaus, in collaboration with a local catering consultancy. Although I lacked catering experience, I used their expertise along with some common sense and guesswork to design the layout and purchase all the necessary equipment and units.

However, the opening of the kaffeehaus was delayed after a surprise expansion opportunity arose. The new St. David's Centre was set to open in October 2009, bringing numerous big-name brands and new visitors to Cardiff. A month before the opening, I was asked if I would be interested in launching a pop-up unit in the Centre. I was keen and was shown various locations. One location stood out from the rest. It was centrally located on the first floor where the two thoroughfares crossed.

I felt on a roll: the new shop was thriving, and I had an overwhelming desire to move forward at pace. I agreed to the deal, and we ended up with a giant blown-up poster of Dad looking down on the entire St. David's Centre, which I adored. I especially liked that we were now operating a stone's throw from the site of the original Bridge Street shop.

Tric, whom I persuaded to manage the shop, was less enamoured with the new venture, feeling it was a "goldfish bowl". However, she gave it her best shot, and the shop was ready in time for the grand opening of the Centre, stocked to the gills with sweets, biscuits, confectionery and chocolates.

The first Christmas was both fantastic and extremely stressful and tiring. I was managing the newly-expanded store, which was busy from the outset, and the newly-opened second store in the St. David's Centre. I juggled between the two shops throughout the day, unsure where to position myself most effectively. It contributed somewhat to fulfilling my early ambition of opening more than one store, but it left me exhausted and didn't help my marriage.

With stress levels at an all-time high, my marriage was under pressure, yet I felt an inexorable drive to make the shop successful now that it was entirely in my hands. It didn't help that I was so preoccupied with the latest developments at a time when both my father-in-law and my father had just passed away. The timing was dreadful but unavoidable – the opportunity for both expansions was a one-off, and I had to grasp it when I could.

Regrettably, our marriage did not last, and after the finalisation of our divorce, I adjusted my work schedule to be available for Daniel, who was 12 at the time. I stopped working every other Saturday for the first time since joining Wally's, something I would never previously have considered.

In the shop, I got on with things. It was more crucial than ever that the shop didn't suffer. In this respect, I was much like my grandfather and father before me. Rightly or wrongly, for better or for worse, the shop always came first. It was all-encompassing in its own way for each of us: whether it was my grandfather working when he was unwell and should have been at home resting; my father sacrificing time with his children and compromising his health; or me, devoting myself to the business and solely focused on making it a success. However, I had to scale back some ambitions as the strain was too much, and I promptly abandoned my franchising aspirations.

If one shop at Christmas was a lot to deal with, it became even more challenging after the opening of the St. David's Centre shop, which celebrated its second Christmas with a happier Tric than the first time around. When she first took the helm in the new store in the run-up to Christmas 2009, she was frustrated that the shop didn't look festive. She recalls:

"The first year, it looked very bland without any Christmas decorations. People were coming in saying they thought it was a Christmas shop, so I got all the stuff the second year and decorated it for Christmas."

I was somewhat surprised when I saw it, but later I called Tric and told her that the shop looked lovely, and I was pleased. Like Dad, I had learnt to bend to the will of the staff.

The St. David's Centre shop was only meant to be a temporary arrangement, and when it finally closed in January 2011, Tric was pleased to return to the Royal Arcade. I reflect on the shop as a wonderful experience from which I gained great satisfaction. However, many of our customers believed it did not represent our traditional brand, and others thought we had closed in the Royal Arcade and relocated there.

Following the closure of the St. David's Centre shop, I was able to resume work on the kaffeehaus. The equipment was already in place, under wraps, so I now needed to plan the menu and establish the processes. I visited Vienna to explore all the kaffeehäuser there and returned with numerous ideas that we would incorporate into the design and processes to replicate an authentic Viennese kaffeehaus as closely as possible.

My trip was akin to a journey back in time to the heyday of the Viennese kaffeehaus culture. I dined at renowned and stylish kaffeehäuser, such as Café Central, Café Demel, and Café Sacher, where celebrated artists, scientists, and politicians, including Gustav Klimt, the Austrian painter, Theodor Herzl, the Jewish founder of modern political Zionism, Sigmund Freud, the Austrian neurologist and founder of psychoanalysis, and Leon Trotsky, the Russian revolutionary and communist leader, were patrons. Chillingly, a young Adolf Hitler may have also frequented cafés like these, potentially formulating his radical racial ideology. Café Sacher is said to be the birthplace of the famous Sachertorte (a chocolate sponge cake covered in chocolate glaze with an apricot jam filling). However, I was intrigued to learn of a dispute that continues to this day between Café Demel and Café Sacher regarding its true origins. I also visited less ornate but equally captivating kaffeehäuser, such as Café Hawelka, which opened in 1939 – when my grandparents were forced to emigrate from Vienna – where the lighting was dimmer and the atmosphere more artistic.

I envisioned the scene in a turn-of-the-century kaffeehaus: elegantly suited gentlemen wearing dinner jackets with wing-collared white dinner shirts and black bow ties, seated around round marble-top tables in a smoke-filled room, engrossed in reading newspapers and engaging in heated discussions about the affairs of the day. Perhaps a young, budding composer, following in the tradition of Beethoven, or Strauss, entertained the guests on a grand piano in the corner. Waiters, smartly attired in tailcoat tuxedos, carried silver trays laden with coffee and cake to the patrons.

My visit evoked mixed emotions. On the one hand, I marvelled at the grandeur and style of the Viennese kaffeehäuser, hoping to emulate them in the best way I could. On the other hand, I couldn't help but reflect that many, if not all, of these same establishments had refused to allow Jews to enter just 70 years earlier.

Upon my return, I developed a coffee menu in the Viennese style, with the coffees featuring German names such as *verlängerter schwarzer*, meaning extended black (americano), and *milchkaffee*, meaning milky coffee (latte). Our food menu included typical kaffeehaus small dishes like smoked sausages, as well as desserts, cakes, and tarts. We also played classical music (albeit on a CD player rather than a grand piano), served our coffees on a silver tray with a glass of water, purchased authentic Bentwood-style chairs, and displayed our newspapers in traditional Austrian newspaper holders. These are found everywhere in Vienna, but our customers struggled to figure out how to use them, so eventually, they had to be removed. I drew the line, however, at asking the staff to wear tuxedos.

Ironically, decades earlier, the unit had served as a café. While stripping out the first floor in preparation for refurbishment, the builders discovered a disused dumb waiter concealed behind some partition walls. It was gratifying to restore the unit to its former function.

Wally's Kaffeehaus finally opened in September 2011. I considered naming it 'Wally's DeliCAFEessen' as a play on words, but ultimately I decided this was far too much of a mouthful.

I wasn't sure what to expect, especially as it was out of sight on the first floor. However, customers flowed in from the outset, drawn by its unique menu of teas and coffees, continental open sandwiches, charcuterie and cheese platters, soups, salads, and desserts.

The first Christmas was chaotic. I worked in the kaffeehaus, clearing tables, washing dishes, and taking orders, to keep things running smoothly. I hadn't anticipated how busy we would be, and we didn't have enough staff.

I concealed some clues about the shop's heritage in the menu. The open sandwiches are named after Austrian provinces or large cities, but two are called Eisenhüttl and Rohrbach, the villages where Otto and Wally were born. The platters are referred to as *aufschnitt*, meaning cut-offs, in homage to the ever-popular meat bundles sold in the deli, comprising the sliced end pieces of meat.

Wally's Kaffeehaus.

The kaffeehaus has attracted a new clientele to the shop. Our older continental customers adore its European atmosphere, as do those who have travelled extensively in Europe, like Huw Davies and his wife Audrey – Welsh folk from the Valleys, who visit Cardiff weekly for German food and to enjoy the kaffeehaus. It evokes memories of the food they experienced when Huw served in the army in Germany and of their time spent in Austria on holidays.

An added benefit is the showcase that the kaffeehaus provides for the products sold in the delicatessen, as almost all the ingredients used in its menu are sourced from the deli counters and shelves. Customers can eat in the kaffeehaus and then purchase the food they have enjoyed to take home.

The kaffeehaus has received some glowing feedback from customers over the years. Here are just a few comments that encapsulate their sentiments towards it:

"I love how it's not loud; it's super clean, has amazing service, and has a great staff. I love it here, it's great."

"Really nice, amazingly tasty food and drink. We love it here; we will come back."

"A wonderful place to come and relax and eat. All the food is delightful."

Aside from the obvious benefits, I'm proud to have opened and run a hospitality business, as I know it was always an ambition of my parents. They would have made excellent hosts, given their creativity, flair for design, and personal touch. I hope I have made them proud.

Following the closure of the St. David's Centre shop, my appetite for further expansion remained strong. I opened a Christmas shop in 2012 at the St. Mary Street end of the Royal Arcade. Although I was apprehensive about opening another shop remotely, I believed I could manage another unit locally. I always remembered how, during Christmas times past, Dad would open the storage unit next door as an overflow unit for selling nuts; I thought this would be a similarly clever idea.

The shop was managed by the husband and son of one of my employees, Nicola Gainey, exemplifying our family-oriented approach. We stocked it with all the best-selling Christmas items: *panettone*, *stollen*, *lebkuchen* (German iced or chocolate-coated honey cakes, plain or filled with fruit filling), nuts, and dried fruits. Unfortunately, the shop only operated for one Christmas; I realised it was better to attract customers to the delicatessen, where they could purchase a wider range of products and visit the kaffeehaus. I was disappointed, but not excessively so. I understood that experimentation was necessary, and it was better to try and fail than not to try at all. This was one area where I differed from my father.

15

Different Directions

Wally's Delicatessen 2013-2018

2013 was a pivotal year for me both personally and professionally. I found myself at a crossroads, uncertain of my next step. I could seek opportunities to expand, maintain the status quo, or even sell the shop and venture into something new. With plenty of time on my hands now that I was living alone, I took up jogging to keep fit and successfully completed my first half-marathon.

I also enrolled in a part-time Executive MBA at Cardiff Business School. Some of the content was similar to my degree course, which made the transition easier, but it also introduced me to new areas. Each month, a different aspect of the business was analysed, and recommendations for improvements would be made.

While the lectures were somewhat dry and uninspiring, the coursework and interaction with fellow participants were exciting, challenging, and rewarding. Ultimately, the business benefited from a few subtle changes.

At the end of the course, I wrote a 20,000-word dissertation titled, "Has the High Street Run Out of Road?" It examined the rise of online retail and questioned whether this signalled the end of the high street.

I concluded that it was not the end, but a fork in the road. One could decide which path to follow – traditional bricks-and-mortar retailing, or the online model. I concluded that it would be preferable for small independent businesses to pursue the bricks-and-mortar route.

I graduated from the course with a distinction, and partly because of my dissertation conclusions, I set aside ideas to expand Wally's remotely and focused on optimising the performance of the shop and kaffeehaus.

I had come full circle: 22 years after joining the business, I was now on the same page as my father, although he had intuitively known what I took ages to discover.

The connections I made during the MBA opened several intriguing new avenues, and I was invited to give a lecture on my dissertation to the Cardiff Business School Innovation Network. The lecture was attended by a Chepstow Chamber of Commerce representative, who subsequently invited me to speak to its members.

Following that, I was invited to consult on the Chepstow town centre and organised a visit, touring the town centre with a member of the Chamber and making notes of my observations. My findings, which seemed obvious to me, were well received, and the modest fee I earned sparked the idea that I might one day establish myself as a consultant, business coach, or mentor.

The MBA also led to me being asked to put Wally's forward as a case study for master's students on the marketing course at the Business School. For three years, groups of students spent their summers examining a particular aspect of the business under my guidance.

I asked them to review both the delicatessen and the kaffeehaus. Each group offered numerous excellent recommendations, many of which I have implemented. I was amazed, and somewhat humbled, that students with no prior knowledge of the business could identify aspects I couldn't, being immersed in it as I was and lacking the time to take a step back and view the business from a distance.

The most noticeable change was in the logo: the design remained the same, but the original wording was replaced with the words: "Quality, Authenticity, Variety" to reflect our vision, along with a newly-extended shop name, "Wally's Delicatessen & Kaffeehaus", with "Since 1981" added below to highlight our heritage.

Wally's Delicatessen & Kaffeehaus logo.

As mentioned, I recognised 1981 as the year the current business started. Of course, I knew the shop on Bridge Street and its history, but I wanted the logo to reflect when Wally's began. Upon reflection, I think this may have been a mistake. For my father and many customers, as I have since discovered, the shop's history is a long-running saga that dates back to 1949, when my grandfather first opened in Bridge Street. The delicatessen has been a constant presence in their lives, through good times and bad, and amidst changing social, economic, and political landscapes. For them, the move to the Royal Arcade was merely a change of location, not the start of a new business. Perhaps 1949 would have been a more suitable date to include in the logo; my father would have thought so.

*

Changes in the shop weren't the only new developments in my life. In the years following my divorce, I remained single. I had been chatting with a woman named Michelle on a dating site, but I felt she lived too far away at the time. Michelle was a bookkeeper and a photography enthusiast. She had been divorced four years earlier and was a single mother to two young boys, Oli and Scott.

In October 2013, just as I decided to consider a long-distance relationship, Michelle returned to the dating site and spotted my profile. "Still on here then, I see," she messaged me. I replied, and the energy shifted; we did not stop talking this time. Michelle recalls:

> "We became good friends, but we both realised it was more than friendship. However, he couldn't come to London because of Christmas in the shop, so he thought I wouldn't wait for him. Yet I felt I'd be cheating on him if I started chatting to someone else, so I told him it was fine: I would wait, and he eventually came to London."

Eager to spend time together but hindered by geography, work obligations, responsibilities towards our children, and the scars of past wounds, we proceeded cautiously. As the relationship progressed, we then introduced ourselves to our respective children.

As we established a happy, lively social life in London, we both fell into a double life – one together, the other apart. Michelle was too rooted in London to consider a move to Cardiff, and the shop required too much commitment for me to relocate to London. A long-distance relationship would have to suffice for the time being.

*

At this point, my decision to concentrate on the Cardiff store was yielding results, and alcohol was becoming a more significant component of the overall offering. The business was on the verge of pursuing a new direction.

The shop had always sold alcohol, initially just Polish spirits, the most popular of which was *wiśniówka*, a Polish cherry brandy. Over the years, the range had expanded, first with the addition of South African wines, beers, and ciders, followed by Italian liqueurs such as limoncello and amaretto. Next came Penderyn whisky, one of many Welsh products Wally's has promoted.

After that, we introduced a kaleidoscopic range of world beers and lagers, beginning when we stocked beers from all the countries competing in the Eurovision Song Contest. The selection expanded from there, driven by a subsequent beer campaign linked to the football World Cup, and complemented by Welsh beers from brewers including S.A. Brain, the iconic Cardiff brewery.

The shop encountered a setback following a Trading Standards "sting" operation, where authorities sent an underage girl, who could pass for 18, to purchase alcohol. A Saturday sales assistant covering extra weekday shifts sold her a bottle of wine without checking her age, which led to me being summoned to City Hall, where I was interviewed on tape by Police Licensing Officers. The sales assistant received a caution and a fine. Naturally, I paid the fine on her behalf. After outlining our impeccable record regarding underage sales and store policies on the issue, as well as agreeing to implement several procedural improvements, I was issued a warning and permitted to continue retailing alcohol.

This was a tremendous relief, as increasingly more of the shelf space was being taken up by alcohol and sales were strong. The sentiment was that people were consuming less quantity but of higher quality.

I had placed the expanding alcohol range into the narrow unit at 44-46 Royal Arcade. However, as alcohol sales soared, a new problem arose: the limited space allocated for alcohol was insufficient for the shop's growing selection of spirits. For a couple of years, we struggled to manage the demand; we couldn't accommodate enough people in the area, and shopping became uncomfortable for both customers and staff.

In 2017, I was approached by a local letting agent who suggested opening a second Wally's shop in another arcade, Castle Arcade, which is the most beautiful of Cardiff's seven Victorian arcades. Built in 1887, it is located opposite Cardiff Castle. Although I wasn't initially interested, I soon became involved in the Cardiff Business Improvement District (BID), which was set to launch soon.

BID areas are designated following a ballot of local businesses, which pay a mandatory levy to fund the BID's work aimed at enhancing the area. This encompasses a full range of activities, from marketing and promotion to sustainability initiatives. During my MBA, I studied BIDs as a method to rejuvenate high streets, so I was keen to get involved when a BID was proposed in Cardiff. I joined the board of directors, contributed to the BID prospectus, and took responsibility for the independent retailers in the area, canvassing support for the vote on implementing the BID. The BID prospectus pledged to invest £5million over five years in city centre improvements, with £100,000 per year specifically allocated for independent businesses. This was an incredibly exciting prospect for the city centre.

I contacted independent businesses in the BID area as part of my remit. Most of these were concentrated in various arcades. During a conversation with an owner-managed retailer in Castle Arcade, I learned that the landlords were offering retailers pop-up units to utilise unoccupied space.

This was also an opportunity for me, for the second time, to open another outlet – a long-held dream of mine. I particularly liked that it was in an arcade, as I believed an arcade brand could be established.

During the summer of 2017, while Michelle and I were on holiday, I negotiated the pop-up lease from my poolside sunbed. I agreed on an acceptable rent and lease for one year and applied for an off-licence.

The only things left were the new store's name, the fit-out, and the staffing. I considered various names, like The Angel's Share and The Devil's Cut, references to the evaporation process occurring in wooden whisky barrels during maturation. However, I opted for Wally's Liquor Cellar, as it was part of our brand alongside the existing Wally's Delicatessen and Wally's Kaffeehaus – and it kept my father's name front and centre.

I wanted to fit out the store affordably, as I wasn't sure if it would last more than a year. Staying true to Dad's thinking, I purchased modular Ikea shelving units that displayed the products well. Aside from tidying up, I didn't spend much on the fit-out and was ready to open by October 2017.

Another crucial decision was deciding who would manage the new store. I wanted someone I could trust, and I recalled Dad's warnings about the risks of having a second store and the potential for being cheated by the manager.

My first port of call was Clive Sims – a man I had worked with for many years. Clive had designed Wally's website, and I knew I could trust him. Clive managed the shop for its first Christmas but didn't want to stay long-term, so I was once again hunting for trustworthy recruits. The solution presented itself in the form of Bethan Owen, a former manager who had just returned from travelling, and Matthew Webster, the partner of one of Wally's long-term employees, Lynne. Matthew had worked in the drinks industry as a cocktail bar manager for many years, and I knew he possessed a good knowledge of spirits, especially whisky. This continued Wally's practice of recruiting from within the families of staff.

Wally's Liquor Cellar opened in October 2017, enabling sales of a much larger range of artisan wines, beers, and spirits than could be achieved in the Royal Arcade. It was a success from day one. I was proud of my achievement and envisioned expanding the concept to other cities.

Wally's Liquor Cellar, Castle Arcade, 2017.

*

Christmas 2017 was an unforgettable time for me. Both the delicatessen and kaffeehaus were thriving, and I was now faced with the added stress and workload of the Liquor Cellar. Desiring to be in two places at once, I devoted considerable time and energy walking along St. Mary Street to the Castle Arcade to check on the Liquor Cellar's progress. This was only feasible because the deli was in capable hands, managed by David, with valuable support from Tric, Dai, Stuart, and Mark.

But then something happened that would shake Wally's world to its core. One afternoon, about a week before Christmas, David suddenly felt unwell, experiencing burning sensations in his legs and neck. He went upstairs to the staff room to rest, and a short while later, he told me he needed to go home because he was feeling so poorly. I immediately realised this was serious, as David would never leave the shop at such a busy time unless it were absolutely necessary.

David stayed away during the week, visiting the doctor for tests. The team and I managed as best we could and somehow made it to Christmas Eve. He stayed home recovering for the next few months and ultimately decided to retire. This must have been an extremely difficult decision for David, who had worked in the business for 47 years. Although he had retirement plans in mind for the not-too-distant future, this came too soon and was not how he had envisioned things.

David's departure in this manner was a considerable shock. There have been moments in my career when I felt I couldn't manage in the shop without him. Certainly, Wally's would not be where it is today without David, and I owe him a tremendous debt of gratitude, just as my father did before me. He remains a great friend of the family today.

I remember David's strong work ethic, which saw him spending up to two hours in the mornings perfecting the fresh display, never resting until it was full and looking appetising to customers. He was an ideas man, too, always suggesting innovative ways to improve the shop. But perhaps his greatest strength lay in his relationships with customers.

David and Tricia Pike.

With my most stalwart colleague gone, I was forced to adjust quickly. I promoted Dai to manager, with Tric, who had stayed on, Stuart, and Mark as his assistants. Fortunately, the experienced management team was able to take up the reins and drive the shop forward.

As the New Year approached, I had a conversation with the St. David's Centre manager, whom I already knew from my earlier stint there in 2009 to 2011. A brief exchange led me to believe that opening a unit in the St. David's Centre to sell Welsh artisan spirits might be feasible. I felt this would attract a different clientele than those who frequented the two arcade businesses. The footfall in the St. David's Centre was around 40 million per year, and the prospect of capturing some of that market was very tempting.

I could not afford a permanent unit, as the costs were prohibitive, but I wondered if a kiosk in the mall's centre might be feasible. I was offered several locations, but the one that stood out was at the foot of the main escalator, outside three of the Centre's flagship stores – Disney, Currys, and Hamleys.

The excitement of a new opening was building. But then tragedy struck.

*

On May 1, 2018, Michelle received a call from the police. They had found the body of a teenage boy and were calling regarding the phone discovered with the body. "They told me the phone's number, and it was Oli's," she says.

The police arranged to meet her at home, where she would need to identify the shoes found on the body. They were Oli's.

Michelle called me in the shop, and I immediately got in the car and drove to London. Our world had shattered. Oli was just 16 when he died. He had left two notes for Michelle, and their brevity was devastating.

It was clear that Oli's suicide had not been impulsive. He had planned it, and Michelle had been forced to watch the tragedy unfold as if in slow motion, hoping that things would improve, that she would find the right help for him, that brighter days lay ahead.

Michelle still lives in the house she shared with Oli and his brother Scott. She cannot imagine moving. "Oli is there," she says simply. However, she has not allowed herself to be frozen by grief;

she is determined that those left behind should continue their own life stories while remembering Oli's.

While the loss was unbearable for Michelle, she was determined not to let it affect Scott's chances. She did everything she could to make his world as normal as possible, including returning to work after six weeks, as that was his norm. Furthermore, she wished for me to return to work and continue with the new project in the St. David's Centre.

*

Back in the shop, I finalised the kiosk design and wrapped up lease negotiations. I named the business Wally's Spirits from Wales, adding another Wally's-branded venture to the portfolio, and the kiosk opened in September 2018. I moved Bethan from the Liquor Cellar to be the manager and stocked it to the brim with Welsh gins, whiskies, vodkas, rums, and other liqueurs.

Wally's Spirits from Wales kiosk, St. David's Centre, 2019.

Around the same time, the short-term lease on the Liquor Cellar was set to expire. Following a successful first year of trading, I negotiated a new six-year lease for the unit.

But my life was also set to take a new turn. My mind was still very much with Michelle in London. I suggested establishing a charity to do something constructive to remember Oli and give Michelle a focus.

Michelle and I founded The Oli Leigh Trust the year after Oli died, with a simple yet momentous aim. Michelle had lived through the nightmare of her son's suicide, and we hoped that the Trust would help prevent other families from experiencing similar tragedies by working to reduce the rate of suicide among young people. Michelle says: "We remember Oli as a person, but it's a bigger picture now: teenage suicide prevention. There are too many children in this world taking their lives, and there's not enough support or training available to prevent it."

Michelle and I are trustees, along with Scott and two others. The Trust's original strapline, "Helping teenagers to see through the fog", came from a drawing found in Oli's room after his death. It depicted a young man with his head stuck in a fog cloud.

The Trust has gained momentum year on year. Michelle is the face of the charity, organising fundraising events, giving talks, conducting training and presentations, and maintaining its presence on social media. Meanwhile, I manage the finance and compliance and act as Michelle's sounding board and support. "It helps that he is very methodical, because I'm not methodical at all," says Michelle. "That's what he's like in his business, and that's why it succeeded."

The Oli Leigh Trust has naturally become the nominated charity for Wally's, with all our customer collections and fundraising efforts supporting its vital work. Alongside the business, I now had another focus and had to ensure I struck the right balance.

Losing Oli in this way was a tragedy, and nothing Michelle and I have done since in his name makes it any easier. However, establishing the Trust has given Michelle a sense of purpose, and if even one life is saved, Michelle will know that something good has come out of Oli's passing.

16

Challenging Times

Wally's Delicatessen 2018-2024

In April 2019, while watching the London Marathon on television, I surprised Michelle by announcing that I would run the marathon the following year to raise funds for suicide prevention.

I wasn't a great runner, although I had completed my first half-marathon in my early 50s. I felt I needed to undertake a challenge outside my comfort zone to raise a significant sum. I was also eager to inspire Michelle to do something positive in Oli's name and to give her a focus in life, as she was grappling with her grief while struggling to find a way to move forward.

Initially, Michelle advised me against undertaking such a monumental physical challenge. Yet she was, at the same time, filled with admiration for my desire to do something positive in the name of suicide prevention.

My fitness was building nicely, and the event was on the near horizon, but on the other side of the globe, troubles were brewing that would stop the 2020 London Marathon in its tracks.

Covid spread rapidly. By March 23, the UK had officially entered lockdown, and all non-essential businesses were forced to close. Inevitably, businesses began to struggle. Amidst panic and uncertainty, all mass participation events were cancelled, and my marathon challenge was postponed.

*

At Wally's, trading remained normal until the lockdown, even as the virus approached. I remember thinking there was no huge sense of doom or foreboding at the time.

I opened the kiosk in St. David's Centre in September 2018, and trade was brisk during the first 15 months. However, the business struggled to show a return on investment. It was also difficult to manage, with little storage space, security concerns, and extended opening hours necessitating multiple shifts. Reluctantly, I decided to invoke the break clause in the lease and closed the business in January 2020. The kiosk unit was donated to a local charity.

I gained immense satisfaction from trading in the St. David's Centre again, and it aligned with my expansion plans, but it wasn't financially successful. I was unaware of what was to come at the time, but the decision to withdraw from the St. David's Centre proved very fortuitous.

As Covid spread, panic buying began, and our online trade soared, particularly the sales of pasta, which was in limited supply.

As a food and drink business and a key retailer, the deli would have been within the rules to remain open. However, I knew this was a loophole not intended for non-essential food businesses like Wally's. Additionally, I was concerned about doing the right thing by the staff, who were apprehensive and wanted to adhere to lockdown rules. Furthermore, footfall was non-existent anyway, since much of the city centre comprised offices and non-essential businesses.

With Wally's closed, I had to deal with all the leftover stock. I had a large quantity of perishable items and Easter products, bought ready for the forthcoming season, including beautiful Italian *colomba* (Easter cakes in the shape of a dove) and decorative Easter eggs, including a giant seven-kilo Easter egg which was due to be raffled for The Oli Leigh Trust.

Eager to ensure the eggs didn't go to waste, I donated the giant egg and some smaller Easter eggs to the Noah's Ark Children's Hospital at the University Hospital in Cardiff, and drove through unnervingly quiet streets to deliver them.

Meanwhile, a local café owner devised a plan to help feed the many doctors and nurses at the University Hospital, who were working tirelessly and under immense pressure during the early days of the Covid crisis. The University Hospital holds a special place in my heart as it's where my three children were born and where they received treatment over the years, including two major operations. Other local hospitality businesses joined the initiative, preparing and delivering meals to the hospital daily. Eager to contribute, I donated all my perishable products, which included hundreds of kilos of cheese, along with takeaway packaging and all the remaining Easter eggs and chocolates, which served as treats for the hospital staff. The community's response was incredible, and a substantial amount of money was raised to purchase provisions for this relief effort.

I then set about working out how best to support my staff and business through the pandemic, spending the first few weeks of lockdown at home, desperately trying to find out more about the various assistance schemes available and writing Covid procedures. I had to do this for three businesses – Wally's Delicatessen, Kaffeehaus, and Liquor Cellar.

The lease for the deli expired at the end of March 2020, and a few weeks into lockdown, I was contacted by the landlord's agent, who was eager for me to sign a new lease. I had no idea what the future held, as we were still in lockdown and closed, so I allowed negotiations to drag on until I could see how things unfolded with the pandemic. All the staff were furloughed for the duration of the first lockdown, although some kaffeehaus staff who were from abroad hastily left to go home as events transpired.

As the news about Covid started to improve, we opened for a few hours each day and set up a takeaway menu, but there weren't enough customers coming in to make it worthwhile.

Meanwhile, Michelle and I hadn't seen each other in person for some time. I was aware that Michelle was at high risk if she contracted coronavirus, having a low immune system following aggressive chemotherapy for non-Hodgkin's Lymphoma years earlier, and I didn't want to take any chances.

At last, news began to filter through about the lifting of the lockdown. I needed hand sanitiser to reopen, which was difficult to source due to the high demand. I spoke with various spirits producers I had worked with who had adapted their businesses to produce hand sanitiser. We eventually purchased our hand sanitiser from Penderyn, the Welsh whisky distillery, and had the best-smelling sanitiser around!

By late June 2020, the shop reopened, and the kaffeehaus followed suit in August 2020. Summer gradually turned to autumn, but trade remained subdued as people were cautious. Nevertheless, after lengthy negotiations with the landlords, I opted to sign a new 10-year lease. Like many others, I believed the worst was behind us and things would gradually recover.

At that point, I was planning Wally's Christmas campaign and needed to decide which products to order and in what quantities. I had no idea what the Christmas trade would be like, but at least we would be open. I assumed trade would be down by 50 percent compared to the previous year and ordered accordingly.

I was right to be cautious; soon enough, Covid cases began to rise again. Trade remained at the predicted levels during November and December, with footfall significantly down on prior years. We implemented a social distancing policy, agreeing on a maximum number of people in the shop for safe social distancing, and made people wait at the door. This felt strange, as I had spent a lifetime trying to get as many people into the shop as possible, and now I was keeping them waiting outside.

I wasn't overly worried as December progressed. However, in the late afternoon of December 19, I was shocked when the owner of the shop next door informed me that a national lockdown had been announced with immediate effect.

The panic was palpable, and Stuart, Mark, and I hurriedly discussed what this meant for us. Fortunately, Stuart and Mark kept a clear head while I rushed around in shock. That is one of their many strengths; they take a matter-of-fact approach and prioritise the business. Stuart said: "The deli is our highest priority right now. Let's focus on that, sell as much Christmas stock as possible, and decide what to do after Christmas." So, we closed the kaffeehaus and the Liquor Cellar at once, but kept the delicatessen open, as an essential food business, until Christmas Eve.

*

A second shockwave, though expected, struck Wally's on December 31, 2020, when the United Kingdom formally withdrew from the European Union's single market and customs union.

Since the Brexit referendum was announced, I had been worried about the potential impact on Wally's. The distinctive feature of the business was that it sold European products. I didn't know how the changes would affect product availability and pricing, but I sensed it would not bode well for the business. My concern was such that I accepted an invitation to appear on Sky News to participate in a live panel discussion about the upcoming campaign.

When the referendum results were announced, I was devastated. A member of staff put up a sign in the kaffeehaus and shared it on social media, stating:

> "Brexit Breakfast: stale bread and a glass of water
> – £10!"

The post went viral.

*

Although Wally's remained open until Christmas Eve, trade was quiet, resulting in a significant impact. The last week of December is the busiest period at Wally's: two weeks' worth of normal sales can be achieved in a single day, and the week can contribute up to 10 percent of annual turnover.

FROM THE ANSCHLUSS TO THE ARCADES

The usual late-night seasonal hours weren't required, and for the first Christmas since I joined the shop, everyone went home before dark.

In April 2021, the lockdown for businesses was lifted, and the two shops reopened. The kaffeehaus followed in May 2021, when hospitality businesses were permitted to reopen. Trade remained quiet, and once more I had to consider my Christmas buying. This time, the news appeared more positive, so I planned to purchase at 75 percent of pre-Covid levels, up from the previous year. I am naturally cautious, so I believed it was better to buy less and sell out than too much and have stock left over.

I also had to consider my training, as the London Marathon was looming again, having been rescheduled for October 2021 after two further postponements. It had been over two years since I first decided to enter, and my training had to be continuously wound down and built up again during that period. According to my training diary, I ran 1,500 miles over those two-and-a-half years!

I finally completed the marathon in October. The day was emotional for me and my supporters: Michelle, Benjamin, Natalie, and Daniel. Towards the end, I felt exhausted, but the cause I was running for and the support I had received drove me to the finish line. It was a marathon effort in every sense, and I explored every avenue to raise funds, including a Tree for Life sale in the shop, an Easter Egg raffle, and even standing outside the shop in full running kit seeking donations. I was thrilled with the total of £12,000 raised to support the vital suicide prevention work of The Oli Leigh Trust, which was by then in full swing.

*

Things were gradually returning to some semblance of normality in the shop, but another momentous change was on the horizon. As Christmas approached, Tric decided it was time to retire. She recalls her thoughts:

"I was going to do another year, but when Covid came, it changed my outlook completely, because we were on furlough for so long," she says. "David was home, and I just didn't want to be in the shop anymore. Being home made me think, *What am I missing?* My nieces were having babies, and I thought, *It's time to go.*"

This was another significant blow, following David's departure a few years earlier, but it was not unexpected. I had anticipated that this, or the next one, would be Tric's last Christmas; however, we all shed a tear or two when she announced it. I knew she would be difficult to replace, if not irreplaceable. Yet, like all the challenges I had faced over the years, I had to get on with it.

If David was like a brother to me at times, Tric was the shop's mother figure. Everyone would go to her with their troubles, which she always managed to sort out. Tric provided the glue that held the shop together, and I knew that I could turn to her for any job that needed doing, whether it was serving on the counters, shelf-filling, window decoration, cleaning, taking in stock, chasing out shoplifters, counselling staff, or organising rotas. She fulfilled all these roles admirably and cheerfully, and I am so grateful to her.

That Christmas, Wally's stayed open and trade was strong. Our longevity meant that we had many loyal customers, and they seemed pleased to return and find that we had survived the pandemic and were still open. This allowed us to quickly pick up where we left off after each lockdown.

It was incredibly gratifying when familiar faces started filing through the doors. They appeared relieved and happy that we were still there, and the shop looked just as it always did. We were welcomed like long-lost friends, even though we had only been closed intermittently for 15 months. I recall one customer, Mr Witts, expressing his gratitude that we were still open, saying: "I don't know what I would have done without my curry ketchup." Another customer, Mrs Kolmar, shared that she had been visiting the shop with her husband, the son of Viennese refugees, every

Tric and Dai, on Tric's last day at work, December 24, 2021. The sticker on Tric's overall reads "This is my last day after 40 years."

Christmas since they arrived in Cardiff, and now that she had lost her husband, she was frightened that "the Wally's cold meat Christmas meal we shared for so long would be no more".

In such troubling and uncertain times, the shop, which had been a constant presence in the lives of so many customers, stood as a grounding point and a link to normality, a reminder that life would go on as before and that the bad times would pass. Initially, many customers wore masks as a precaution, and indeed, older customers took longer to regain the confidence to return, but before long we saw all the familiar faces again.

Seeing customers return has been one of the most satisfying experiences in my business career. I faced the most challenging circumstances I have ever encountered, or am ever likely to, and emerged intact. People often describe the Covid period as a "war", and I concur with that sentiment. In my lifetime, military conflict has not crossed my path, but this was a battle that I fought, along with the rest of the UK and the world – and won. Although not comparable by any means, I regard coming through this period as my contribution to the survival of the family business. My grandfather fought in real wars three times, lived to tell the tale, and started the business. My father also served in the army, albeit in peacetime, and faced his own battle with the business's survival when he was forced to relocate to new premises. The business has endured for three-quarters of a century due to the perseverance, dedication, and commitment of three generations of Salamons. I am proud to have played my part.

I am also proud that no-one was made redundant during the pandemic. However, during the second lockdown, I took the opportunity to restructure the management team. Up until then, following David's retirement, David Richards had been the manager. Dai is quiet and unassuming; he excels at his job and gets along well with customers, many of whom he has known since they came in as children with their parents. He says this is the bit about the job he enjoys the most, serving the customers: "I have served one family for four generations; I've served Carlos, his mother, his daughter, and I've just served his granddaughter."

Dai is the longest-serving member of staff, but just before the first lockdown, he requested to reduce his hours to four days a week, to which I agreed. After 40 years in the business, this was the least he deserved.

However, the shop needed a full-time manager. The assistant managers, Stuart Meyer and Mark Pask, were already handling most of the purchasing and effectively managing the business. Stuart is very focused and determined. He began jogging during the Covid lockdown and has run every day since, even after extremely long hours in the shop leading up to Christmas, and including on Christmas Day. Stuart has become my right-hand man and is invaluable to me. He is to me what David Pike had been to my father and me for years previously. Not only does he handle a substantial amount of the purchasing, but he also manages the alcohol side of the business and packages our online orders. He supervises all the maintenance for the shop as well. This element of the business is vital to its success, and most people aren't aware of what occurs behind the scenes to keep the shop running. We have a lot of ageing refrigeration and other equipment, and we are situated in a Victorian building with the associated challenges that come with it.

I wanted Stuart to be the manager, so I went for a walk with Dai and explained all of this to him. Credit to him, he understood and even agreed that Stuart would be best placed to be manager.

I don't know how my relationship with Michelle would have flourished as it has without Stuart at the helm. I worked closely with him at first as I trained him to be the manager the business needed. Now, Stuart sees the business as I do. He makes the same decisions and deals with issues as I would – whether they be staffing, customer, or equipment related. Above all, he appreciates the effort I have put into the business over the years, recognises how hard I still work, especially at Christmas, and encourages me to take time to be with Michelle.

*

Another shock hit the business when Russia invaded Ukraine on February 24, 2022, and economic sanctions were imposed on Russia by the world's largest economies. This led to an almost immediate surge in energy costs and inflation, resulting in a cost-of-living crisis in the wider economy. The timing was particularly brutal, coming at a point when businesses worldwide were trying to resume "business as usual" after the gruelling years of the pandemic.

Wally's, like other businesses around the world, faced a triple whammy of falling demand, chaotic supply chains, and increased costs, as suppliers passed on rising production and distribution expenses. The impact was particularly severe in the food industry, as Ukraine and Russia are the world's largest exporters of wheat and sunflower oil. While inflation in the overall economy rose to double digits, I estimate it surged to between 20 and 25 percent in the gourmet food sector. I faced the difficult decision of how much of these cost increases I could pass on to customers and, as is often the case in such times, had to strike a careful balance between maintaining profit margins and risking loss of business.

Although the war in Ukraine persists, the pressure on energy and goods prices has diminished. Nevertheless, soaring inflation has resulted in prices being significantly higher than before the invasion, consequentially impacting consumer demand.

We are currently living in uncertain and rapidly changing times. President Trump's tariff deals and counter-deals are wreaking havoc on global markets and upsetting the established international economic order. I wonder if this will be the next challenge that Wally's will face.

17

Taking Stock

Wally's Delicatessen 2025

It is 76 years since my grandparents first welcomed customers to Bridge Street Stores, 44 years since an exhausted Wally, David, and Tric mopped up spilt honey the night before opening Wally's, and 32 years since I joined the business. Wally's is now a Cardiff institution. It has received many awards, most notably Cardiff Life Retailer of the Year 2014 and Cardiff Family Business of the Year 2017, among many others. It is loved by its regular customers and visitors to Cardiff alike.

My children still enjoy frequent reminders of this. "I will never tire of people's reactions when they hear my grandfather was Wally, or the tingle of pride I feel when I see a stranger walking around Cardiff with a Wally's bag," says Ben.

While Wally's has undergone some huge changes over the years, its appeal lies in its timelessness. This is embodied not only in the shop's signage and old school interior, but also by the long-serving staff who provide continuity and a consistent welcome to the shop's many regulars.

Dad would always greet customers with a smile and a "Sir" or "Madam"; that is how we still greet customers. The style is quite formal, even old-fashioned, but I'm sure it is appreciated.

It's not by chance or habit that I keep so much of Dad's original vision for the store intact. Wally's *is* Dad. I know this will always be the case and do not fight it. Instead, I embrace it and fill the shop with markers of our heritage, be it photos on the wall, the style in which we conduct business, the stories we tell, or the culture we create.

I wonder what character traits I have inherited from my father and grandfather. Undoubtedly, their experiences will have shaped their outlook and behaviours, some of which will be passed down to me. I don't believe, however, that I have any "inherited trauma" – a feature affecting some second- and third-generation descendants of Holocaust survivors. Studies have shown that the trauma experienced by Holocaust survivors may be passed down to future generations, affecting them psychologically and behaviourally. This can be reflected in anxiety, depression, or a tendency to worry that their parents' trauma could be repeated. If anything, I would say that being the descendant of Holocaust survivors has been a source of strength and resilience for me.

The one thing I sometimes wish I had not inherited from Dad is his work ethic! I am a workaholic like him, often to the detriment of my personal life. But of course, that is at the core of what has made the business successful and enduring. There is a lovely photo of Dad hanging on the stairs to the kaffeehaus, and I always say he is still checking that I'm working hard!

After Dad died, I had to deal with his death while striving to keep things running seamlessly, and I had to show the world I could run the shop as well as my father had, now that he was gone. Having sole responsibility for everything, all the results of my decisions, and all the risks on me was a huge challenge. As Michelle says: "The shop is not just successful because it's Wally's; it takes a huge amount of work and effort to keep it that way."

Retailing – buying and selling – is easy; everything else is hard. I sometimes feel that I'm not a retailer but a maintenance manager, and at other times a personnel manager. When employing so many people, you must deal with their issues and understand their domestic situations. And when staff leave, it's always upsetting and difficult; staff retention in the shop has been excellent over the years, although in the kaffeehaus it's more difficult due to the age and ambitions of the staff.

Throughout it all, I have experienced highs and lows, stresses and elations, from opening new businesses to letting staff go (thankfully only twice for disciplinary reasons). My grandfather, father, and I have had to contend with economic, social, and political shocks – post-war depression and rationing; three-day weeks and power cuts; legislative changes and several bouts of inflation. I think all three of us faced these challenges in much the same way: with stoicism and a realisation that the only way through them was to put our heads down and work hard.

Like any food retailer, the shop has been subject to regular Environmental Health inspections over the years. I'm pleased to have kept an extremely high food safety standard amid increasingly stringent regulatory requirements. Some years ago, the Guild of Fine Food Retailers (GFF) invited me to share my expertise in a working party set up to work out practical issues around the retail of perishable fine foods, resulting in me being credited as an industry advisor in the GFF's Assured Code of Practice for Deli Retailing.

Today, the delicatessen and kaffeehaus have settled back into a dependable rhythm. Trade during the year is steady, and Christmas trading has been robust. I have recruited excellent staff in the delicatessen to replace those who have left, but many long-term staff remain. The employees in the shop nowadays tend to come from the local population rather than from immigrant communities, where my grandfather and father would have looked for staff. Perhaps that is because I do not have as close a connection with those communities as they had. But this also reflects the changing customer demographic. As immigrant communities have assimilated, the customer base is markedly more local than my grandfather and father would have experienced, with second- and third-generation immigrants adopting local cultures and eating more typically British foods.

The availability of staff for the kaffeehaus – a big problem following the pandemic and Brexit, as European workers returned home to their families for the lockdown and then found they couldn't return following post-Brexit border control changes – has improved. However, the staff are now supplemented by students from India and Asia rather than Europe.

Unlike the delicatessen, the Liquor Cellar did not recover so well after the pandemic. Trade did not return to pre-Covid levels and, despite trying everything to grow the business, things didn't improve, and it ceased trading in April 2024. With great sadness, I made Matthew and the other two staff redundant – the first redundancies I had made in my career.

There are still significant challenges to face, and I believe the full impact of Brexit on the business is just starting to be felt. Following Labour's victory in the General Election of July 2024, I would like the new government to alleviate some of the difficulties of importing goods from Europe. At the time of writing, a new UK-EU deal has been announced, and there is even talk of a pan-European single market, so I will watch that space with interest.

*

Now that no other family member is working at Wally's, Michelle has become my sounding board and an essential partner for discussing ideas, letting off steam, and discussing work-related issues. She is a fresh set of eyes on the business, and because she is not involved on a day-to-day basis, she can often see things from a unique perspective. She has even been my official tester for sample products, which I take to London for her to try or use in a dish and give me feedback.

When her mother visited the shop for the first time, she was very impressed, saying: "There's nothing like this in London." Michelle's friends constantly ask her whether I would set up a Wally's in London. It's an idea I had been toying with, particularly as it would have enabled me to spend more time with Michelle.

However, what had looked like a plausible idea before Brexit and the pandemic, when business was booming and the future looked bright, no longer seemed so clever afterwards. In common with many other people, the lockdown experience reset my outlook. My ambition to expand the business has faded; my focus is now firmly on my relationships with loved ones, my work-life balance, and on keeping my stress levels to a minimum.

I have this saying: "It's either steak or salad" as a code for whether it's been a good or bad day's takings. Every Saturday night, Michelle will ask me, "Is it steak or salad tonight?" Fortunately, it's more often steak than salad.

Steven outside Wally's Delicatessen & Kaffeehaus, 2024.

*

I would describe myself as a Welsh Jew. My national identity is non-negotiable, unlike my grandfather and father, for whom identity was confusing. I was born in Wales and didn't suffer the ignominy of alienation and naturalisation. I do not feel European, although

I acknowledge my roots and know they have made me who I am today.

I think this is mainly the case for second- or third-generation immigrant Jews. Most have assimilated and reconciled with their family's past. Some have even assumed German or Austrian citizenship to "close the circle". One of Wally's customers, Zoe Morris-Williams – the granddaughter of Joachim Koppel, who founded the Aero Zipp factory where my grandfather worked when he first arrived in Wales – is a fluent Welsh speaker and has raised her children the same way. Although I do not speak Welsh, I find it remarkable that in just three generations, the descendants of German Jewish immigrant families are now speaking Welsh, when their grandparents could barely speak English.

Like Ignatz and my father, my Jewish faith is also of paramount importance to me, and I have tried to maintain this aspect of my identity all my life without being overtly religious, and pass it down to my children, as it was passed down to me.

An Israeli friend told me recently that he is Israeli first and Jewish second. That's how I feel: Welsh first, Jewish second. I would pass the 'Tebbit test' (a controversial phrase coined in 1990 by Conservative politician Norman Tebbit about the perceived lack of loyalty to the England cricket team among South Asian and Caribbean immigrants and their children). Would my grandfather have done so? I'm not so sure.

Now aged 62, I spend more time considering the past and the future of Wally's. My research for this book has been a part of that process, a chance to reflect on the extraordinary story that created today's iconic shop.

I feel gratified to have uncovered aspects of my family's story that were previously unknown, continuing the process that my sister Rochelle had begun years before when she started researching the family tree. When I recently picked up the baton to investigate my grandparents' story further, I discovered that in December 1949 my grandfather had written to the Army Records Office asking for his 1939-1945 Star Medal – awarded to him for serving overseas for a minimum of six months in the conflict – to be forwarded onto him, as he had only received the ribbon in July 1944. It was unclear whether this was ever received, so in October 2023, I wrote to the War Office and got both his Star Medal and his 1939-1945 War Medal sent. By a twist of fortune, however, whilst searching through a box of Mum's old documents, I found a small drawstring bag containing the original Star Medal and ribbon sent to my grandfather.

Researching my family's wartime history has permanently altered my sense of identity. As a country, Austria did not acknowledge or address the horrors and shame of its conduct during the Second World War until 1991, when Chancellor Vranitzky acknowledged Austrian collusion with the Nazis. Before this, Austria maintained it had been a victim, not an accomplice, of the Nazi regime. Vranitzky told the Austrian parliament:

"We acknowledge all the facts of our history and the deeds of all sections of our people, the good as well as the evil. And just as we take credit for the good, we must also apologise for the evil to survivors and relatives of the dead."

This statement opened the way for wartime refugees to apply for an Austrian State Pension, and Otto and Wally completed their applications in the early 2000s. They had to prove that their family had fled Austria due to persecution from National Socialism. Dad wrote to various Austrian state archives and organisations to obtain the relevant documentation, and in 2002 he lodged a claim with the National Fund of the Republic of Austria for Victims of National Socialism. In August 2005, he was awarded 7,630 euros as compensation for property losses in the category: "apartment and small business leases, household property and personal valuables". He also received 1,000 euros as a final distribution of the fund set up for this purpose. The award letter read:

"We are conscious of the fact that the injustice that you and your family have been subjected to cannot be made up for.

Yet, we close with the deep hope that through its work, the National Fund has succeeded in expressing the efforts towards a reconciliation rendered by the Republic of Austria."

Dad was also granted Honorary Membership of the IKG – the *Israelitische Kultusgemeinde Wien,* the representative body of the Jewish community in Vienna – in recognition of "the difficult personal fate" he and his family had experienced.

I regret that Dad did not share any of these endeavours with me when he could. He had been sent the same files from the state archives that I discovered in February 2023, when I was researching this book. I had thought this was the first time this file had been opened in 80 years.

I wanted to know what Dad made of the compensation, these expressions of reconciliation. Had he viewed them as empty words and inadequate gestures, or a genuine attempt to make up for past wrongdoings? It seemed to me that my grandparents' unwillingness to speak about the past extended to my father.

The only story I remember him telling me was of a trip back to Austria with my mother a few years earlier. They visited Rohrbach an der Teich and wandered about the village. Dad had little information about the family's life there at that time. They spoke to one or two locals and enquired whether anyone remembered the Salamon family. One man, about Dad's age, motioned for them to wait while he went inside a house. A few minutes later, he came back out, followed by an elderly woman, bent over double, with a headscarf and walking stick.

Dad asked her again in his broken German whether she remembered the family. She replied that she could remember the young boys playing in the road and pinching apples from the cart. But then she said something that stuck in my father's mind for the rest of his life: after the family left, she had to go in and clear up the stinking mess left by the rotting fruit and poultry. She showed no regret or sorrow at the circumstances of their hurried departure, just bitterness that they hadn't cleared up after themselves.

Further appeasement efforts have followed, including a 2022 act enabling the descendants of Jews who were driven out of the country by persecution to apply for Austrian citizenship.

I did think for a while that I would apply for citizenship, partly as my children could apply too (which might be helpful for them in a post-Brexit world) and partly as a closing of the circle of forced departure and then return. However, while researching this book, I became increasingly aware of how the Austrian state and people treated my family and began questioning whether I wanted to become an Austrian citizen.

These feelings were reinforced by the sentiments I experienced when I visited Rohrbach an der Teich in February 2023 with Benjamin and Natalie. We didn't know what we would find; all we had to go on was the one photograph of the original family store. This photograph was ingrained in the whole family's deep consciousness. It hangs proudly in the shop today and has even been used as the label design for Wally's own-label range of gins. It is a link to another world, a peaceful world before it was shattered by the events of the Anschluss and its aftermath.

In Rohrbach an der Teich in the 1930s, the family store was next to an inn. On our visit in 2023, when we first entered the building we thought was the family shop, we were entering the building next door, which was the inn; from the photo, it looked exactly like the shop. Inside, we met the current owner, an unremarkable woman about my age. I shall never forget her reaction on hearing the name Salamon once we explained why we were there and that we were researching the family story. She froze and went white as a sheet, her mouth fell open, and she bellowed our name: "Salamon, Salamon!" She seemed friendly enough, putting to rest my fears that we would be treated suspiciously as Jews returning to reclaim their assets.

She then called out to someone at the back, and an elderly, bespectacled, white-haired lady hobbled towards us, staring incredulously. She was the owner's mother and, remarkably, the daughter of the people who had run the inn in the 1930s – she was the young girl in the old shop photograph, sitting on the steps outside with Sigi, Otto, and Wally. I showed her the picture, and without prompting she remembered the names of my uncles, Sigi and Otto, and *"das kind"* (the child) Wally, whose name she could not remember, probably because he was just a baby at the time and she was a bit older.

The owner explained how the Salamon's shop was next door and that the building had been remodelled and looked quite different now. The building, where the shop was located, has now been absorbed into the inn, housing the *fremdenzimmer* (guest rooms). As she explained this, all I could think of was how or when the neighbours had taken possession of the building, whether any monies had been paid for it, and to whom. Did they move in once my family had been evicted? All this remains unknown, but it was commonplace throughout Nazi Germany after Jews were expelled for people who were once friends and neighbours to take away anything they could lay their hands on and occupy the properties.

What concerned me most was that the owner didn't show any acknowledgement or remorse about what had happened to my family, although she knew their fate very well, as shown by her reaction on seeing us turn up like ghosts from the past. I wondered how the story of the Jewish family, probably the only ones in their small village evicted from their home by the Nazis, had been communicated and passed down over the intervening years.

Whilst talking, I mentioned that we were staying in Vienna. The owner responded by saying how much she disliked Vienna as it was full of Turkish immigrants who were lazy and didn't work or integrate. I thought to myself that this was precisely the sort of attitude shown towards Jews in the 1930s, and how tragic it was that nothing had changed.

I had a thousand questions, but our broken German and her little English made conversation difficult. We exchanged email addresses, and I subsequently wrote with a few pertinent questions, hoping for some answers. I have not received any response to my enquiries – the enduring silence perhaps a powerful indictment.

While Austrian citizenship would now seem a tainted legacy, Wally's endures as a positive embodiment of the resilience of a family of survivors, and the determination and pride of three generations of men who have carried the business through all its challenges, heartbreaks, and triumphs.

*

Since its earliest days in Bridge Street, the shop has catered for the specific demands of various immigrant communities who settled in and around Cardiff: Russian Jews fleeing pogroms at the turn of the 20th century; Continental Jews fleeing fascism in the 1930s and 1940s; Czechs, Hungarians, and Poles fleeing communism in the 1950s; Spanish and Italian economic migrants in the post-war period; Somali seafaring families who lived and worked in the docks from the 19th century, and later Somali refugees fleeing the civil war in the 1980s and 1990s; Greeks, seeking a better life; South Asians, including from India, Bangladesh, and Pakistan, deeply connected to the UK through British colonisation; East African Asians escaping discrimination and persecution from newly independent African countries like Uganda; Black South Africans seeking employment in the health sector; White South Africans seeking new opportunities following the end of Apartheid; Poles seeking work in the UK after Poland's EU accession in 2005; and, more recently, international students from around the world studying at Welsh universities.

These communities have grown and shrunk over the years, and some of these markets have now disappeared altogether, due to competition and assimilation. But Wally's has always been one of the beating hearts of Cardiff's vibrant immigrant communities, whether for an everyday requirement or just an occasional taste of home.

Ignatz, Wally, and I have faced the challenges of constantly shifting migration trends. We have had to move with the times, indeed try to stay ahead of the times, and this is one of the secrets of our success. While the Bridge Street shop could rightly be described as a Jewish shop (or a shop for Jews), by the time my father opened in Royal Arcade that was no longer the case. Today, it's even less so. Most customers would not even know that the shop is Jewish-owned, which is how I like it. We have a wide and varied customer base and cater to all people who live, work in, or visit Cardiff – regardless of ethnicity, race, or religion.

Cardiff now has a cosmopolitan population of around 365,000. In 2024, it was voted the best city in Europe for young families to live in, according to the European Commission's Quality of Life in European Cities report. I want to think Wally's is an integral part of the city's retail landscape. It is known as a "destination location": people will visit the city centre just to visit the shop. Indeed, Wally's is often highlighted in tourist packages as a must-visit destination on their trip to Wales.

The redevelopment of the former docks area, started in 1999 with the construction of a barrage to create a freshwater lake, and the establishment of shops and restaurants, boating trips, and other tourist attractions, has undoubtedly boosted the city's appeal.

The shop is more than the sum of its parts; in a sense, it's a "living being" with its own personality, stories, and friends. For many of those who had lost their extended families in the war, it became a pseudo-family member. This feeling is nicely summed up by long-standing customer Janina Kuczys, who says: "I went so often as a child I thought I was part of the family." It has provided food, community, and continuity for its customers, who at the outset included many who had been displaced by the war and longed for a taste of home. It has brought the excitement of difficult-to-source international foods to the people of Cardiff. It has ridden trends ranging from whole foods, to fancy Italian pasta and Polish meats, to US confectionery and South African staples.

Many families have been coming to the shop for decades, initially as children with their parents, then as adults, and later with their children and grandchildren. As research for this book, I started a project to collect the memories of customers who remembered the Bridge Street shop, my grandparents, and Wally and Otto. I asked them how they felt about the shop and what they remembered about it. By way of thanks, I gave them a pin badge, reading: "Shopping at Wally's for 50 years."

There is a keen sense of family pride in Wally's. While many family members have moved away, particularly to London, the shop remains a treasured port of call for all of them. Belinda sums this up:

> "When we go to Cardiff, the kids still want to go into the shop – and they're not young kids anymore, either; they are grown-ups. It means a lot that a family member is still in the shop to see. We used to go and see Dad, and now we're going to see my brother. It means the children can experience the same emotion of seeing a family member in a shop I had when I visited Dad. It's that same continuity and a feeling of pride. Wally's is just part of our DNA."

Dan uses that same phrase: "Wally's is in our DNA." The shop has been a constant rock in a sea of change for him. "I call Dad weekly," Daniel says. "I want to know how the shop's doing, because if it's not doing well, I know Dad's not doing well."

The question that hangs in the air is whether any of my children will want to take on the business. It's something I haven't demanded of them and never will. They have all started their careers, taking them away from the shop.

Natalie sums up the feelings of all three siblings when she says:

> "I would love for the shop to stay in the family; however, I have now found myself in London at the start of a very long career. All we've ever known in this family is the shop; everything revolves around it, whether holidays to Austria for research, an exhausted Dad at Christmas, or a cold meat and cheese Christmas dinner.

"Even now, when I return and visit Cardiff, I'll first visit the shop to see the long-term staff members and eat some delicious food. Often, wherever we are in the world, if we cross paths with a Welsh person, they or their family know the shop. That is a feeling you can't beat."

I remain committed to running Wally's, but it can be a juggling act, especially with my desire to spend more time with Michelle in London. So, undoubtedly at some point, my ties to Cardiff might loosen further.

Will Wally's one day stand alone, with no Salamon family member at the door? It seems possible, but as long as the shop endures, so will its founders' legacy.

Started as a grocery store by my grandfather, the store soon changed into a delicatessen serving the needs of the Eastern European immigrant community. Taken on by my father and his brother, they added health foods and wholefoods to the range and introduced more Western European foods. Today, under my direction, we offer gourmet foods from every continent, and we may be considered not just a continental but a global delicatessen.

I am proud of my achievements and how I have maintained my grandfather's and father's legacies. What brings this home to me more than anything else is when customers come up to me and say: "Your father would be so proud." I hope so.

The product mix may have altered, the prices increased, and the trading style adapted over the last 76 years. However, one thing that has remained constant throughout is my grandfather's, father's, and my determination to offer our customers a wide variety of authentic, quality gourmet foods from around the world.

The business has borne the Salamon family through three-quarters of a century of highs and lows, births, marriages, and deaths, and their stories are in its very bones. The Salamon family made Bridge Street Stores, Continental Delicatessen, and Wally's Delicatessen, and they in turn were the making of the Salamon family.

Steven in Wally's Delicatessen, 1995, and standing in the same place in the shop, 2023.

Wally's Delicatessen at night, Royal Arcade, 2024.

Epilogue

The Holocaust stripped my grandparents of most members of their respective families. What follows are the details of those in their immediate families who perished in the Holocaust – and the few who, like them, found a way out.

Ignatz's parents – Jozef and Karolina Salamon

In his old age, Sigi recalled the last time he saw his grandparents. It's a fond, funny memory that reveals a lot about them.

Karolina and Jozef had been the pillar of the Salamon family; their children and their offspring continually looked to them for support and guidance. Not long before the events of the Anschluss, Sigi had been sent from Austria to live with his grandparents in Poland for a year, so that they could give him some religious guidance and mentoring – or, as he put it: "Get some *yiddishkeit* (a Jewish way of living) into him."

The experience changed his appearance and his way of relating to the world. "I was wearing *tzitzit* (prayer shawl), let my sideburns grow, and my grandmother instilled in me a love of Torah and Yiddish," he later recalled.

If he saw a rainbow, which some Jews take as a sign that God considers the world to be deserving of destruction, it would strike fear into his heart. "I would be shaking at night and praying to God, saying: 'Oh please God, did I miss anything?'"

While Karolina was proud to have cultivated religiosity in her grandson, his parents felt she had put the fear of God into him. He tried to get his parents to follow the *mitzvot* (Jewish laws) and struggled to readjust to secular life once he returned to his family. "I was only with my grandmother for a year," Sigi recalled. "She wanted me to become a rabbi; she had great but crazy plans. When I went back to Austria, I continued for a while. My newfound love of God and Torah made my parents despair."

Over time, his religious fervour died down, much to the relief of his family. Life settled back into a comfortable pace. But he never saw his grandparents again.

While their son was making his escape from mainland Europe, Jozef and Karolina found themselves living in fear. They were vulnerable, not only because of their Jewishness, but also because they were elderly. Following the German invasion of Poland on September 1, 1939, events quickly took a turn for the worse. Deportations and shootings were commonplace, and Jews were violated and forced into ghettos. For whatever reason, Jozef and Karolina had remained in Poland before the German invasion. We will never know whether this was because they chose to stay, believing things would get better, or tried to leave but couldn't due to their age or insufficient funds. Along with millions of their fellow Jews who remained in Poland, this proved to be a fatal error. By 1940, Karolina had died in Suchej, probably because of the harsh conditions she was forced to live in, although the precise cause of her death is not recorded.

Jozef, meanwhile, had been deported sometime between 1939 and 1941 to the Sosnowiec Ghetto, which the Nazis had set up to house Polish Jews. Most of its inmates, estimated at over 35,000 Jewish men, women, and children, were deported from there to Auschwitz, where they were murdered. Jozef died in the ghetto in 1942, probably murdered or worked to death, although the precise cause of his death is not recorded.

Jozef's older brother, Leon Salamon, emigrated to the US at the turn of the century and had 12 children. These included Gussie Levin and Harry Salamon, who my grandfather listed as cousins on his visa application to the US Consulate in Vienna in 1938. Another brother, Moses Salamon, perished in the Holocaust in 1942, although the precise date and location are unknown.

Karolina's brother, Heinrich (Joachim) Reichenbaum, who was an innkeeper in Suchej before the war, and his son, Jakob Isak Reichenbaum, a doctor, were both murdered in Auschwitz in April 1942. Both men were hanged within a month of arriving, after having their mugshots taken. It appears from the mugshots that Joachim and Jakob were sent to Auschwitz not only for the "crime" of being Polish Jews but also as political prisoners.

The Auschwitz mugshots, according to Helen Tichauer – a survivor who worked in the Auschwitz *bauleitung* (site office) – were taken only of inmates (Jews as well as non-Jews) who arrived in Auschwitz through the penal system. The photographed Jews had at some point been "arrested" and were regarded in the first instance as criminals. However, they may have been arrested for as marginal an offence as violating curfew, posing as Aryans, or appearing on a membership list of a Zionist organisation. All the mugshots predate the mass deportations of the autumn of 1942 and therefore have no bearing on Jews who were or were not selected for forced labour rather than the gas chambers. Ironically, none of the people photographed would have been sent to the gas chambers. They were called "*karte indiziert*" (card indexed). Those who arrived as "prisoners" were "sentenced" and could not be discharged, but neither could they be gassed. Often, however, they were shot, hanged, or beaten to death, sometimes only days or weeks after arriving at Auschwitz. The photography was done under SS auspices in a police-like environment through the *Erkennungsdient* (identification department). Of a total of 38,000 mugshots that were taken at Auschwitz, less than 10 percent were of Jewish prisoners; the vast majority were of Polish, German, and Czech prisoners.

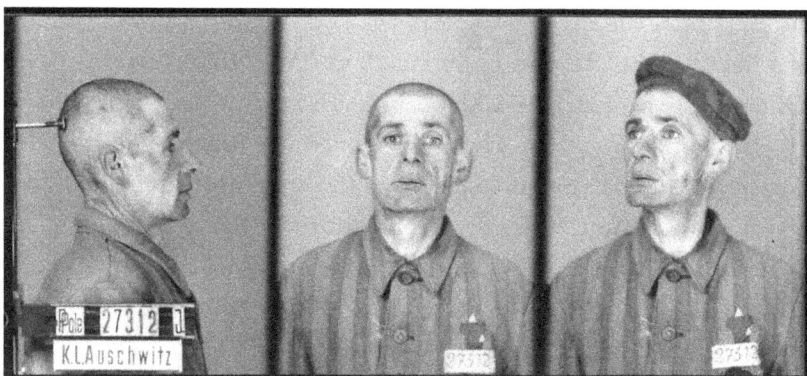

Joachim Henryk Reichenbaum mugshot – Auschwitz-Birkenau, 1942.

Frieda's parents – Moses and Rosa Stein

Frieda's father, Abraham Moses (Moishe) Stein, was murdered in 1943 in a camp in Transnistria, South-West Ukraine, after being deported there following the German conquest of the region and the capitulation of the Romanian government.

Her mother, Rosa (Rivka) Stein, was murdered in the same camp in 1942. Pages of testimony exist at the Holocaust Memorial, Yad Vashem, in Israel, written by a cousin of Rosa's, David Geffner, the son of Frieda's cousin Hermann Geffner, who was a witness at Ignatz and Frieda's wedding.

Frieda's mother had two brothers, Hermann and Nathan Kohlreiter, who had emigrated to the US before the war, and who are referred to as relatives in my grandfather's visa application in 1938.

Frieda's brother, Yaakov, escaped from Nazi-occupied Vienna towards the end of 1939, with his wife Zila and their children, Yitzhak and Ruthi. They undertook a gruelling four-month journey back to Romania, through Czechoslovakia, Hungary, Bulgaria, and Yugoslavia, and arrived at the port in Sulina, Romania, where they endured a week-long wait in freezing conditions with very few amenities until their vessel, the SS *Sakaria*, arrived.

The SS *Sakaria* sailed for Palestine on February 1, 1940, with 2,175 refugees aboard. Conditions on board were horrible, with little shelter, overcrowding, and insufficient food and water. The ship was intercepted at sea off Tenedos Island by HMS *Fiona* on February 9, and taken to Haifa with a guard on board, arriving on February 13. The British police interned all the illegal immigrants from the ship at Athlit – a prison camp for illegal arrivals, just south of Haifa. Zila and the children were released after a couple of weeks, but Yaakov was kept there for around three months.

Following his release, the family built a life together in Tel Aviv, where Yitzhak's wife Dalia and their sons, Amir and Yuval, live with their families.

Ignatz's siblings

Ignatz's only brother, Maks Salamon, came to Cardiff with his wife Irka to work for Aero Zipp Fasteners in June 1939. They brought their son, Roger, who was born in Poland, with them. Their second son, Edgar, was born in Cardiff in 1943.

Maks rose to a senior management position with Aero Zipp and often travelled to their factories in Holland after the war. They lived in Lisvane, Cardiff, and spent a peaceful retirement tending their beautiful garden, where my sisters and I would occasionally visit them.

Maks died following a stroke in 1991, and Irka followed several years later, in 1996. They are buried in the Orthodox Jewish cemetery in Ely, Cardiff. Roger and Edgar continue to live in Cardiff.

Ignatz's sister, Ruzia Gutfreund, was my grandfather's only sister who survived the war. In 1939, she lived in Bielsko-Biala – a small town close to Suchej, where she was born – with her children, Manek (Maurice) and Anna (Nusiana), while her husband Roman (Romek) was in the Polish Army.

With the looming threat of a Nazi invasion, Polish Jews didn't know what to expect; many feared the worst, that they would be arrested, tortured, and killed. They had heard tales of the Nazis' racial policies towards Jews in Germany. Others thought that the situation couldn't get that bad and that the Allies would have the military might to defeat Hitler.

Those in the former camp, including Romek and Ruzia, made plans to leave. When the Soviet Union signed the Ribbentrop-Molotov non-aggression pact with Germany in August 1939, many understood that Poland would soon be divided between the two powers, with the Soviet Union taking eastern Poland. They felt that they would be safer in the hands of the Soviets than the Germans as, unlike the Nazis, the Russians were not overtly opposed to Jews.

Ruzia and Romek left their parents, brothers, and sisters behind and headed eastward with their children, until they arrived in Soviet-controlled eastern Poland. On their way, they passed through Bochnia to say farewell to Romek's brother. Whilst there, Romek changed out of his army uniform into civilian clothing, because he would have been treated as a deserter if he had been stopped still wearing his army uniform.

The Soviet Union had invaded Poland from the east 16 days after Nazi Germany had invaded from the west. Hitler wanted Russia to provide *lebensraum* (living space) for the German people. Despite Romek and Ruzia's earlier optimism about life under Soviet rule, things didn't turn out as they had expected. Around June 1940, hundreds of thousands of Poles, including Ruzia and her family, were deported to gulags in Siberia to become slave labourers, often having been charged with a made-up crime, or not having been charged with any crime at all. This was at the order of the People's Commissariat for Internal Affairs, the interior ministry of the Soviet Union, abbreviated to the NKVD. This organisation was headed by Nikita Khrushchev, an ideologist, who would later replace Stalin as general secretary of the Communist Party. The mass deportation was all part of Stalin's plan to consolidate his power and economically exploit eastern Poland.

What happened next is not clear. It appears that Romek, Ruzia, and their children spent at least a year interned in Siberia, where they experienced forced labour, freezing conditions, lice, and near starvation. Ruzia later recalled that they subsisted on scavenged raw potatoes. In July 1941, following Hitler's invasion of Russia in Operation Barbarossa, an accord was signed between the Polish government-in-exile in London and the Soviet Union, as part of a wider British-Soviet pact designed to bolster the united front against the Germans.

The accord provided for a Polish army to be formed from the ranks of released Polish citizens. The army was to be under the command of a Polish government appointee, General Wladyslaw Anders, a former Soviet prisoner himself, but to be subordinate operationally to the Supreme Command of the USSR.

Romek, as an enlisted Polish soldier, was conscripted into this army, known as Anders Army. At first, the army remained in the Soviet Union, with the men undergoing rehabilitation after the harsh conditions of the gulag, as well as military training. Stalin wanted to send the units to the front much earlier than General Anders thought was proper, given the fighting state of the men. Tensions and suspicions, including what had happened to the thousands of Polish Army officers who had been imprisoned (and massacred by the Soviets), ensued on both sides to such an extent that, eventually, between March and September 1942, Anders Army was evacuated with the blessing of the Soviets.

They made their way – Romek amongst them – to Tehran, Iran, via Krasnovodsk on the Caspian Sea. From there, they spent time in Palestine (where many men deserted, including Menachem Begin, who became Prime Minister of Israel in 1977), where they were passed under the British Middle East Command and became part of the Polish Second Corps, which fought in the Africa and Italy campaigns. From the later testimony of Romek's nephew, we know that Romek fought in the Battle of Monte Cassino between January and May 1944 – one of the bloodiest battles of the Second World War.

Stalin had agreed to allow the families of the soldiers to be evacuated with them if they weren't Soviet citizens, and many wives and children joined the evacuation. Stalin had earlier granted amnesty to all Polish citizens in Russia and allowed the refugees not evacuated with Anders Army to leave for different parts of the Soviet Union. However, permission to leave the country completely wasn't granted until 1946. It's unclear, however, whether Ruzia and her children were among the Anders Army evacuees, or where they lived the rest of the war years.

What is known is that by early June 1946, Ruzia and the children were in Szczecin, a city in northern Poland, close to the German border. From there, she appealed to the American Joint Distribution Committee (JDC) in New York, which was charged with assisting displaced persons in Europe and reuniting them with their families, saying that she and her two children were "in dire need of assistance" and pleading "for assistance immediately". The JDC contacted their Warsaw office, asking them to investigate and help if possible. They, in turn, sent the enquiry to the Jewish Relief Committee in Szczecin. The investigation revealed that Ruzia had previously received aid on June 4 by way of clothing, including a ladies' overcoat, one garment, one pair of ladies' shoes, and one men's overcoat.

However, they now assigned further clothes: one pair of old men's half-boots, one ladies' overcoat, one cloak, one pair of men's trousers, one men's coat, one men's shirt, one garment, two chemises, and two sweaters.

In March 1947, Ruzia and the children were sent to a Displaced Persons Camp in Linz, Austria, run by the JDC in Vienna. This was a temporary facility for displaced persons hoping to reconnect with their families. After the war, some 850,000 people lived in such camps around Europe for up to two years.

Meanwhile, in Cardiff, Ignatz and Maks worked hard to discover what had happened to their families. With the help of the International Tracing Service, run by the Red Cross, they managed to track down Ruzia and arrange to bring her to the UK. Her index card at the Displaced Persons Camp closed on July 1, 1947, suggesting that is when she finally managed to leave for the UK.

It would have been an emotional reunion when Ruzia eventually arrived in Cardiff. It's not clear when her husband, Romek, also came, although they had settled in Clare Road, Grangetown, before long. Sadly, I do not remember much of Ruzia; I can only recall the unusual pull-knob doorbell they had at their house when we visited. Ruzia and Romek received their naturalisation certificates in 1948, with my maternal grandfather, Ernie, acting as referee for their application. This was unusually quick, as there was a five-year residency rule, but Romek's service under British Army command may have speeded up the process.

Romek later worked for Lionite, a factory owned by another refugee. This might have been difficult, as Romek never learned to speak English; Edgar, Ruzia's nephew, can remember him having Polish newspapers delivered and fondly recalls enjoyable evenings spent at their house playing cards.

Both Romek and Ruzia suffered a lot of ill health during their later lives; Edgar can remember Ruzia being almost bent double with rheumatoid arthritis. Romek died in Cardiff in 1970, and Ruzia in 1974. Maurice worked for a while at Aero Zipp before becoming a taxi driver, dying in 2009, three years after Nusia, who had married and settled in London. Maurice is survived by two children, with a third child having died in Cardiff in 2021.

Ignatz's other sisters, Manya, Josefina, Anna, and Sabena, remained in Suchej in the lead-up to the outbreak of war, and perished in 1940, either in a camp or a ghetto. Perhaps they were amongst those who thought it would be safe to remain in Poland, although the exact circumstances are unknown. Their precise causes of death are not recorded, but it may be assumed that they were either murdered or worked to death, in common with the millions of Polish Jews who suffered the same fate.

Ignatz's sister-in-law, Irka Reichenbaum, lost her brother, Ernst, and his wife, who were both murdered at Auschwitz in 1942. Ernst's son, Eduard, was murdered, aged 10, at a subcamp of the Neuengamme concentration camp, near Hamburg, in 1945, after being one of 20 Jewish children from Auschwitz selected by Dr Josef Mengele for a cruel medical experiment by Nazi physician, Kurt Heissmeyer. With little medical or scientific knowledge of the subject, he injected live tuberculosis bacilli into the lungs and bloodstreams of Jewish children, trying to prove his hypothesis that this would act as a vaccine. With the Allies advancing, the children and their four adult caretakers were murdered by being hanged in the basement of Bullenhuser Damm School, thus destroying most of the evidence. Fortunately, a Scandinavian prisoner held at the same camp recorded the names, ages, and countries of origin of the victims. Heissmeyer was eventually tried for his crimes in 1966. At his trial, he said he saw no difference between Jews, whom he regarded as *untermenschen* (subhumans), and guinea pigs.

A bronze relief stele commemorating the children of the massacre was placed at the site in 2001, paid for by Hamburg citizens. Eduard's brother, Itzhak, survived the war and emigrated to Haifa, Israel. He is still in contact with his first cousins, Roger and Edgar.

The brutal reality is that all family members who stayed in Europe post-1939 were amongst the six million Jews murdered by the Nazis. Before the Second World War, over three million Jews were living in Poland. By 1945, this number was around 100,000. In 1938, approximately 190,000 Jews were living in Austria. By May 1945, some 70,000 had been murdered and another 120,000 had fled as refugees.

Today, no-one from the Salamon or Stein families is left in Poland, Romania, or Austria; we survive only in the US, UK, and Israel, where family members escaped.

Wally's brothers

After their retirement, Otto and Maureen lived out a peaceful existence in Cardiff. Otto enjoyed pottering in his garden, playing bowls with friends, watching football on television, and the occasional trip to Ninian Park to watch his beloved Cardiff City play. Maureen enjoyed cooking, entertaining, and communal activities.

They died within a year of each other – Otto passing in 2003 and Maureen in 2004 – and are buried next to each other in the Reform Jewish cemetery at Ely, Cardiff. They are survived by their two children, Karen and Michael, who live in Cardiff, and their five grandchildren.

Sigi, the oldest of the three brothers, emigrated to Israel after his National Service ended in 1951, after having struggled to settle in the UK since first arriving there. In Israel, he felt he belonged. He learned Hebrew and served in the Israeli Army, including during the 1973 *Yom Kippur* War. He married an American, Nina, and together they had two children – Debbie, who was born in the US, and Rafi, born in Israel.

Sigi followed soon after the 1973 war. He was heartbroken about leaving Israel but chose to stay with his family. While living in America, he struggled to make a living and was troubled by antisemitism

Sigi had left his friends in Israel and never really connected with anyone else. The friends he had were either Israelis or people who shared a deep love for Israel. Sigi and Nina eventually divorced, and Sigi met Ellen, who became his longtime companion. He still contemplated moving back to Israel at times, but he decided his life was in the US with his family and friends.

During these last years, he found true happiness and contentment. He spent time caring for his grandchildren, whom he loved very much, and he no longer struggled with himself or with not being in Israel. He died in 2010, the last of the Salamon brothers to pass, and is buried in New York. He is survived by his children, Deborah and Rafi, who live in New York, and five grandchildren.

The Salamon brothers, 1989. Left to right: Sigi, Wally, Otto.

My mother

Following Dad's passing in 2008, Mum stayed in their marital home for a few years. She sold their villa in Spain and bought a bungalow in Mill Hill, London. This allowed her to spend time in London visiting her growing number of grandchildren and enjoying cultural visits to art exhibitions and the theatre.

She got a puppy called Chuchie, who became her much-loved companion. She enjoyed taking Chuchie out for walks, where she would engage with the other dog walkers.

In 2015, she sold the Cardiff family home, which was becoming unmanageable, and bought a bungalow in Rhiwbina, Cardiff. Here, she designed a beautiful garden, where she enjoyed pottering and built an art studio where she could indulge in her love of painting.

Unfortunately, Mum's health started to deteriorate when she contracted pneumonia following a hip operation, and she was not the same thereafter. She was diagnosed with atrial fibrillation and COPD, probably the result of a lifetime of smoking. Getting to

London was becoming increasingly difficult, and reluctantly, in 2022, she sold the London bungalow.

Following a series of hospitalisations with severe breathing difficulties, my sisters and I took the difficult decision to register Mum with a private assisted-living care home in Cardiff. She couldn't manage alone at home, and we were concerned that we could not get there quickly enough in an emergency. We found a dog-friendly home, and Mum went for a respite stay, which became permanent. At first, Mum hated it there, despite the first-class facilities, and wanted to return home. But she gradually warmed to the place and appreciated the improvement in the quality of life it allowed her.

Chuchie adapted to life in the care home well and quickly became a firm favourite of the staff and visitors. She died in early 2024, leaving a huge void in Mum's life.

Mum continues to miss Dad every day, and no visit to see her is complete without listening to one of her stories about Dad and their exploits together.

My sisters

After finishing school, Belinda trained as a secretary and moved to London. At the age of 26, she left for Israel, where she fulfilled her dream of going to university. After four years away, with a war brewing, she returned to London, where she married and raised three children – two girls and a boy.

Belinda misses Dad immensely and is enormously proud of his achievements. After Dad's passing, I gave her one of our father's handwritten signs (for dried prunes), which today has pride of place in her home.

Rochelle graduated from Sheffield University with a degree in English Literature and Philosophy. She then moved to North London, where she worked as a counsellor and fundraiser before marrying and raising four boys.

Rochelle has a strong bond with the shop, having worked there for many years in the 1980s, and from her childhood, sitting around the kitchen table while our parents formulated their plans for the new shop.

Rochelle continues her family research and hopes to produce a wider family tree showing all branches, including on our mother's side.

My children

After finishing school, Benjamin studied History at the University of Exeter. He then worked in the charitable sector in London. Today, he is a philanthropy manager for Macmillan Cancer Support.

While working at Wally's, Natalie discovered a knack for retail, so she applied to work in Cardiff's Apple Store. In January 2017, she moved to London to work in the Regent Street branch. While working there, she became a special police officer with the Metropolitan Police. In 2019, she joined the Met full-time, where she now works in the Response Unit, responsible for driving herself and her fellow officers to 999 calls on "blue lights".

Having studied business studies at the University of Birmingham, Daniel now lives in London and works for the Walt Disney Company as a supervisor on the marketing team.

Scott, Michelle's son, attended the University of Leeds Medical School and graduated as a doctor in the spring of 2025, fulfilling a lifelong ambition.

In total, 20 great-grandchildren of Ignatz and Frieda Salamon live today to continue their legacy.

Acknowledgements

To my sister Rochelle, who supplied most of the information on the family in the pre-war years through her painstaking research, much of it conducted before the internet made things much easier. My family's survival story might never have been told without her connecting references in family documents to Kitchener Camp and my grandfather's escape from Austria. Boxes of papers and letters that she handed me shone a light into a previously unexplored world.

To my mother, Laraine, who was there alongside my father for much of this journey, supported him, and allowed him to follow his passion. Without her memories of Dad and his parents in the early years of their marriage, this book would not be what it is.

To my sister Belinda and my cousins Edgar Salamon, Karen Coulter, and Michael Salamon, who supplied documents and photographs that helped thread the story together, and for their recollections of working in the family business.

To my cousin Debbie Raymond, who wrote her father's memoir, *Daddy's Life*, after his death, which offered invaluable insights into the family's life before and during the war years.

To Ron Gutfreund, who provided his father's wartime testimony, which was not easy reading, but which opened previously unknown aspects of the family's wider story.

To Clare Weissenberg, curator of the Kitchener Camp website and exhibition, who provided extracts from publications about the Auxiliary Military Pioneer Corps, which helped piece together my grandfather's service years in the British Army.

To Jenny White, who showed a real passion for this project from the start and convinced me there was a story worth telling.

Jenny interviewed family members and former staff and helped me write the first draft of this book. Her advice on style, presentation, and the level of detail that should be included was invaluable.

To David and Tricia Pike, without whom Wally's would not be where it is today.

To members of staff, past and present, who have contributed to the success of the family business over nine decades.

To Wally's customers, old and new, without whom we have no business.

To my children, Benjamin, Natalie, and Daniel, who gave me the will to keep going when times were tough. This book is for you.

To my partner, Michelle Leigh, the most amazing person, who keeps me grounded and gives me strength and purpose.

Sources

This book is the result of an amalgamation of diverse sources.

My experiences and research, layered on family stories, recollections, and photographs passed down over the years, provided the initial background. This was supplemented by more detailed accounts and research into the family's history. Most important were the family tree, documents, and photographs supplied by my sister Rochelle, collated from family members and the result of meticulous research.

Debbie Raymond's account of her father's life story opened a new window on the family's early years. Crucially, a video taken in Spain not long before Wally died, showing an often-heated discussion between Wally and Sigi about their parents and their childhood, shed previously unrecorded light on the family's story.

Alexander Gutfreund's testimony at the Yad Vashem archives included vital clues as to what happened to Ignatz's sister, Ruzia, and her husband during the war years.

Old files kept in the office of Wally's Delicatessen revealed more vital information, as did boxes of cuttings, cards, and other memorabilia kept by my mother, Laraine.

Jenny White interviewed family members and former employees, notably David and Tricia Pike, for their recollections.

The following resources were consulted for important family documentation and historical information:

The National Archives
The Ministry of Defence
The War Diaries 69 Company Auxiliary Military Pioneer Corps

The Ministry of Defence Medals Office

The Israelitische Kultusgemeinde Wien (Jewish Community of Vienna)

The Burgenlandisches Landesarchiv (Burgenland State Archives)

The Wiener Holocaust Library

The Jewish Telegraphic Agency archives

The Leo Baeck Institute archive

The International Tracing Service archives

World Jewish Relief

The Association of Jewish Refugees

The National Life Story Collection, British Library

In-house magazine clippings, Aero Zipp Fasteners Limited

The following websites were accessed:

www.kitchenercamp.co.uk
www.thejc.com
www.ancestry.co.uk
www.kinder-vom-bullenhuser-damm.de
www.bfpg.co.uk/2020/04/covid-19-timeline/
www.lbi.org/1938projekt/9/fake-generosity
www.jta.org/archive
www.ikg-wien.at/en/about-the-jewish-community-of-vienna
www.en.wikipedia.org/wiki/Kristallnacht

Extracts from the following publications were referenced for background information on historical aspects of my family's story:

Norman Bentwich, *I Understand the Risks* (Gollancz, London, 1950)

Norman Bentwich, *They Found Refuge* (Cresset P, 1956)

Leonard H. Ehrlich and Edith Ehrlich, *Choices Under Duress of the Holocaust* (Texas University Press, 2018)

Helen Fry, *The King's Most Loyal Enemy Aliens* (The History Press, 2007)

Helen Fry, *Jews in North Devon* (Halsgrove, 2005)

Yisrael Gutman, *Jews in General Anders Army in the Soviet Union* (Yad Vashem Studies, 1977)

Peter Leighton-Langer, *The King's Own Loyal Enemy Aliens* (Vallentine Mitchell & Co Ltd, 2006)

Cai Parry-Jones, *The Jews of Wales* (University of Wales Press, 2018)

Major E.H. Rhodes-Wood, *A War History of the Royal Pioneer Corps 1939-45* (Gale and Polden Ltd, 1960)

Taube Foundation for Jewish Life & Culture, *1,000 Years of Jewish Life in Poland* (2009)

Milka Zalmon, *The Forced Emigration of the Jews of Burgenland* (Yad Vashem Holocaust Remembrance Centre, 2003)

The following books provided historical context for the story:

Nick Barlay, *Scattered Ghosts* (I. B. Tauris & Co Ltd, 2013)

Tammy Bottner, *Among the Reeds* (Amsterdam Publishers, 2017)

Bettie Lennett Denny, *In the Wake of Madness* (Amsterdam Publishers, 2024)

Daniel Finkelstein, *Hitler, Stalin, Mum & Dad* (William Collins, 2023)

F.J. Fishburn, *On the Basis of Hearsay* (Grosvenor House Publishing, 2018)

Michael Fox, *Through It All* (Michael Fox, 2023)

Georgia Hunter, *We Were the Lucky Ones* (Allison & Busby, 2017)

David Joseph, *Burgenland* (Amberley Publishing, 2023)

Rena Lipiner-Katz, *A Life Inherited* (Concierge Publishing, 2023)

Claire Ungerson, *Four Thousand Lives* (The History Press, 2014)

Photo credits: